State Power and Democracy

State Power and Democracy

Before and During the Presidency of George W. Bush

Andrew Kolin

palgrave
macmillan

First published in hardcover in 2011 by PALGRAVE MACMILLAN® in the United States—a division of St. Martin's Press LLC, 175 Fifth Avenue, New York, NY 10010.

Where this book is distributed in the UK, Europe and the rest of the world, this is by Palgrave Macmillan, a division of Macmillan Publishers Limited, registered in England, company number 785998, of Houndmills, Basingstoke, Hampshire RG21 6XS.

Palgrave Macmillan is the global academic imprint of the above companies and has companies and representatives throughout the world.

Palgrave® and Macmillan® are registered trademarks in the United States, the United Kingdom, Europe and other countries.

ISBN: 978–1–137–03561–5

The Library of Congress has cataloged the hardcover edition as follows:

Kolin, Andrew, 1955–
    State power and democracy : before and during the presidency of George W. Bush / Andrew Kolin.
        p. cm.
    Includes bibliographical references.
    ISBN 978–0–230–10935–3 (alk. paper)
        1. United States—Politics and government. 2. Federal government—United States—History. 3. Democracy—United States—History.
    4. Power (Social sciences)—United States—History. 5. United States—Politics and government—2001–2009. 6. Bush, George W. (George Walker), 1946– 7. War on Terrorism, 2001–2009—Political aspects.
    I. Title.

E183.K67 2010
973.93—dc22   2010021790

A catalogue record of the book is available from the British Library.

Design by Newgen Imaging Systems (P) Ltd., Chennai, India.

First PALGRAVE MACMILLAN paperback edition: July 2012

10 9 8 7 6 5 4 3 2 1

Transferred to Digital Printing in 2012

For Ellen

CONTENTS

ACKNOWLEDGMENTS

I dedicate this book to my wife, Ellen. It was her endless support and enthusiasm that made this book possible. She put in countless hours, over many months, editing the manuscript and was instrumental in clarifying many of the book's central themes.

My friend and colleague, Professor Gordon Snow, made many important contributions to the book. He had invaluable insights and suggestions as to how I could strengthen my arguments.

I also want to express my appreciation and thanks to attorney Sallie Randolph, who provided essential legal advice and guidance on all aspects of publishing and writing in general.

Introduction

The expansion of state power over the course of U.S. history came at the expense of democracy. As state power grew, there developed a disconnect between the theory and practice of democracy in the United States. Ever-greater state power meant it became more and more absolute. This resulted in a government that directed its energies and resources toward silencing those who dared question the state's authority. Such questioning of state power had emanated as a response to mass-based political movements striving to further democracy with an increase in freedom, especially for the downtrodden. This put mass movements in direct confrontation with the elite politics of policy makers.

So, over time, as the U.S. government continued on its course of seeking to increase state power by extending ever-greater control over people and territory, it also meant it worked toward a goal to diminish mass-based political movements. This tendency began not long after the end of the Revolutionary War, starting with the conquest of North America and by the start of the twentieth century, continuing with the expansionism outside of North America. Throughout the nineteenth and twentieth centuries, the U.S. government initiated policies intended to eliminate democracy inside and outside the United States. It is no coincidence that as the state enacted measures to crush democracy, there appeared federal agencies with an antidemocratic mission. Also developing throughout the nineteenth and twentieth centuries in relation to crushing democracy was the state unleashing political repression. Nonetheless, political repression ebbed and flowed, often determined by historical factors and the ability of progressive movements to affect social change during periods of unrest. Still, despite some success in making America more democratic by including the excluded, overall state power was becoming more absolute, above the law and the U.S. Constitution. The achievements of progressive movements were being overshadowed by the state's measures, which eventually wore them down and then eliminated them as a social force for the advancement of democracy. In the latter part of the twentieth century, when mass-based movements for all intents and purposes were eliminated through persistent and intense political repression, what remained for the most part was procedural democracy, which in a short period, would also be eliminated, to be replaced by a form of absolute power in which the government had been made into a permanent police state. Much of this took place after the attacks of 9/11, during which the administration of George W. Bush, in a very short period of time, was able to put in place many of the essential features of what is now an American police state. Consider some of the key features of the Bush administration police state, many of which have carried over and have become part of the Obama administration. For example, the central idea, very much a part of all police states, that the nation is in an ongoing state of emergency, which during the Bush administration, was due to this so-called war on terrorism. Another key aspect of police states also present in America is that security always trumps civil liberties; there is to be no balance between security and rights, since in the name of national security, all state actions are justified. What we also have prior to, during, and after the Bush administration, found in all police states, is an extreme concentration of power within parts of the government, especially within the executive branch. After 9/11, and all throughout the Bush administration, for the most part, the president had assumed dictatorial authority, making the power of the president absolute in many ways; the implication was that an American police state has functioned to sidestep the rule of law and the U.S. Constitution. Supporting the executive branch's absolute power as an essential feature of this American police state is the use of various intelligence gatherers. Even prior to the final formation of the American police state, these federal agencies were in the business of mind control through arbitrary surveillance and as a vital cog of the repressive machinery of the government. The end result is that the state's perceived enemies are identified, and action is taken against them without much semblance of due process; they are confined, made examples of, and put into preventive detention for indefinite periods. Once again, such actions, in particular—the use of preventive detention—are a hallmark of police states. In addition, these actions during and even after the Bush administration are the methods used to manifest the power of a police state. As with all police states, the American version is, above all, obsessed with excessive and unnecessary secrecy. For a government to operate outside the law, it will often engage in criminal behavior, committing violations of international law so that extreme secrecy is essential. Such secrecy also serves to reinforce the collective actions taken by the police state, that is, of an authoritarianism that functions in accordance with a rigid chain of command, meaning a prohibition is placed on any questioning of authority. So, the U.S. government, especially during the Bush administration, functions in accordance with a mindset in which most of the key participants followed orders with few or no questions asked. Another attribute found in all police states, including in the United States, is that in its never ending quest to extend its power and make it more absolute, the state will manufacture reasons to go to war, and in so doing, will commit war crimes, not only in the waging of an aggressive war but also in committing torture.

Throughout the history of how U.S. power grew, there was no reversal of antidemocratic initiatives or most of all, the government's determination to diminish mass democracy. Also, as these antidemocratic measures were implemented, most of them became permanent. The upside of this for state elites, especially in the executive branch during the middle of the nineteenth and throughout the twentieth century, was of an executive branch that understood the advantages of concentrating power. To understand how the U.S. government became more and more a police state, look no further than how it freed itself from colonial rule. For the American Revolution was, by and large, the result of a mobilization of the masses by the elites to liberate the colonized from a colonizer. It was also the starting point of the myth of how the post-Revolutionary government was to be an embodiment of democracy. The truth of the matter was that after the American Revolution, the thinking among economic and political elites was that America had become too democratic, especially as mass democracy was expressing itself on the state level. After the adoption of the Constitution, a central aim of political elites in the government was to diminish mass democracy; in service of this goal was state repression. In so doing, another goal was being met—increasing the government's control over people and territory as a measure of the government's power. On the other hand, with the appearance and growth of democratic practices, this was perceived by elites as a threat to the expansion of state power. As such, the government responded primarily through the use of force and violence, seeking to extend ever-greater control over people and territory within North America. This meant that state repression was being unleashed on a grand scale against whoever stood in the way of the state's goal to increase its power. As a result, throughout much of the nineteenth century, U.S. government policies would result in genocidal and ethnocidal measures taken against American Indians. Slavery was also increasing in importance to the economy, in service of the expansion of state power; it is no coincidence that American Indians and slaves were the earliest groups that were defined by the government as political outsiders. Groups that are depicted as enemies of the state throughout U.S. history and described as "others" served as a convenient justification to enlarge state power at the expense of democracy. The ability of the government to expand its power through political repression was affected by the relative strength and weakness of political movements. Another factor was the extent to which such mass-based movements could advance democracy in relation to the state's goals. For example, American Indians were looked upon as an obstacle to state expansion and, therefore, had to be eliminated. On the other hand, the Abolitionist movement had some degree of success in shaping government policy because of the national division between free and slave states. Like the Abolitionists, the women's movement had, over time, some degree of success due to its reformist emphasis. This does not mean there was no state repression, but the repression was more moderate to the extent that government policy was not fixated with the goal of destroying these movements. The reason was that these movements could have some degree of success against more moderate state repression because their goals did not represent a fundamental challenge to the overall goal of state power, which was at the time, and still is, seeking control over more and more people and territory.

The government's policies toward the labor movement was another matter altogether. Organized labor, especially its more radical elements, such as the IWW, was a greater challenge to elite rule. The history of state repression against organized labor through the nineteenth and twentieth centuries has been fairly well documented. Most striking was the extent to which the full scope and scale of political repression was turned loose against Labor-Socialist parties and organizations. If this example points to anything, it is that the government's repressive machinery would be let loose against a broad-based movement that would not only, in greater numbers, include the excluded, but in so doing, it challenged the state in representing elite or mass interests. In spite of the persistence of political repression against these and other political movements throughout the nineteenth and twentieth centuries, many of the key features, which were cemented during the Bush administration, had not yet appeared. In other words, a full-fledged police state had not yet developed, in part because of the existence at the time of viable political movements. But in surveying U.S. history, it becomes clear that the actions of the government in the end were intended to disrupt and eliminate progressive, mass-based political movements. As the state applied repressive initiatives against Labor and Socialist organizations, the state viewed these organizations, too, as political outsiders, in that they were seen as seeking to subvert the government in relation to an alliance they had allegedly formed with external enemies of the United States. Whether applied to organized labor, Socialists, Communists or terrorists, state ideology remained the same in perceiving the threat as coming from political outsiders who had formed an alliance with an external threat, hence the need to employ emergency measures, which in the end, made state power more and more absolute. Although state repression was consistent against mass movements, there was no police state because the emergency measures brought to bear ebbed and flowed over time, as state elites believed the threat was over. A much clearer path toward an American police state develops in the first two decades of the twentieth century, with the appearance of antidemocratic federal agencies, in particular, the Federal Bureau of Investigation, which defined its bureaucratic mission as a response to a perceived permanent threat to state power from political outsiders, especially Communists.

While this was taking place, another key development was leading to the creation of an American police state as the government sought to further extend control over people and territory outside of North America. At the start of the twentieth century, the United States takes its imperialist goals outside of North America, with the result that in the twentieth century, it becomes a major colonizer, destroying—as other police states did—democracy overseas. Whether it's the destruction of democracy at home or overseas, the actions of the U.S. government, which were increasingly consistent with the practices of a police state, resulted in policies intended to stamp out diverse viewpoints and instill mass conformity. As police states are, by their nature, hostile to rule of law, political repression is accomplished through the use of essentially illegal measures, such as the Alien and Sedition Acts and the Espionage Act. This outlawing of political thought and alternative viewpoints persists as an ongoing theme throughout much of the twentieth century and became one of the key features of the Bush administration police state. The FBI and other federal agencies, which were created to act as thought police, put in place bureaucracies whose mission it is to search for and persecute individuals and organizations that do not follow state policy and whatever the state identifies as its version of official truth. As the pioneer intelligence gatherer, the FBI understood all too well that if you can control people's thoughts, essentially outlawing dissident thought, you can also control their activities. From the 1920s and for most of the twentieth century, the FBI and other federal agencies identified the Communists as enemy aliens, in part, because they harbor patterns of thought that did not conform to those of the state.

With the early Red Scare and later, the Communist hysteria in various decades, the U.S. government was becoming more antidemocratic, for it was not just Communism but all thought and dissent that became suspect. All police states seek absolute control throughout society, and therefore it is no coincidence that as the FBI was on its witch hunt against political outsiders, state power was being extended downward, in the search for ever-greater control at the state and local levels. Consider that what appears in the 1920s was consistent with what appears in many police states: the formation of a political police force. From the 1920s onward, in order to combat political outsiders, many state governments form a partnership with local police officials with the goal of stamping out grassroots democracy. These Red Squads, a political police force, engage in surveillance; disruption; and, in many instances, the destruction of political organizations often active in nonviolent political expression. The Red Squads acted in similar ways as the FBI did, as agents of the state seeking to instill in American society social and political conformity.

Yet in spite of political repression on the federal, state, and local levels, for much of the twentieth century, many mass-based movements persisted for two reasons: one, they appealed to many Americans, and two, as political repression was mounted against these movements, eventually the government believed that the political crisis that triggered such movements had ended. The police state that came to fruition during the Bush administration was in some ways different from other ones; in the police states that appeared, for example, in Germany and Italy, the destruction of democracy that precipitated them was rapid. On the other hand, the police state in the United States developed after various historical twists and turns, some of which, for a time, slowed down the growth of the police state. One important reason why it took longer for a police state to develop in the United States than it did in other Western countries is the interplay between the government's response to key events and the viability of political movements as the events unfolded. For example, consider what took place in response to the shock and impact of the Great Depression. In contrast to Germany of the 1930s, progressive political movements reappeared in the United States and were able to shape policy making, while in Germany, by the 1930s, a contributing factor, no doubt, to the rise of Hitler and to Nazi Germany was the political Right's success in having vanquished the Left. Nonetheless, even though progressives had achieved some degree of limited success during the Great Depression, as seen in Roosevelt's adoption of Socialist measures, political repression did not entirely disappear. The reflexive action taken by the state at the height of the Depression and during World War II was the mounting of political repression against political outsiders. Appearing as part of this twisted path toward the American police state was what took place in the 1950s through the 1970s. As mass-based political movements began to reappear, making for a transition from the Old to the New Left, so did the bureaucratic means to eliminate these newly emerging political movements. The development of other essentially political police agencies within the federal government, which would supplement the work of the FBI, such as the CIA, NSA, and a host of other intelligence gatherers on the federal and state levels were an ominous sign, paving the way for the growth of the American police state. So throughout the 1930s and 1940s, the FBI was engaging in surveillance of various alleged political outsiders; by the end of World War II and the start of the cold war, state repression was accelerating during the Truman administration with the passage of the National Security Act, as well as the growth of the CIA. Inside the federal government, there was an increasing subordination of the legislative branch to the executive branch, which would spell the eventual end of procedural democracy in the United States. Coinciding with this development, the increasing concentration of power in the context of what was being expressed as a permanent emergency—the Communist threat—the government became more determined to eliminate mass democracy. For instance, prior to the Truman administration, during World War II and in the name of a national emergency, Roosevelt ordered the internment of Japanese American citizens. This targeting of outsiders identified as an internal and external threat continues throughout the twentieth century, associated with the alleged menace; first Communism, and later, terrorism, was propelling America forward to create a police state. With an ongoing national emergency being made permanent over the course of many decades, along with creating an atmosphere of national hysteria, political repression was unleashed without restraint. At the same time, while mass democracy was being crushed in the United

States, foreign policy in the postwar period remained consistent: to extend control over more people and more territory, resulting in the formation of alliances with dictatorships so as to crush democracy overseas as well. With the reorganization of the military after World War II, the military industrial complex became another key component in the twisted road to police state practices, based on the premise of permanent war making, with a cold war arms race, the sending of troops, and the establishment of military bases across the globe. This is another defining feature of a police state: a nation placed in an ongoing state of mobilization to prepare and fight wars throughout the globe. Police states, such as the one developing at this time in the United States, incorporate war making into normalized state functions. Permanent war making translates into the global subversion of democracy. Supplementing the military in undermining democracy overseas, the CIA was one of many federal agencies during the second half of the twentieth century that was carrying out an essentially antidemocratic mission in the name of national security, which was brought to bear on those countries that aspired to be self-determining or which mounted a campaign to remove their colonizers. But for U.S. policy makers, all this was equated with Communism. Whether anti-Communism was applied to domestic or foreign policy, the notion of political reality as an either/or scenario manifests an authoritarianism often associated with police states. There is only one view and one truth—the state's official truth—which is not to be questioned. On the other hand, for mass movements from the 1930s to the 1970s, their overall goal was to uplift the downtrodden, which meant questioning the uses of state power. Whatever can be said in assessing the successes and failures of progressive movements in the United States, there is no doubt that in many ways, their limitations can be attributed to the intensive scale and scope of political repression.

Consider the extent to which the FBI made use of the Cointelpro program against many political organizations, clearly diminishing their effectiveness and in most cases, fundamentally undermining the organizations. In many ways, the Cointelpro program was significant in paving the way for a police state, for progressive movements that developed after Cointelpro were much smaller and less effective in advancing mass democracy; for without viable political participation, there is no democracy in the United States. What the government had in mind by eliminating these mass-based movements was to have as complete control as possible over peoples' minds and bodies. It is no coincidence that from the 1950s, the CIA was using a clandestine torture program through the MKULTRA program. Here again, a creeping authoritarianism is prominent within the federal government in that the CIA is also exporting mind control and torture overseas. American foreign policy in many parts of the world had this antidemocratic aspect in that U.S.-backed dictators had the assistance of the CIA in order to suppress any form of dissent.

On the domestic front, from the 1960s, another precondition for a police state was emerging in that the Red Squads were exhibiting an authoritarianism that was becoming more a part of American political culture as well. Such Red Squad activity amounted to a strategy in which democracy was subverted at the grassroots level. In service of this goal, the surveillance by the Red Squads appears on a broad scale, covering both political and nonpolitical activities. So by the early 1970s, there appears a pattern of undermining democratic opposition to state policy.

The ending of procedural democracy was yet another step toward the establishment of a permanent police state. The Constitution is supposed to place legal limits on the concentration of power within parts of the government. Instead, with such wholesale political repression of mass-based movements through the use of national emergency, the government was consistently stepping outside the legal boundaries contained within the Constitution. As a result, by the early 1970s, as large-scale political movements were on the wane, the government was moving a step closer to a police state, in particular, as the events of Watergate unfolded, which became in many ways, a dress rehearsal for a police state. Watergate represented a political assault, not just on the supposed external threats to the Nixon administration, but political repression was extended to its internal enemies. That meant taking action against the Democratic Party by seeking to rig an election and resulting in one of the most blatant attempts to destroy procedural democracy. The fact that the Nixon administration had plans to imprison its enemies is indicative of an ongoing historical pattern in the ways in which the U.S. government deals with its perceived opposition. As it had done in the past, the government employed antidemocratic federal agencies to spy on, infiltrate, and undermine various organizations.

On the surface, it seems that in the post-Watergate era, the Church Committee Hearings initiated various reforms, and the tendency toward a full-blown police state had been halted; but instead, the twisted path toward a police state continued. If the post-Watergate era represented anything, it was a response to tone down some of the more extremist initiatives undertaken by the U.S. government and, as in previous periods, there was a temporary relaxation followed by reformism. The reason for such reformism was that the extremism of the Nixon administration, as had been the case with its predecessors, drove the government to become dysfunctional. But ironically, the end result of these reforms was that they made the march toward a police state inevitable. Consider one of the most important post-Watergate reforms, the FISA court. While the court appeared to be a reform intended to end illegal surveillance, in the end, it had the opposite effect, making government surveillance legal for the first time and over time, functioning to rubber-stamp requests for surveillance.

In addition, in the post-Watergate era, the government continued to take advantage of opportunities to enhance its power. It did so by making the government more authoritarian as part of an effort to reassert its control in response to the Watergate scandal and the defeat in Vietnam. The reassertion of state power at home and overseas was yet another contributing factor that would lead to the eventual formation of a permanent police state. A factor in this reassertion of power was the absence of mass-based political movements in the decades that followed the 1970s. Also at this time, the concentration of power within one branch of government had been manifesting itself increasingly in terms of an imperial presidency. Postwar presidential administrations define their power in relation to foreign policy initiatives. This explains, in large part, why the foreign policies of post-Nixon administrations (Ford, Carter, Bush senior, Clinton, and George W. Bush) centered on a continuation of a foreign policy that was outwardly anti-Communist and antiterrorist but in reality was driven by the maintenance and extension of an American empire around the globe. Such antidemocratic foreign policies, which continued to equate nationalism with support for Communism and terrorism, increased the role and power of presidents, federal agencies entrusted with intelligence gathering, and policy makers, who sought to remove anti-American regimes from power, replacing them with undemocratic ones. Post-Watergate administrations were largely successful in finding various ways around the so-called Watergate reforms, in seeking to enlarge the powers of presidents at home and overseas and continuing to erode what remained of procedural democracy.

Another factor that contributed to the erosion of democracy in America was the replacement of political movements that challenged the power of government with those that, by and large, supported its goal of becoming more authoritarian. As progressive movements declined by the mid-1970s, they were replaced by their much more extremist counterparts on the Right. Coupled with this reassertion of state power was a developing right-wing political movement and a culture more and more reflective of a police state in which surveillance has become a way of life. Some of the surveillance was justified on the grounds that it was essential in order to combat terrorism, and yet, so much of the surveillance was unrelated to any possible terrorist threat. To this day, an ongoing surveillance of daily activities takes place in many social settings from the shopping mall to the supermarket to the workplace in which the bottom line is that Americans are all regarded as suspects because we are all deemed to be criminals without having committed any crime. In addition, surveillance is employed against individuals and organizations who are often engaged in what should be considered lawful association and who are viewed with great suspicion not just because of what they might do but because of what they think. This helps lay the groundwork for a police state, which by definition, functions to monitor and essentially infiltrate all social activities. Intelligence gathering through such surveillance becomes an end in itself because the government can always manufacture what appears to be a good reason for gathering as much intelligence as possible about everyone. This is the mindset of intelligence gatherers in the federal government with an authoritarianism, which expresses itself as seeking total control in terms of dominating all thought and action. Underlying such extensive surveillance is a fear of democracy; a fear of diverse viewpoints; and finally, of those who take issue with the actions of policy makers. As a result, the United States has developed a sophisticated national security apparatus, which was being bureaucratized during the Truman administration and which has grown throughout various administrations since then as a result of their obsession with excessive secrecy. In its final form, a police state not only spies on everyone, it seeks to monopolize and control the flow of information and its sources. This allows policy makers to enact policy without mass participation.

With the decline of mass movements, all that was left for the United States to do to form a police state was to get rid of what remained of procedural democracy. The first attempt to do this occurred during the Nixon administration. Consistent throughout all post-Watergate administrations was the effort to establish clear links between internal and external threats. In other words, the state's power must become more and more absolute in order to combat this terrorist threat. The other victim in this war on terrorism is rule of law, for a police state is a manifestation of absolute power exercised in the absence of legal limits. One prerequisite for a police state's exercise of absolute power is the concentration of power in one branch of government, and so in the latter part of the twentieth and twenty-first centuries, presidents operate with ever greater frequency outside of the U.S. Constitution and according to their arbitrary will. So by the time we reach the presidency of George W. Bush, the executive branch had become a branch that saw itself as above the law while making law. The state came to embody the will of George W. Bush and his inner circle. In this regard, the Bush administration functioned as other police states have, in Germany, Russia, Italy, and Spain. Most indicative of a police state mentality exhibited by recent presidents from Nixon to George W. Bush was that they truly believe they did not break any laws because of their belief that they had sole authority to act as lawmakers. The spark that ignited the transition toward the final form of an American police state was the attacks on the World Trade Towers in 1993 and 2001. At the same time that this permanent police state came into being, what took place was the elimination of what remained of procedural democracy and rule of law. In response to these attacks, the Clinton and both Bush administrations had the opportunity to twist law in such a way as to make diverse viewpoints illegal. Any and all opposition to this war on terrorism would unleash the unquestioned power of the federal government through wholesale surveillance, roundups, and preventive detention as well as political trials.

Overall, the formation of an American police state was the end result of establishing a link between internal and external terrorist threats in a time of national emergency. Afterward, the government acted outside the Constitution by passing the Patriot Act, the Military Commissions Act, and a host of other measures, which produced a direct assault on civil liberties. By using an abstract definition of terrorism, the government had all the rationale it needed to consider all citizens and noncitizens terror suspects. The clearest example of an American police state that acted like so many other police states is its use of preventive detention. In one example—extraordinary rendition—all the government has to do amounts to accusing anyone of anything related to terrorism, and this was a sufficient reason to seize and ship individuals elsewhere to be tortured. The use of torture, unfortunately, is an all-too-common practice used by democracies that have degenerated into police states. Torture as state policy simply means that a police state is exercising total domination over the minds and bodies of those identified as enemies of the state. The U.S. government also used torture to justify the maintenance of a state of permanent emergency. Torture as state policy was also employed as a propaganda tool in the Bush administration's campaign to rationalize an aggressive war against Iraq. All too common in many police states is the tendency to manufacture reasons to go to war so as to create mass mobilization to support the war. Police states also function in a state of permanent war in part through the use of shock troops, specialized forces used to instill terror on a conquered nation, such as the use of mercenaries, like Blackwater Corp. in Iraq. Such corporate warriors fit well into the idea of a police state that operates outside the law. The twisted and extensive use of signing statements also indicates that an administration is functioning outside the law. In a distorted extension of the theory of a unitary executive, President Bush's excessive use of signing statements resulted in giving him dictatorial powers.

One obvious question must be asked: what is the future of the American police state? If history tells us anything about police states, it is that they all eventually crumble, in large part, because over time, they become dysfunctional. The same can be said of the police state of the Bush administration. During the second term, there were indications of a breakdown in how this police state functioned. Some of the clearest symptoms of this dysfunction were the revelations of torture at Abu Ghraib, the National Security Agency's surveillance program, and the large number of prisoners released from Guantanamo Bay. In addition, opposition mounted to the reauthorization of the Patriot Act and the Supreme Court ruling in the Boumediene case, which called into question the use of the Military Commissions Act. In the early days of the Obama administration, the trend seems to point toward an American police state that will be modified, not eliminated; the evidence appears in the mixed messages of the administration.

CHAPTER 1

Growth of State Power and the Assault on Democracy

The American police state, which developed during the George W. Bush administration, has historical roots in post-Revolutionary America. A key theme that emerged during the Revolution was the gulf of interests separating wealthy colonial elites from laborers, servants, slaves, and Native Americans. The possibility of unrest and rebellion concerned elites: if alliances formed, they would be the common enemy. Mass mobilization in support of elite rule had proven useful in ridding the colonies of the British: in a brilliant example of political sleight of hand, colonial upper classes had effectively shifted lower class outrage to their British counterparts. Taxation, which impacted the profits of rich colonialists, was portrayed as harmful to all. From the revolt against taxation to the political revolt, mass mobilization in support of democracy, against the British Empire's aristocratic principles, made the Revolution possible. In the name of democracy, an armed force was created, consisting mostly of white males deemed reliable, with steady employment and a little land. Indians, Negroes, white servants, and unemployed males were left out. Nonetheless, appeals to mobilize in the name of democracy raised expectations and demands to incorporate novel, political principles—equality, equal representation, and checks and balances on the power of government by establishing legislatures whose membership didn't favor elites. Still, women, African Americans, and Native Americans were excluded.

Pennsylvania was the state that most embodied democratic principles. During the Revolution, it strongly advocated extending democracy to all social segments and requiring its militias to represent that diverse mix. But soon, new leaders emerged, opposing mass-based politics. Robert Morris, a wealthy Philadelphia merchant, promised to provide badly needed financial assistance requested by Congress and Pennsylvania if he could also control state and federal financial systems and official appointments.[1] He helped organize the Constitutional Convention, where elites warned that the current state structure created "excessive democracy." So New York, Massachusetts, and New Hampshire strengthened the Senate and the executive, "to tame the lower house."[2]

In Western Massachusetts in 1786, near-destitute farmers facing increased taxation and debt unsuccessfully sought relief from the legislature. To prevent the seizure of their farms, they armed themselves and organized under former Revolutionary War Captain Daniel Shays, who ordered them to capture the Springfield arsenal. Despite the suppression of the rebellion, the political impact favored the rebels, who received general amnesty. Many won seats in the state legislature. Elites at the Constitutional Convention concluded that the Articles of Confederation couldn't stem excessive democracy from the states. Elite rule was becoming a characteristic feature of American politics, diluting democracy and using state power to confront and control democratic forces.

Nevertheless, the democratic surge had a lasting impact on the U.S. Constitution. The framers needed to establish a government that could promote and protect property, regulate the economy, create an elaborate infrastructure. and acquire native Indian lands, adhering to the policy of North American expansion, while allowing the democratic surge from below to be both expressed and contained. The framers removed the people's direct access to government, constructing a large, federal policy-making body, removed from the masses. The federalist principle of government was based on assumptions about the nature of the masses. Madison's idea of a majority faction ruled by its passionate nature fits well into elites' antidemocratic thinking. Still, the framers knew that strong democratic sentiments among the masses had to be expressed within government's structure. The antifederalists feared the power of a federal government; hence, the incorporation of a Bill of Rights into the Constitution. Another concession involved granting some independence to state and local governments. These measures worked, manufacturing popular support, but while most white males supported ratification, other segments had no voice. The Constitution was silent about women, African Americans, Indians, the poor; more striking is the weak role of the masses in federal policy making.

Democratic participation is, at best, indirect. Constitutional arrangements defined the legal functions of each branch, weakening popular participation: Congress and the president are elected by delegated representatives; senators are chosen by state legislators; elections are staged at different times; Senate membership is based on equal representation; and while the people elect representatives to the House, there are two-year term limits, all of which weaken popular participation. The concept of dividing power between two houses further limits democracy, erecting institutional roadblocks to efficient passage of legislation that could benefit the masses. Lifetime appointments for Supreme Court justices help the Court resist democratic pressures from below.

Policy makers would follow a consistent direction, enlarging state power and pursuing territorial expansion while confronting opposition, while official ideology stated that such expansion increased liberty. The Northwest Ordinance of 1787 expressed the government's intention to acquire Indian property from the Ohio River and the Great Lakes to Mississippi,[3] insuring that its power would grow. Once settled by whites, that land would be served by representative government, a key element in American empire building, so long as the United States could keep expanding without foreign interference. By creating a powerful nation, the United States could face Europe from a position of strength. In his farewell address, Washington communicated that America should avoid foreign entanglements and foster the economic and territorial goals that the Monroe Doctrine expressed. Its main premise was to stay out of European affairs and preserve America's liberty of movement within North America. While reassuring Europe that it would remain neutral, America also sent the message that Europe should neither seek new colonies in North America nor transfer any to America. America had declared its right to promote its national interest in the Western hemisphere.

Collectively, unilateralism, exceptionalism, and the Monroe Doctrine facilitated the federal government's use of various means against those resisting the land grab, primarily Indians. In the name of liberty, that is, a liberty to expand, they were identified as an alien race, the essential "other." They hindered the growth of government's power, whose expansion was partly justified by a racist ideology portraying them ironically, as enemy aliens: outsiders in their native land. In Texas, government offices paid bounties for Indian scalps. The antidemocratic nature of the American state begins to reveal itself as the government confronts a group hostile to its goals of expansion and empire building. Acquisition of land through "Indian removal" became a fixation. It was a massive population transfer. In the late eighteenth century, most Americans lived approximately 50 miles from the Eastern Seaboard; by 1840, nearly five million had traveled through the Appalachian Mountains.[4] While in 1820, 120,000 Indians lived east of the Mississippi, by 1844, there were less than 30,000.[5] Contact with Europeans had a devastating impact, especially as Indians were exposed to diseases to which they had no immunity. There also were examples of intentional exposures; smallpox-infested blankets, distributed to Indians by the U.S. Army, caused a pandemic from 1836 to 1840.

Some actions were intentionally genocidal. Between 1790 and 1915, the War Department recorded 52 wars with tribes.[7] By destroying Indian agriculture, the government's methods had the effect of ethnocide, causing many Indian casualties from disease and starvation; of the 17,000 Cherokees forced to march up to 1,000 miles in the "Trail of Tears" to allow white settlement east of the Mississippi, a quarter perished.[8] Indians surrendered huge tracts of land that later comprised much of Arkansas, Ohio, Missouri, and Michigan.[9] In the West, the Army waged campaigns to destroy whole tribes when Indians resisted. During Andrew Jackson's administration, the Indian Removal Act of 1830 allowed whites to take over much of Alabama, Florida, Tennessee, Georgia, Mississippi, and sections of Kentucky and North Carolina through the forced signing of 94 treaties.[10]

State power in service of empire building was also used against another group identified as "the other," African Americans, who were exploited as a labor source. Slavery institutionalized extreme political repression as a way of life. While the Ordinance of 1787 prohibited slavery, territories to the South were allowed to have it. Kentucky, Tennessee, Mississippi, and Alabama joined the Union as slave states. Slavery was already established in Louisiana and Florida. By 1830, it existed as a cradle-to-grave system of social control over African Americans. Considered "tools that talk," slaves were brutally treated because they were seen as subhuman—purchased, like any commodity—from the moment of their arrival in the United States. Slave state codes gave the states legal authority to grant property rights to slave owners, eliminating any notion of equal treatment under the law. Slave codes protected the owner's property; when slaves escaped, governors used militias called Slave Patriots to capture them.

Throughout U.S. history, a tug of war has continued between political movements and the government's antidemocratic policies against excluded groups. A political movement can slow down or even reverse repressive measures by disrupting and reorienting state policy, pushing back against repressive measures, challenging official labels of otherness, while pressuring the government to enact reforms. Perhaps Indians failed to stem the government's expansionist policy because they couldn't effectively disrupt the government's agenda or its extremist measures.

By contrast, African Americans have had some success challenging their otherness, partly due to the forms of resistance they chose and social conditions before the Civil War. State policies were geared toward preserving slavery, rather than perpetrating ethnocide or genocide against African Americans. Passive resistance was possible; slaves damaged property or worked especially slowly or not at all. Some resorted to arson, which terrified slave owners. The ultimate and most dangerous resistance was escape. Captured slaves faced severe punishments. Less frequent and less successful was armed rebellion, such as the one led by Denmark Vesey, who attempted to initiate a large-scale rebellion by burning Charleston. Although heavily armed, Vesey and his coconspirators, betrayed by an informant, were captured and hanged. Nat Turner's revolt resulted in the killing of over 60 whites, but retaliation was swift and brutal, resulting in a bloody massacre.

The Abolitionists prove that political movements can disrupt repressive state policies and advance democracy. To promote their cause, they exploited the emerging political rift between free and slave states. Their efforts to assist slaves contributed to the Democratic Party's fragmentation between North and South. Southern states were determined to halt the exodus of slaves with the Fugitive Slave Act. The Kansas-Nebraska Act allowed settlers to choose to be free or slave states. Abolitionists pushed party politics and the nation to finally settle the question. In addition to the bold but failed John Brown Raid, the continued flight of slaves to the North inflamed an already charged political atmosphere. Divisions within the Republican Party surfaced over the Kansas-Nebraska Act, eventually turning it into the antislavery party of Abraham Lincoln. What tipped the Civil War in favor of the North was the value that black volunteers brought to the Union cause. Slaves had fled the plantations, denying the Confederate Army sufficient supplies. Abolitionists simultaneously exerted legislative pressures; before the war's end, slavery had been banned. In 1866, Congress passed the Tenth Amendment and the Civil Rights Act.

The success of the Abolitionists suggests that the government can accommodate reformism, providing its core interests remain unaffected. The movement settled the question of whether the American economy would favor free or slave labor. Even without the Abolitionists, the issue would have had to be resolved. So political movements with a democratic outlook can disturb and affect policy making. American government can accommodate itself to pressure from political movements which strive to make America more democratic. That was because the reformism of the Abolitionists did not interfere with the government's primary prerogative: to enlarge state power.

Feminism was another political movement which shaped policy making without challenging the state's primary interest. The movement organized around the goal of gender equality, drawing inspiration from women who wrote about the bias of male revolutions. In "Vindication of the Rights of Women," Mary Wollstonecraft responded to Edmund Burke's statement that "a woman is but an animal and not of the highest order," replying that gender differences were nothing more than the prejudicial reflections of a male culture and were culturally, not biologically, rooted. The otherness of women, she argued, was manufactured. Boys are socialized with positive ideas: men are dominant, controlling, and assertive; girls are taught to be submissive. Such cultural prejudices are reinforced with legal ones. According to John Stuart Mill in "On the Subjagation of Women," legal invisibility appears in the marriage contract, locking a woman into a relationship with an intimate oppressor. For Lucy Stone, it illustrates that gender relations are charged with issues of power and control, granting men legal authority to control women's bodies and possessions. The bottom line for feminists was legal reform. The Seneca Falls Convention attacked the prejudiced notions of otherness and transformed women's rights from an idea into a political movement: a call to action to fight for the right to vote. The movement began practicing tactics used by Abolitionists, as feminists had fought alongside them to eliminate slavery. By the end of the Civil War, Abolitionists stood with Republicans, organizing support for black male suffrage. The thinking was that it would be the Negroes' hour. Feminists were told they would have to wait their turn. Abolitionists justified their rejection of women's suffrage, claiming the vote at this time was more important for blacks.

Ultimately, feminists would succeed by engaging in the disruptive electoral politics that had proven successful for the Abolitionists. The period 1890–1920 marked a shift in emphasis of the National American Women's Suffrage Association. Under Susan B Anthony's leadership, it originally advocated a strategy of winning a constitutional amendment but then chose to pursue a state-by-state referendum, a strategy that was partially successful. In 1910, Washington became the first state to pass a women's suffrage amendment in 14 years, igniting victories in California, Oregon, Arizona, Kansas, Montana, and Illinois. Still, the movement fell short of the 36 states needed. The movement then adopted the confrontational style of British suffragists, who used violence, such as burning down buildings, vandalizing artwork, invading the House of Commons, and blowing up mailboxes, to bring attention to the cause and to pressure the government.[11] Under Alice Paul's leadership, the Congress Union was formed, pressuring the Democrats, and holding President Wilson responsible for women not having the right to vote. Paul used the Congressional Union to promote the message, bolstered by the fact that women had the vote in a quarter of the states in the electoral college.[12] They stepped up the pressure to add key Western states. The combined federal and state strategy was more aggressive. Paul employed her understanding of electoral politics, using the newly formed women's party to threaten Wilson with defeat in states that had granted women suffrage; he was reelected with their support. The suffragists maintained the pressure, picketing the White House until some were arrested and imprisoned, whereupon they began lengthy hunger strikes, another British tactic. Alice Paul was force-fed and underwent psychiatric examination. This generated sympathy, as the courts invalidated the suffragists' imprisonment. The public viewed them as heroines, and their tactics paid off. Congress's rules committee, which had tabled a suffrage amendment, now released it to floor debate. Jeannette Rankin, the first woman representative, introduced it to the House, where it passed. After another year and a half, it moved to the Senate where it won approval. On August 26, 1920, the thirty-sixth state, Tennessee, ratified the amendment, allowing every American woman the right to vote.

Reformist victories by women and African American males notwithstanding, the U.S. government continued to pursue its related goals, expansionism, and attacks on democracy. Having settled the question of free versus slave labor, the government attacked social forces that embodied economic democracy, the Labor and Socialist movements. As broad-based democratic movements and examples of political dissent—the lifeblood of truly democratic societies—they were threatening economic and political elites. Repression was ramped up. Political repression was now the response to any perceived crisis that threatened the reproductive functions of state power. State repression of organized labor usually happened during an economic downturn. The American Labor movement in the late nineteenth and early twentieth centuries sustained some of the most intense forms of American political repression.

Tactics against organized labor were all-encompassing, and the company town was a prime example. In Pullman, Illinois, the company owned everything, from factories and stores to schools and churches, hiring and controlling everyone who worked there. Private security forces were employed to suppress labor organizing and to control peoples' movements, a hallmark of political repression. Corporations could count on the government—police, militias, even federal forces—to combat labor organizers. Labor's major weapon, the strike, faced the labor injunction, a legal means of identifying labor actions as criminal. The use of injunctions illustrates how legal means are used to repress workplace dissent. They would bar regular union activities, such as picketing and meetings, and were so arbitrary as to prevent strikers from assembling within a certain number of blocks from their employers. The use of restraining orders threatening immediate arrest also was widespread; judges would issue them without due process, on the word of the corporations' attorneys.[13]

Like Labor, the Socialist movement began in the decades following the Civil War. Drawing upon the writings of Karl Marx and the activities of the First International Workman's Party, the Socialist movement became Americanized. Eugene Victor Debs popularized Socialist ideas and connected them to the Labor movement. The 1870s provide evidence of how crises drive state repression against broad-based democratic movements. The growth of Labor and Socialist movements coincided with the depression of 1873–1878. Unionism was reaching a fever pitch; many new unions, some national, were created, with membership at several hundred thousand. Strikes were increasingly common over working conditions and the eight-hour workday. With unemployed workers taking to the streets, the gulf between the haves and have-nots became palpable; police were called in to break up demonstrations.[14] Demonstrators became targets. Nationwide attacks and arrests were common against striking workers and demonstrators. Fearing loss of power and control, state elites fixated on doing whatever was necessary to suppress what they perceived as excessive democracy. Consider the 1877 railroad strike; at issue were working conditions and wage cuts. The strike went nationwide, affecting freight and passenger trains. State elites feared the democratic surge of support for striking workers. The government called in tens of thousands of militiamen and federal troops to crush the strike. It set the pattern for the government's response against perceived, internal-external threats. State elites had made a connection between the labor unrest of the 1870s and the 1871 uprising of the Paris Commune, confirming their fears of foreign-inspired Socialist influences, inspiring derogatory references in newspapers to aliens and the commune. It was the first of many Red Scares. This manufactured perception of Red influence created a reactionary tide against social change. Efforts to uplift the masses through labor reform were seen as the work of enemy aliens with Red inclinations, dismissed as un-American or Communist. From then on, the government would consistently overreact to such events, producing hysteria among political elites, accelerating antidemocratic measures against radical-democratic movements that developed in response to political and economic crises.

Although less severe than the 1873 depression, the 1882–1886 downturn was noteworthy for its nationwide impact. Again, state elites believed that foreign influences caused the reemergence of labor activism and the growth of Socialist parties, although these activities were largely homegrown. The use of the strike as the democratic weapon of choice by the Knights of Labor, for example, and a splinter group of the Socialist Labor Party, the International Working Peoples Party (IWPA) angered economic elites. The Knights, which had won a notable victory in 1883–1884 against Union Pacific Railroad, was highly democratic, offering membership to any worker, regardless of employer, nationality, or race. They presented a real challenge to the interests of economic elites, advocating government takeovers of transportation and communications as well as workers' cooperatives and the elimination of "wage slavery."[15] The IWPA was prepared to employ violence to defend activists, and both organizations used strikes and reformist measures to uplift workers' living standards, particularly by advocating for the eight-hour workday.

The U.S. government seized on the events of May 1–4, 1886, as an opportunity to respond with excessive measures. To achieve the eight-hour workday, workers held the largest nationwide strike ever on May 1, resulting in the granting of shorter hours to tens of thousands of workers. But this was achieved at great human cost; in Milwaukee, five were killed when the Wisconsin National Guard opened fire on peaceful demonstrators.[16] Government violence was also employed against Chicago's unions in the Haymarket bombing. Tensions had been brewing over a strike at the Cormick-Harvester factory, where local police and a private police force led regular attacks on workers and picketers. On May 3, Chicago police fired into a crowd of strikers. The next day, a peaceful meeting was held by the IWPA but when it ended, a bomb was thrown into a crowd of police, setting off a poisonous national backlash against labor and radicals.[17] The incident demonstrates how state repression strives to thoroughly eliminate perceived threats, using ideology to create conformity of thought and action. In the aftermath of the bombing, the essence of law, which should ensure equal treatment, is made into its opposite, the instrument for implementing arbitrary treatment. Chicago police arrested approximately 150 people, held for hours without warrant or charges.[18] Political trials were held, another effect of political repression. Any semblance of habeas corpus was absent; the judge was anything but impartial, and no believable evidence connected the defendants to the bombings. But the trial had its intended outcome: it suppressed democratic movements. The state unleashed a propaganda campaign to rationalize its extraordinary actions during what it described as a nationwide emergency. This campaign, largely directed toward immigrants and union members, communicated the idea of the threat posed by the alien "other." Soon, state legislatures were developing anti-labor bills, while local police forces, militias, and the Army were strengthened.

The government's primary goal was eliminating those who questioned state power, especially expansion through territorial acquisition. This expansion, pursued with increasing vigor by the early twentieth century, coincided with the development of bureaucratic agencies within the federal government, which would become self-perpetuating through the identification of perceived threats to state power. They would eventually assume the character of political police organizations, promoting political mind control, with the goal of mass conformity. The Federal Bureau of Investigation would become the pioneering federal political police agency, growing along with the government's efforts to extend power and territorial control.

Beyond North America, military intervention became the new tool for subduing nations that resisted American influence, creating an American mission to suppress democracy abroad as well as at home. The government sold these interventions to the American people as an effort to promote democracy while using military force to neutralize nationalist/democratic urges overseas. This policy of Unilateralism was often successful, beginning with America's first attempt at regime change, the removal of the Hawaiian monarchy in 1893. Queen Liliuokalani's democratic initiatives within the framework of a new constitution proved unacceptable to America. It would have, in many ways, negated Hawaii's status as an American protectorate. By fostering resistance to reforms and with the dramatic appearance of American troops, the Hawaiian experiment with democracy was over.

The Spanish-American War of 1898 set a pattern of selling expansion as a means of furthering democracy, while actually suppressing it.

Global expansionism was the cover for spreading antidemocratic practices worldwide. It marked the beginning of presidencies whose power derived from foreign policy, starting with McKinley. There was growing concern within his administration over the Cuban independence movement and the possibility that Cubans might one day be self-governing. An independent Cuba would not be at America's beck and call. Reforms, especially land redistribution, would threaten more than $50 million in American investments, primarily in agriculture.[19] Like other interventions, the Spanish-American War needed a provocation—it was the sinking of the Maine. The theme was established: American political repression continued at home while, overseas, the government claimed to advance democracy. This ideology projected a noble democratic image for America while its real intent was extending power. To get Congress to support military intervention, McKinley agreed to the Teller Amendment, a statement of American support for a democratic Cuba. But soon, America rejected it, favoring instead the antidemocratic Platt Amendment, which promoted a U.S. takeover. After the Spanish surrender, the American government revealed to the Cubans that the Teller Amendment was no longer valid. The United States had passed a law giving it the right to determine Cuba's domestic affairs, including maintaining bases there and the right to veto any treaties it wanted to forge with other countries. Under the Platt Amendment, Cuba existed as a sovereign nation only if it conformed to undemocratic guidelines that the United States had established.

This antidemocratic, expansionist ideology relied on racism to justify foreign interventions. Perhaps the arrogance of the colonizer drives it to resort to racist doctrine. In the Philippines, U.S. racism was also a response to Filipino nationalism and its resistance to the McKinley administration's idea to extend an American presence beyond Manila. The Philippine people wanted independence and resisted becoming another American possession like Cuba. The new Philippine nation established a constitutional, self-governing framework. Days later, it declared war against American forces on the island. The Philippine resistance viewed itself as engaged in a struggle to repel a foreign invader while American officials used racist contempt, referring to the Filipinos as "goo-goos." Faced with the overwhelming superiority of American military might, the Filipinos resorted to guerrilla tactics. American colonizers did not expect the violent scope of resistance. Consider the Balangiga incident: "A few remained on sentry duty while the rest ate breakfast. The town's police chief strolled up to one of the sentries, said a few pleasant words and then suddenly produced a long knife and stabbed him. . . . scores of rebels who had infiltrated the town poured out of their hiding places. They fiercely set upon the unarmed Americans stabbing and hacking them to death."[20]

There was a violent American backlash. American forces were directed to "take no prisoners." Soldiers killed indiscriminately. Villages were razed. Filipinos were depicted as the "other," objects targeted for inhumane treatment and methods of torture, including "the 'water cure,' in which sections of bamboo were forced down the throats of prisoners and then used to fill the prisoners' stomachs with dirty water until they swelled in torment. Soldiers would jump on the prisoners' stomach to force the water out, often repeating the process until the victim either informed or died."[21] The Philippine people eventually succumbed to U.S. rule, having sustained more than 200,000 deaths.[22] Mass democracy, the foundation of the United States, was at odds with a government seeking to extend control over people and territory in North America and overseas. The example of ancient Rome teaches that the power of the state grew in direct proportion to its seizure of territory: militarism became the true measure of political success. Roman rulers became dictators. The irony is that the Constitution established the United States government to function as a democracy, yet it acts in practice as an empire.

This trend, in which foreign policy and military intervention defined success, was reinforced through the administrations of Roosevelt and Taft. Their public descriptions of America as a beacon of democracy masked their intentions to undermine and conquer the sovereign authority of governments that stood in the way of America's imperial designs. Nicaragua, for example, was building a canal. At first, all was well with President Zelaya, but things changed when U.S. policy makers decided to pursue a Panama route, which for Roosevelt necessitated creating a Republic of Panama. But Panama was a province of Colombia. With experience gained from overthrowing Hawaii's government, Roosevelt formulated a plan to create a nationalist movement seeking independence. With the support of American troops, these so-called rebels were depicted as emerging leaders who would create a Republic of Panama. Zelaya accepted the loss of the canal and America's role in the new republic's creation. The "Roosevelt Corollary," essentially the Monroe Doctrine extended to Latin America, set the stage for an eventual overthrow of Zelaya during the Taft administration. So when Zelaya attempted to prevent American business interests from interfering with national goals, a plan was hatched to oust him. As in the United States, mass-based popular movements overseas resisted antidemocratic measures; soon, Nicaraguans rose up in defiance of the occupation. Although Cesar Sandino's rebellion succeeded in removing a U.S. military presence, he was overthrown by General Somoza. The Somoza family dictatorship was finally overthrown by the Sandinista National Liberation Front in the late 1970s. In Nicaragua, as in the United States, democratic movements had the capacity to push back against repression. But the overall trend persists: state power expands, and with it, comes territorial acquisition through militarism, producing political repression, the ultimate aim of which is to destroy democracy. Yet, America still projects an image of fostering democracy, demonstrating the influence that political movements have had in framing and adhering to democratic ideals. Democratic principles are taken seriously only when there is consistent pressure from below. The trend toward increasing state power and repression inside and outside the United States cannot be understood apart from the American presidency's expanding power, facilitated by a growing federal bureaucracy, in particular, the State Department's foreign affairs bureaucracy. The military also was key, expanding in size and sophistication. The Army, for example, had 30,000 men in the 1890s, while 70,000 troops would later be committed to the Philippines alone.[23]

The enormous resources now at the presidency's disposal and perceived threats posed at home and overseas caused the office of the president to begin to rely heavily on military force. In intervention after intervention, first against Spain and then in the Philippines and Europe, presidential power grew through the aggrandized role of commander in chief. After the war with Spain, McKinley "held the reins of military governments in Cuba and the Philippines without Congressional oversight."[24]

The Wilson ideal of exporting democracy developed as a response to World War I and the demise of traditional empires, while preserving a dominant presence for the United States, which initiated policies against what it saw as noncapitalist democratic ideals. The Wilsonian idea of democratic capitalism underlay his well-known Fourteen Points, a grand vision of global affairs in which the ultimate goal is uninhibited free trade. Democratic capitalism would function on a level playing field on which nations conformed to a fixed set of rules. While Wilson's vision was portrayed as idealistic, advancing democracy, in reality, it was a reaction to alternative visions of democracy. When colonized nations took self-determination seriously, Western powers fiercely resisted. Self-determination was not for non-whites. Wilson disliked democratic movements and was intolerant of dissent. He advocated a

paternalistic democracy unequivocally supportive of American interests. This meant stopping democratic revolutions from below, which is
why Wilson sent troops to Mexico, Haiti, Cuba, and the Dominican
Republic. But his greatest concern was the Bolshevik Revolution. At
first, he believed it would fail. When it didn't, he sent troops to Russia,
using military intervention to halt a democratic revolution. He sought,
above all, to prevent the spread of Bolshevism to Europe.

CHAPTER 2

Eroding Democracy in a Time of Crisis

Anti-Bolshevism translated domestically into political repression against the so-called Reds. The "Red Scare" that unfolded from 1917 into the 1920s had the ripple effect of suppressing many forms of political expression. A social climate of fear manufactured by those in power exaggerated political expression as threatening the status quo. Dissent was regarded as threatening the growth of state power. The U.S. government created a state of emergency to justify its actions. The Red Scare of this period led to the creation of the first state bureaucracy, driven by the need to recreate the ideology of a permanent threat to state interests. Although the Reds were the main targets, methods used against them were eventually employed against other political organizations. After the Haymarket Affair, federal and state laws were passed, making people's opinions and associations grounds for arrest; thought control became legal repression. Anarchists were targeted, especially after McKinley's assassination. Suspected meeting places were raided, anarchists were rounded up, and publications shut down. These initiatives began at the federal level with Roosevelt's announcement to Congress of "the waging of war" against anarchists and sympathizers.[1] Legal repression was next: in 1903, immigrants who believed in or promoted the idea of overthrowing the U.S. government by force were barred from entering. Several states outlawed the promotion of anarchist views. It became illegal to have and/or express a particular political viewpoint. For the first time, federal and state governments worked together to control social thought. Laws applied to members of groups affiliated with anarchism. The Departments of Commerce and Labor, the Secret Service, and the Post Office launched campaigns to deport alien anarchists or prevent circulation of their publications.[2] Meetings were disrupted, and members and speakers were arrested. Political repression spread to the International Workers of the World (IWW). "Wobblies," who pledged to represent all workers, questioned capitalism and used the general strike, especially threatening to capitalist elites. Efforts by the mostly nonviolent IWW to organize and express civil disobedience were sometimes met with violence from local law enforcement on the basis of new local ordinances that suddenly outlawed street speaking. In Spokane and Fresno, hundreds of arrests were made, even of newsboys who sold the IWW paper, and headquarters were raided. When they wouldn't stop singing and shouting, jail authorities turned 150-pound pressure fire hoses on them and kept them standing in the cold water for the night.[3] The IWW case demonstrates why movements become targets. Its success as a mass-based labor movement, capable of effectively utilizing the strike, was an exercise in worker democracy that threatened capitalists. IWW strikes were met with fierce resistance. President Wilson led the government's repression efforts, concerned that dissident views could slow or end America's involvement in the war, that was unacceptable to an administration determined to expand its presence overseas. But opposition was widespread. Despite government's patriotic drumbeat, hundreds of thousands resisted the draft, and progressive political movements led the opposition.[4]

Wartime provides governments with opportunities to operate outside legal boundaries. Wars allow state power to expand in scope and scale so that government can create a steady, permanent erosion of civil liberties and the rule of law. The Wilson administration embarked on initiatives designed to eliminate political opposition by identifying liberals, labor leaders, and Socialists in the United States as nothing more than puppets of Germany. The Espionage Act of June 1917 severely sanctioned any action or the expression of any viewpoint contrary to government's official view. One could not mail materials advocating acts considered treasonous. The Sedition Act of May 1918 made it illegal to criticize the war or the government and outlawed the issuing of statements favoring any country at war with the United Sates or opposing America's participation in it. It also outlawed misstatements hindering the war's progress. The Supreme Court also participated, issuing its first landmark ruling interpreting the First Amendment. Defendants were charged with violating the Espionage Act. They circulated a pamphlet that attempted to prevent armed services recruitment, urged non-compliance with the draft, identified war profiteers, advocated writing to Congress, and encouraged readers to join the Socialist Party: all examples of lawful, nonviolent political dissent. But Supreme Court Justice Holmes uttered his famous remark that the defendants were "shouting false fire in a crowded theater," providing legal cover for political repression. By oppressing such speech, authorities squelch what should be in the country's best national interest, the expression of political truths during wartime.

Not surprisingly, the nationally known Socialist Party leader Eugene Debs was targeted. Debs was a vocal opponent of the draft and U.S. involvement in the war and received nearly a million votes in the 1912 presidential election. He was arrested, tried, and found guilty of Espionage Act violations. Again, the Supreme Court rejected the defense claim that the act violated Debs's First Amendment rights. Given the wartime atmosphere, it is hard to believe Justice Holmes's contention that Debs's Socialist views were not on trial. Rulings in these and similar cases failed to address whether or not wartime emergencies provide government a blank check to suspend rights and take any action in the name of national security. Failure to address the government's ulterior motives in waging war allowed it to engage in political repression, which thrives in settings where questioning the government is deemed unpatriotic.

Legal repression during the Wilson administration also unfolded through the creation of organizations that functioned as thought police. Early in the war, Attorney General Gregory "asked loyal Americans to act as voluntary detectives and to report their suspicions directly to the Department of Justice. The results were staggering. Each day, thousands of accusations of disloyalty flooded into the department."[5] Repression flourished with the rapid rise of citizens groups, like the American Protective League, with more than 200,000 members reporting on supposedly disloyal individuals in their communities. Governmental and nongovernmental efforts were coordinated. Gregory said they had received thousands of complaints and put thousands of individuals under surveillance, fostering an atmosphere in which these organizations were unrestrained and often went beyond the pale in turning in alleged disloyal Americans.

With implicit immunity, they engaged in wiretaps, breaking and entering, bugging offices and examining bank accounts and medical records. Vigilantes ransacked the homes of German-Americans. In Oklahoma, a foreign minister who opposed the sale of Liberty bonds, was tarred and feathered. In California, a brewery worker who had made pro-German remarks was tarred and feathered and chained to a brass cannon in a city park.[6]

These citizen groups were tolerated, even encouraged, by the federal government. Without legislation and judicial rulings to back them up, they could not have operated as they did. This intent to engage in thought control was especially effective because it united grassroots efforts with those of the highest levels of government.

The federal government sought to seize and control those identified as political outsiders through deportation. The Alien Act of 1918 allowed deportation of anarchists, without due process. No evidence had to be provided, investigations were secret, and defendants could neither retain counsel nor appeal a decision. State and local governments followed suit with new sedition and antidissident legislation passing in 11 states and numerous cities. States created "councils of defense," which vigorously supported the war, circulating names of individuals who didn't buy Liberty bonds, sometimes seizing their property and business licenses.[7] Only a small number of individuals and organizations need be targeted for political repression to function effectively. The majority becomes afraid to express alternative perspectives and remains silent. What became deeply ingrained throughout American culture was a fear of those described as hostile to America's war aims, who, it was believed, might subvert these aims by forming alliances with enemies. In the *Abrams* case, the Supreme Court coined the phrase "clear and present danger," which would serve as cover to legislate against political dissent in wartime. The *Abrams* ruling shows what can happen to those who question foreign policy; its disturbing moral is that state power shouldn't be questioned, whether the threat or crisis is real or manufactured. It strengthened government's growing authoritarianism at a time when seditious speech was the pretext for tightening government control so that any notion of free speech became nonexistent. According to the Wilson administration, the war was a national crisis that had transformed many Americans into potential suspects engaging in un-American activities. Rational political discourse was banished, replaced by paranoia. One man was jailed for stating that he wished Wilson would go to hell.[8] All citizens could be suspected of being un-American; only those whose thoughts conformed to those of the administration were recognized as loyal. Wilson made similar criteria grounds for firing federal employees; new applicants could be denied if there was a "reasonable belief" that they were somehow disloyal. Political repression diminishes the influence of democratic movements as government undermines the ideas that drive them. Targeting membership in these movements was a key legal tool and in 1918, Congress passed legislation aimed at doing that.

Federal agencies became more powerful, assuming the tasks of intelligence gathering, mass surveillance, infiltration, and the undermining of political organizations. Between 1917 and the end of the war, the number of employees serving in the government's security agencies in the Department of Justice, the Treasury, and the Post Office exploded, with some federal employees charged with the job of spying on U.S. citizens.[9] The bureaucracy was becoming more specialized, increasing repression by identifying dissenters. The FBI would become a key tool of the American police state, beginning to function during the Red Scare as intelligence gatherer, regarding diverse viewpoints with great suspicion; all ideas were potentially dangerous. According to this view, democracy is a disease, and dissent is an infectious symptom, which can spread throughout the body politic. It is entirely inconsequential that dissenters are engaging in lawful activities. Communism, seen as an internal-external threat, fits well into this model. This is how state repression grows, out of fear of "alien radicals" whose first allegiance is to foreign countries.

Since domestic unrest in the United States was seen as the work of foreigners, laws targeted aliens: the Alien and Sedition Acts, Foreign Agents Registration Acts, the Alien Registration Act, and the Internal Security Act. What better way to discredit political dissent than to claim that it is the product of foreign influences? In 1919, workers striking for higher wages and shorter hours were painted as plotting to overthrow the government; public panic ensued.[10] Allegations of thwarted bomb plots were followed by the discovery in April 1919 of as many as 34 bombs in the U.S. mail addressed to government officials, after an explosion at the home of a former U.S. senator. Other events ignited an already charged atmosphere; major cities experienced riots during May Day protests. The final spark was a simultaneous explosion of bombs in eight cities; one destroyed part of the home of Attorney General Palmer, who declared they were attempts by anarchists to terrorize the country. Intelligence gatherers concluded that Bolshevism was responsible, and a Senate Judiciary Subcommittee called Bolshevism "the greatest current danger facing the republic," which, it said, would require stringent sedition legislation.

Responding to this "disease of radicalism," Palmer established the General Intelligence Division, GID, part of the FBI. J. Edgar Hoover was put in charge, gathering material on radical organizations, monitoring political ideas. He created a detailed card system on over 200,000 persons believed to be radicals. From the beginning, the GID sought to enlarge its power and importance, manufacturing and distorting allegations of radical activity. GID agents exhibited fanaticism, exaggerating through ceaseless propaganda the threat posed by radical activities. Most of the public was supportive, caught up in the message that harsh methods had to be taken. A national political police force of undercover agents and informants had been let loose to round up and deport so-called enemy aliens. "Approximately 650 people were arrested on suspicion of radicalism, many of whom merely happened to be at the wrong place at the wrong time."[11] In January 1920, in more than 30 cities, 4,000 more suspected radicals were taken in, in raids conducted in cafes, bowling alleys, and other ordinary gathering places.

The Red Scare was also a response to an increasingly progressive labor movement in which economic democracy had become an issue. In 1918, the AFL advocated for public ownership of utilities, more regulation of corporations and government funding for low-cost worker housing. Strikes became far more common; during 1919, there were more than 3,000, involving millions of workers. Unionism became a broad-based democratic movement, growing in strength and numbers in numerous industries. Political elites also were troubled by events in Europe in 1918 and 1919. Bolshevism threatened to spread to Austria and Germany. While leftist policies were shaping Europe's Socialist parties, American political and economic elites responded by rolling back programs that benefited the masses, such as the U.S. Employment Service, housing projects, and veterans benefits. Government's anti-labor efforts intensified with the goal of breaking unions that dared to organize workers and go on strike. The steel industry, one of America's most important and powerful, became the object of a major strike. If successful, it would impact other major industries. Across the country, federal and state troops were mobilized. In Pittsburgh alone, steel companies armed and deputized 25,000 men to violently destroy the strike. Gary, Indiana was put under martial law, and private homes were raided in the night.[12]

Hoover's zeal in hunting down radicals translated into a policy and practice hostile to the rule of law, particularly procedural due process safeguards. The Fourth, Fifth, and Sixth Amendments were simply ignored during the FBI's radical witch hunts in 1920 when the Department of Labor issued several thousand blank warrants for Communists that would be filled in later, once identified. In numerous cities, FBI agents and local Red squads conducted raids and searches without warrants, rounding up several thousand suspects, who were arrested and incarcerated for long periods under extreme conditions without arrest warrants.[13] The FBI also was hostile to the Eighth Amendment fundamental due process right to bail, arguing that release of agitators would allow them to continue to promote their propaganda; Hoover ordered immigration agents to refuse bail if an individual refused to answer a question. Hoover's files included detailed biographies of so-called radicals underscoring an obsession to persecute and prosecute individuals for their political beliefs. With the GID, the FBI began a trend, which continues today, in which a secret political police agency within the government operates without effective oversight from Congress or the president.

Local political police were engaged to monitor and neutralize mass-based political movements; they historically worked against the labor movement, not only to break strikes, but to prevent workers from organizing at all. Local police sought control of the streets, preventing the masses from having a public presence, denying them their right to assemble and freely associate, under the pretext that when the masses assemble, there is potential for violence. While local police sought to control outdoor meetings with intimidation and overt violence, indoor meetings were the object of insidious techniques designed to discourage them; organizations were required to provide in advance names of speakers; fire, health, and building ordinances were invoked; owners or renters were intimidated by the presence of officers who would show up en masse.

Local police actions were independent from federal actions, but the ideology was the same: an official offensive against radicalism, through police surveillance and intelligence gathering. Police departments formed alliances with the American Protection League (APL), in many ways, a "cloak-and-dagger" secret citizens' organization designed to report on citizens' loyalty and to bring draft dodgers and other dissidents to the attention of police.[14] APL members were deputized and could make arrests; with police, they would spy on and disrupt meetings of Socialists and Wobblies. Acting on their own, local police behaved as enforcers of antiradical modes of thought. Red flags were banned, and American flags were sometimes required to be displayed. Local police began acting as agents of thought control, arbitrarily preventing radicals from giving speeches. In the 1920s, intelligence gathering became routine as police, collaborating with political and economic elites, increased monitoring, using informants to break strikes and neutralize the labor movement. The rationalization was the need to prevent violence, even though when labor meetings were held, there was no violence.

Despite federal, state, and local political repression, there was not yet a clear direction toward the formation of a police state. There were even setbacks. During the 1920s, there was a backlash against the Red Scare, with major newspapers publicly opposing federal proposals for sedition legislation. Prominent attorneys and members of the clergy, labor, and even some judges agreed, and sedition legislation died in the House of Representatives in February 1920. The U.S. Labor Department, which bore responsibility for deportations, lost interest in these procedures. The expulsion by the legislature of New York of five elected Socialists for no reason also contributed to the outcry against the Red Scare. Overseas, the defeat of the Socialist threat in Germany, as far as political elites were concerned, made Europe safe from Bolshevism. The Soviet Union was essentially contained within its borders, another reassurance that America wouldn't face a competitor as it expanded overseas.

There were clear indications that the repressive atmosphere was receding. Repressive legislation was no longer a priority and some well-known radicals were released or pardoned. The federal Sedition Act was repealed; far fewer individuals were deported for their political viewpoints. Socialists expelled from their seats in the New York Legislature were reinstated, as was the sole Socialist in the House of Representatives, Victor Berger. Even the Communist Party came out of hiding.

But incremental steps had been taken which would, in the long run, serve as a foundation for the development of a police state decades later. The Red Scare greatly diminished the structural and organizational base of mass movements. With the pacification of the labor movement, in particular its more radical elements, such as the IWW, state power grew, destroying the ability of movements to advance democracy. Overt repression was replaced by the increased powers of surveillance of federal agencies, such as the Justice Department and the War Department, still on the watch for foreign radicals. Fear was used to tame political dissent. William Burns, who headed the Bureau of Investigation, called a 1922 coal strike the work of foreign, Communist influences and organizations such as the American Civil Liberties Union and the National Association for the Advancement of Colored People were closely monitored.

While federal political repression against radicals relaxed, the same couldn't be said of the local level. Teacher loyalty oaths passed in 20 states, and textbooks lacking patriotic content were banned. States passed laws still on the books today, requiring the observance of patriotic holidays and the teaching of an officially approved version of

American history. The ACLU was banned for a time from using public schools as meeting places to discuss free speech. University students expressing radical ideas faced censorship, even expulsion. More blatant political repression was reserved for organized labor. The labor injunction denied labor its most fundamental weapon, the right to strike; during the 1920s, more than 900 such injunctions were issued.[15] When legal repression failed to contain organized labor, the National Guard was sent in, even though violence was rare.

The 1930s are a pivotal decade for examining the relationship between state power and mass movements and the influence of historic events. The economic crisis as a systemwide collapse would temporarily weaken state power, presenting an opportunity for mass-based movements to reappear, forcing the government to make concessions and relinquish a degree of social control in the name of political stability, thus expanding democracy. The Great Depression exposed the unrestrained, capitalist economy. Twenty-five percent of the workforce was unemployed. There was no denying the powerful presence of so many people who were down and out, riding rail cars, living in packing crates and the Hoovervilles of every city.[16] Franklin Roosevelt's administration had one goal: to save capitalism. It also hoped to quell political discontent. Political unrest, as demonstrated by the people who took to the streets, was tied to the government's failure to provide some social safety net. Roosevelt realized that a small measure of economic redistribution would stabilize both the economic and political systems. Work relief programs, Social Security benefits for the unemployed and disabled, and the nation's first subsidized housing programs would bring desperately needed assistance to tens of millions of destitute Americans. These measures passed largely because of the pervasiveness of political unrest. Grassroots democracy on this scale had no historical precedent in the United States. In part, it was a mass movement of the downtrodden, whose rising political consciousness and strength in numbers made policy makers sit up and take notice; the fears of local officials and businessmen forced Roosevelt to make relief programs a priority.[17] It was impossible to ignore pervasive protests from such a broad cross section of society. The labor movement was revived. Striking workers saw unprecedented wage increases, the introduction of the 40-hour workweek, and minimum wages in some industries. Mass democracy, representing the working class American majority, advanced its economic interests. The Communist Party's involvement in organizing the unemployed gained extensive support among workers, even those unaffiliated with it, creating a large new constituency of Americans who sympathized with its attempts to help the unemployed.

Federal agencies viewed this rising tide of democracy with alarm, especially in light of events overseas. This tendency to connect domestic and foreign policy would set the stage for political repression, much the way the 1920s Red Scare had. Deportations increased, with leftist union organizers and immigrants the targets. The government met some Communist-led protests with tear gas and violence. Eventually, all political movements and forms of dissent were depicted as either Red-led or Red-inspired. Police clashed with unemployed veterans marching on Washington in 1932 seeking payment of World War I bonuses. Once the White House was informed, Army troops, authorized by Hoover, cleared the veterans from downtown using bombs and tear gas, injuring protesters, their families, and bystanders. The inflammatory response was triggered by an Army intelligence report stating that the protest was supposed to signal Communist uprising throughout American cities, to be followed by revolution.[18]

The incident served as an excuse to accelerate more repressive measures. Troops were amassed outside of major cities by the secretary of war in preparation for the uprisings. In the name of promoting stability against a leftist threat, the government was willing to marshal state power against unarmed hunger marchers, simply because Communist Party members participated. Through the 1930 Smoot-Hawley Tariff Act, the government censored and could confiscate any material it identified as subversive. Local police acted as agents of state repression, preventing groups from exercising the right of assembly and breaking up meetings and strikes. In several instances, in the early thirties, police fired into crowds of unemployed demonstrators led by Communists, resulting in some fatalities. This pattern of using police as agents of federally inspired political repression continued, influenced by the congressional committee known as the Fish Committee, which institutionalized the use of local police and Red squads to act as the state's coercive arm, monitoring and infiltrating political organizations. First targeted against organized labor, they were used against a broader range of left-wing and Communist organizations, gathering dossiers on participants, identifying illegal aliens, and sharing information with police in other cities.

The 1936 meeting between Hoover and President Roosevelt would put the U.S. government on the path toward a true police state. In that meeting, Hoover, who had testified before the Fish Committee, began urging more concerted attacks on radicalism, advocating more intense investigations of Communism and Fascism. The meeting launched an unprecedented partnership between the Office of the President and the FBI, making intelligence gathering and surveillance essential prerogatives of state power. The rogue nature of Roosevelt's decision to work with Hoover to monitor Communists and Fascists would result in political repression against anyone seen as standing in the way of the president's objectives. Thus, the fundamental constitutional relationship between the president and Congress was profoundly altered. "Congress was doubly deceived: the launching of the probe was kept secret, and its funding authority misused. The assignment reflected President Roosevelt's spacious view of his powers as chief executive, a natural affinity for the intelligence process...and a callousness to the claims alike of privacy and free expression."[19] The 1936 assignment lay a strong foundation that other presidents would build on, subjecting the political beliefs of Americans to surveillance. For Hoover, this was a blank check to investigate any political perspective, to gather information from multiple sources to compile elaborate intelligence files. He didn't distinguish between Fascists and Communists, believing that any idea or way of life identified as contrary to the status quo was a threat.

This partnership between the FBI and the executive branch resulted in a further concentration of power in the presidency. In 1938, Roosevelt expanded intelligence gathering and surveillance, in order to keep an eye on subversive elements, which he called the "espionage situation." Domestic intelligence was now a collaboration between the FBI and various military intelligence divisions, involving various parts of government in the business of surveillance. Roosevelt fully agreed with Attorney General Murphy's request, communicated at Hoover's insistence, to share all intelligence information received by state or local law enforcement. He ordered all law enforcement agents to turn over to the closest FBI office any domestic intelligence information potentially related to espionage or subversive activity. This was a profound step: the FBI had been assigned the role of national coordinator for all surveillance matters. It was clear that this role would be permanent.

While the executive branch worked with federal agencies to implement repression, Congress also assumed a central role, establishing the House Un-American Activities Committee, led by Martin Dies, to attack mass-based political movements. It linked the New Deal to Communism, implying that New Deal reforms and advances were a threat because they expanded democracy. The media provided extensive coverage of the highly inflammatory proceedings, which ignited political hysteria and identified hundreds of upstanding newspapers and organizations, including the Boy Scouts, the Catholic Association for International Peace, and the Campfire Girls, as Communist-affiliated.[20] Diverse thought and alternative lifestyles were automatically suspect, so the committee became obsessed with Hollywood, well aware of its influence on popular culture. It spread fear of alternative ideas and organizations and identified thousands of federal employees as alleged Communists or associates. The chief danger of this political paranoia was its propaganda value, creating a society that participated in and supported fanaticism. The committee enjoyed significant popular support.

While political extremism marginalized all mass-based movements, the federal government targeted organized labor above all. Despite the passage of the Wagner Act, a reaction developed against the movement's most progressive elements. Local governments and business owners worked to break strikes and infiltrate unions with the help of local and private police forces. It was a response to attempts to expand worker democracy in the South and in agricultural areas, where workers' rights were still largely absent. Organizers faced the daunting prospect of forming unions in parts of the country where unions were almost entirely absent, and the political culture was reactionary. Police forces in these areas, in alliance with economic and political elites, used legal and coercive repression, including intimidation, surveillance, and armed citizens groups to halt efforts to unionize. Union members' homes were raided. In 1934, when hundreds of thousands of cotton textile workers went on strike from Maine to Georgia, tens of thousands of National Guardsmen and local law enforcement personnel were called out; they beat and arrested many strikers. In Georgia, the governor declared martial law, imprisoning thousands of workers and key strike leaders. To subdue and disperse crowds of thousands of striking California farmers in 1933, heavily armed law enforcement officials shot into crowds and used tear gas. In Arkansas, local authorities, the police, and economic elites mobilized powerful resistance against organizers who formed the Southern Tenant Farmers Union. They were accused of a host of charges, from disturbing the peace to obtaining money under false pretenses; police raided meetings, routinely beating or arresting attendees. Miners had had a degree of success in organizing until they met fierce resistance from local police and the National Guard, who used force and mass arrest, conducting raids, breaking up public meetings, and manufacturing criminal charges. In industry after industry, the goal was to oppress organized labor.

Labor still had enough influence nationally that it could push back some of those antidemocratic forces. Roosevelt, the manager of

America's greatest economic crisis, had to mediate between the forces of repression and democracy. With his reelection in 1936, the administration's goal was to avoid political instability; Roosevelt and the federal government expressed greater acceptance of labor activity and strikers. Union membership spiked to 7 million in 1937, and millions of workers participated in more than 4,000 strikes. The government had stepped back from accelerating repression for several reasons: America was still at peace, the charges of the Dies Committee came to be regarded by the administration as baseless and exaggerated, and the goals of the labor and Left movements were generally reformist, not revolutionary.

At the same time, presidential power was eclipsing the power of Congress. Growth in state power at home coincided with its projection overseas through militarism and stronger institutional ties between the federal government and the military. By the late 1930s, there was increasing concern that Japan's and Germany's interests in Latin America would threaten U.S. export and oil markets. Mexican President Cardenas made it illegal for foreign companies to control Mexico's resources. Washington's concern was that Mexico's actions could spread to Venezuela and Brazil, where the United States had oil interests. Mexico backed off after the United States threatened to withdraw loans. Out of fear of going to war over Latin American markets, the United States created a policy that was low key and nonmilitary, the result of which was in many ways similar to European appeasement.

Japan's attack on China in June 1937 reshaped American foreign policy to favor military intervention. Until then, foreign policy was "Open Door," allowing the United States complete access to Asian markets. China had been viewed as a key export market. The Japanese invasion jeopardized this plan. Some in the Roosevelt administration called for maintaining economic and military threats, but this changed in 1939 when Japan revealed that its strategy of a new order included actions in the Philippines. Roosevelt then embargoed gasoline and iron shipments to Japan. With Nazi conquests of Poland and France, the United States increasingly found itself lending support to colonial powers not regarded as a threat or against the new colonists, Japan and Germany. When the United States formally declared war against Japan after the Pearl Harbor attack, it was out of concern that Japan threatened its interests in the Pacific.

The detonation of the American atomic bomb against Japan illustrates how government/military projects gather momentum and are ultimately deployed. "Atomic Diplomacy" would allow the United States to disguise its antidemocratic strategy by using cold warism to portray the Soviet Union as threatening global democracy. The arms race was predicated on a bipolar view of the world, which served to expand the antidemocratic alliance between government and what Eisenhower later identified as the "military-industrial complex." The foundation of that alliance is militarism, which by its nature is antidemocratic and authoritarian. Militarism incorporated into state ideology depends on the perpetual creation of threats. The arms race demonstrates how militarism, in defining the world as us versus them, makes violence and mass killing the ultimate answer to social problems. Once militarism was built into the federal government through the extensive granting of military contracts to semicivilian firms, the incentive was created not just to fund projects but to manufacture threats necessitating new ones. Militarism opened the way for a much more ambitious expansion of state power overseas, using nationalist and democratic slogans to promote antidemocratic ideals.

The selling of World War II as a great patriotic war served, in the long run, to erode democracy at home and overseas. With new sophistication, war making was mass marketed like any product. No wonder more Americans joined up than had ever before. But it was the antidemocratic ideology of the cold war that produced a militarism in which preparation for, and glorification of, war became the norm. The growth of militarism is troubling because its inherent authoritarianism is based on using force to put down those who dare question state power. It is made possible by the emergence of a specialized, highly trained group of individuals who embody the principles of militarism and the near worship of violence for its own sake.

In the late 1930s, the overly simplistic idea that particular threats, small or large, could be used to rationalize oppressing all Americans became a common theme. The 1939 Hatch Act covers possible actions, constituting a kind of anticipatory state repression; it also includes punishment for one's thoughts, proclaiming that membership constitutes a subversive activity and is sufficient cause for legal action. This is guilt by association. The June 1940 Alien Registration, or Smith Act, had language so broad and abstract as to make it applicable to any person or organization. The government bears no burden of proof except to deem the activity in question treasonous. Since the nation wasn't at war, it amounted to a sedition act.

In a September 1939 public statement, Roosevelt gave the FBI supreme authority in domestic intelligence gathering and surveillance, facilitating its role as political police. All persons entering the country were now profiled as to any potential danger they posed. The FBI was authorized to select identifiable subversives who had expressed incorrect thoughts. It was the perfect opportunity to heighten the supposed danger posed by Japanese and German fifth columns in the United States, socializing Americans to accept the harshest measures against the accused, portrayed as representing an immediate danger to public safety. When identifying internal and external dangers to national security is the priority, the Constitution and the rule of law become obstacles to be pushed aside.

The use of illegal wiretaps by the Roosevelt administration and its alliance with the FBI according to the Federal Communications Act of 1934 demonstrates the degree to which the rule of law was sidestepped. From Roosevelt to George W. Bush, presidential power and control over state power grew steadily. When Attorney General Jackson banned FBI wiretaps, Roosevelt made sure they were reinstated, directing Jackson that they be allowed in order to uncover subversive activities. This was a slippery slope, and soon, wiretaps without court orders could be utilized against any political perspective. These warrantless wiretaps were established when the United States wasn't at war; the FBI now had the authority to monitor and gather information without a court order on anyone.

Roosevelt's partnership with Hoover's FBI established a trend in which antidemocratic agencies defined their mission as attacking democracy and its political movements. Over the course of the twentieth century, during crises when choices had to be made between reconciling civil liberties with security or sacrificing liberty for security, the federal government chooses the latter. The alliance between the executive branch and the FBI made everyone a suspect and a potential enemy. It also created paranoia: in 1940, Roosevelt had the FBI do loyalty checks on his wife's social secretary and implement wiretaps on his closest aides.[21] With war with Japan as a foregone conclusion, the FBI could rationalize extending surveillance and counterintelligence. In that climate, society becomes its own internal policing agent, taking care not to express taboo ideas.

State power worked against democracy, with the Plenary Power Doctrine as a rationalization. Created to empower government to do whatever is necessary in the name of national security, it first was utilized in the 1880s against Chinese immigrant workers; it was later extended to any group that prevented the government from seizing territory. The doctrine, which had legal standing in the courts, targeted identifiable "outsiders," groups defined as noncitizens. Otherness became a means for limiting the expansion of democracy. In the Supreme Court case, *Elk v. Wilkins*, Indians were determined to have the same status as foreign-born individuals. In the 1830 ruling in *Cherokee Nation v. Georgia*, Indians are again deemed noncitizens; by implication, their territories are under U.S. government control. Their noncitizenship status figured in the *United States v. Kagama*, in which land seizures were ruled permissible. The Allotment Act gave the government authority to seize all remaining Indian lands. European settlers used plenary authority to support the slave system and define African Americans as property.

In foreign policy, the doctrine was used to dominate peoples under the guise of meeting national security objectives. Consider how the concept of otherness figured into the American occupation in the Philippines. In a report by the commission led by William Howard Taft and strongly supported by Theodore Roosevelt, the Filipino people were described "as 'weaklings of low stature, with black skin...thick lips and large, clumsy feet. In the matter of intelligence they stand at or near the bottom of the human series, and they are believed to be incapable of any considerable degree of civilization or advancement.'"[22] Otherness set the stage for the internment of Japanese Americans, an example of how, in wartime, the government uses it to connect perceived internal and external threats. After Pearl Harbor, the identification of Japanese citizens as fifth columnists was useful in increasing the dominance of the executive branch at home and overseas. Using the Smith Act, the government initiated registration of all noncitizens under the broader category of "Enemy Aliens." Despite the absence of any evidence of fifth column activity by Japanese Americans, Roosevelt promoted intelligence gathering and surveillance, focusing first on Japanese descendents in Hawaii and on the West Coast. Just being Japanese was sufficient to prompt the government to mobilize special intelligence units. Even prior to the attack, the government was moving toward oppressive actions. As early as December 1941, the FBI began compiling extensive lists of persons of Japanese ancestry, considered possible subversives. The "ABC" list distinguished the Japanese into those seen as immediately dangerous, potentially dangerous, or pro-Japan. Listed were leaders of Japanese civic groups, businessmen, language teachers, Buddhist priests, and martial arts instructors. After thousands of arrests, the attack on Pearl Harbor gave Roosevelt the excuse he needed to employ police-state style tactics. He instituted martial law in Hawaii, which immediately suspended basic due process rights, such as habeas corpus and trial by jury. The hysteria that the attack generated, along with pressure from interest groups, created a groundswell of support for mass evacuations that government and military officials were advocating of the Japanese from Hawaii and the West Coast. Executive Order 9066 authorized the secretary of war and military commanders to place under military control designated areas in which Japanese Americans would be concentrated; it authorized the roundup and evacuation of Japanese Americans from California, Oregon, and Washington. The government had identified an internal enemy. Evacuation was viewed as temporary, but more extreme actions were contemplated. Popular fears grew of free-roaming Japanese in the nation's interior. Under the pretext of heading off possible violence, the Japanese were shipped to "relocation centers." For three years, the internees were, in Roosevelt's own words, placed in concentration camps, complete with barbed wire, guard towers, and armed guards. Camp conditions were far from adequate, providing insufficient shelter; neither adults nor children were provided proper clothing or shoes; conditions were unsanitary; and camps experienced outbreaks of malaria, dysentery, typhoid, and tuberculosis.[23]

The Supreme Court rationalized such measures as required due to "military necessity." The Plenary Power Doctrine facilitated police state coercion against Japanese Americans: "otherness," not military necessity, motivated Japanese American internment, even extending to Latin Americans born to Japanese parents, who were also seized, illustrating how the doctrine overreaches, politically repressing those outside U.S. borders. This group represented no security value; nonetheless, individuals were kidnapped as potential bargaining chips in exchange for U.S. citizens and soldiers captured during the war. In cooperation with the United States, the Peruvian government raided homes of Japanese Peruvians, rounded them up, and turned them over to American authorities, though some had lived there as long as 40 years, and their wives and children were Peruvian citizens. No charges were filed, and no hearings held.[24] Individuals were confined in prison camps, whose conditions, according to a State Department representative, were far worse than at European prisoner of war camps.[25]

These examples demonstrate how the cover of war provided the Roosevelt administration with a convenient rationale with which to extend state power at the expense of law, especially international law. The U.S. government was now in the business of seizing and imprisoning civilians from a country that wasn't at war, on the basis of racial identity, charging them as posing a threat to American national security. This occurred even though there was legal precedent against the kidnapping of civilians and their illegal deportation as far back as Lieber's

Code, which outlawed the military's ability to wage war against civilians and prohibited the enslavement and kidnapping of civilians to distant lands which, according to Nuremberg, constituted a war crime. U.S. citizens also became targets. Sedition was used to send a message, especially against news media and publications. The FBI made examples of various groups, breaking into their offices and stealing confidential material, installing listening devices and more than 1,800 wiretaps on the phones of unsuspecting Americans throughout the war.[26]

CHAPTER 3

Accelerating the Assault on Mass Democracy

When the Truman administration came into office, political repression was still increasing, a result of the continued growth of executive power and the manufacturing of the threat of war. Militarism supported the government's articulation of the internal-external menace of Communism in the context of the cold war. Communism was the official threat, but the government's response to the perceived Communist menace provided a litmus test for all diverse political views. American relations with the Soviet Union had enjoyed an increase in popular American support during World War II, including genuine support for democratic principles and some Communist Party ideas.[1] But when Truman took office in 1945, hopes for cooperative relations with the Soviet Union were in shambles. While American democratic forces strengthened efforts to uplift the downtrodden, by the end of World War II, an antidemocratic backlash was mounting.

The economic downturn in 1945–1946 forced organized labor to resort to the strike. Truman took the lead, breaking strikes by seizing railroad and oil refining operations. Congress passed one of its most powerful pieces of antilabor legislation, the Taft-Hartley Act of 1947. The Communist Party was an obvious initial target; eventually, the Communist Control Act of 1954 would neutralize it as a functioning organization. It was the opening act to a much broader assault on political viewpoints. By the late 1940s, the Communist Party was much smaller than just a decade earlier. Attacks were increasing on a broad range of alternative, especially leftist, political perspectives. Another Red Scare was underway while the government promoted itself as a champion of democracy. In January 1947, the House Un-American Activities Committee (HUAC) embarked on an investigation to identify Communists and sympathizers in government. In the committee's Orwellian view, antidemocratic attitudes were defined as democratic while democratic views were defined as their opposite. HUAC Chair J. Parnell Thomas held that diverse political perspectives threatened the American way of life, as though there was only room for one narrowly defined America in which no one questioned government's authority.

The Truman Doctrine enforced this perverse view, allegedly to protect and defend freedom, while using anti-Communism to attack it. Domestically, it was manifested in the loyalty issue; the federal government mobilized resources to intimidate and silence anyone who dared question its actions. Americans were forced to accept the government's official view of loyal and disloyal behavior in accordance with Truman's executive order. By December 1947, the implication was that persons who expressed independent thoughts would be blacklisted. The Red Scare of the 1950s was fueled by the administration's efforts to manufacture a fear of democracy by making examples of anyone who dared question its anti-Communist policies, orchestrating highly publicized arrests and deportations of union organizers, vocal opponents of the administration, and supporters of the Progressive Party. The majority got the message and lost the courage to speak or act in defiance of the administration.

The Truman administration established detailed categories. Actions that could be defined as suspect and un-American were sabotage or espionage; treason or sedition; advocating overthrow of government; an intention to release classified information; spying for foreign governments; membership in, or affiliation with, organizations with foreign connections or domestic ones identified by the attorney general as Totalitarian, Fascist, Communist, or subversive. These broad categories allowed the government to identify dissenting thought or activity as subject to punishment. The provisions of the sixth category connect any dissenting political philosophy to future acts. The 1947 publication of the attorney general's list of subversive organizations demonstrated that the state viewed membership itself as subversive. Opposition viewpoints were seen as Communist or Communist-inspired. The accusation that Henry Wallace and the Progressive Party were affiliated with Communism worked well, undermining the party's legitimate questioning of foreign policy. Statements by high-ranking officials in the Democratic Party linked Wallace with the Communists; Truman implied that Wallace should go to Russia, assisting the enemy against his own country. Even organizations that traditionally worked to expand democracy, such as labor unions and Americans for Democratic Action, got into the act; the ADA began functioning as an anti-Communist pressure group, currying favor with the Democratic Party by equating Wallace with Communists.

By labeling the questioning of U.S. foreign policy as Communist, such efforts lay the foundation for McCarthyism. Even though the convictions of Alger Hiss and Judith Coplon as Soviet spies were eventually overturned, the allegations firmly established an atmosphere where political "others" were feared. Communism was the ultimate form of political otherness; the questioning of state power was tantamount to a threat. In a larger context, the chief goal of the Red Scare was to subvert democracy and the more democratic measures associated with the New Deal. In an effort to win back the White House, Republicans and proponents of free enterprise sought to reverse gains made by progressive movements and unions.[2]

The military-industrial complex, which requires perpetual preparation for war, also continued to expand, furthering the assault on democracy. Even Eisenhower, one of its creators, foresaw its consequences. In his 1960 farewell address, he used the phrase "garrison state" to describe the flourishing connections between the federal government, the military, and the arms industry. In terms of misplaced priorities, it signifies the loss of alternatives to military production. But the military-industrial complex does more than shift economic priorities from butter to guns; its existence chips away at democracy. In preparing for war, the goal is to increase state power and its repressive capabilities. The needs of the masses take a backseat to the need to produce weapons. Ironically, its economic functioning is antidemocratic and even anti-capitalist, for it engages in parasitic, nonproductive economic growth. Defense firms strive to maximize costs and subsidies, drawing upon the coffers of the federal government for virtually unlimited capital. These firms operate like an insulated monopoly market, without competitors or worries about inflation, productivity, performance, or poor design. For the military-industrial complex, higher costs mean more activity, facilities, employees, and cash flow. There are no built-in limitations to the cost-maximization process.

Defense firms are but one part of the military-industrial complex. Other parts include senior military officers within the Pentagon and the Department of Defense and key members of the executive and legislative branches. A set of working relationships and partnerships developed between the government and weapons-producing firms. While Congress and the president provide final authorization for what to produce and the cost, the Pentagon and the Department of Defense also work with Congress, the president and defense contractors. The relationship between the Pentagon and the firms is symbiotic. The president and Congress see their relationship to the Pentagon and these firms as political, furthering America's need to use military hardware to shape world events. These cozy institutional and social relationships are antidemocratic, locking out the masses from directly shaping federal policy making and increasing antidemocratic institutional tendencies within the federal government. Greater power is equated with ever-greater military might.

The military-industrial complex is antidemocratic because it creates an industrial policy that favors companies that manufacture high-tech weapons. This arrangement, a kind of corporate socialism, severely hampers nondefense industries that must compete within the capitalist market. Such firms lack the powerful advantages of those that participate in the cold war economy, which are protected from declining profits. Unlike civilian firms, they have unlimited research and development funds and lack serious competitors. There is no better example of the negative economic impact that this favoring of military over civilian firms has produced than the steady decline of America's manufacturing base. To some extent, the lack of governmental support has contributed to the decline of the automotive sector, including the drain of top engineering talent away from the automotive industry to military contractors. The absence of government research and development funding for nondefense industries, as well as ineffective trade policies, is another factor. Compare this to Japan, whose industrial policy, including generous research and development funding for the auto industry, over time contributed to wholesale expansion into U.S. markets, promoting cooperation among large manufacturers and initiating export promotion techniques.

The military-industrial complex produces an ideology of militarism within the culture. It emerges primarily in the regions dependent on a cold war economy, known as the Gun Belt. In such a culture, "might makes right," and permanent enemies are necessary. Politics is reduced to the contest of which nation can impose its will by force. Such an antipolitical view results from the arrogance that comes from a license to commit violence without suffering consequences. Inside the federal government, policy makers are captive, willing participants in weapons production. Members of Congress are very careful, as are presidents, not to cut defense spending, which would impact the Gun Belt. "Military spending had...become a form of pork barrel on a huge scale."[3]

The executive branch also was developing a vast national security bureaucracy, made possible by the July 1947 passage of the National Security Act. First, there was a reorganization that incorporated the military within the executive branch. The War Department was split up; in its place, the new Department of Defense would consolidate control over the military with leadership at the cabinet level; the heads of the armed forces would come together in the Joint Chiefs of Staff, under a top military advisor, who would be the chief advisor to the president and the Secretary of Defense.[4] The second key development was the formation of the Central Intelligence Agency (CIA), which would become a critical player in missions to destroy democracy overseas. The CIA would answer to the National Security Council, staffed with members who answered to the president. Anti-Communism was its institutional mindset; nations that didn't embrace this doctrine were subjected to covert operations. Foreign governments had no right to their own sovereignty. The real enemy then was not Communism, per se, but a nation with the freedom to make its own choices.

As with domestic political repression, covert operations contain an element of mind control, as if controlling people's minds will create a political reality agreeable to U.S. global interests. This fixation, characteristic of police states, became the CIA's trademark, making it a fundamentally antidemocratic institution. For example, in Italy in 1948, the CIA had been issued top-secret orders from the National Security Council to conduct "psychological operations" to beat the Communists at the ballot box by supporting the Christian Democratic Party—in many countries, a CIA front. A well-funded, relentless propaganda campaign was waged. Money was a means to use covert operations to shape minds, creating an anti-Communist political reality. Just as the Communists had front organizations throughout Europe, now the CIA would create a network of covert political groups, often staffing them with Russian émigrés. The goal was to overthrow governments and reshape public opinion to support the new government and its pro-U.S. interests.

Practically by definition, the CIA operated outside legal restraints. It had no legal authority to implement covert actions in other countries. Congress had neither provided a constitutional charter nor authorized funds for these purposes.[5] After the CIA Act passed in May 1949, the agency was given free rein to act overseas as an international political police force, with the single stipulation that no such function could be carried out inside the United States. CIA recruitment and use of former Nazis, including those from Hitler's military intelligence unit and the infamous postwar "rat line" underscored its antidemocratic nature; the agency employed some of the most infamous Nazis, including Klaus Barbie, the "butcher of Lyon."

The Eisenhower administration continued to deal with the Soviet menace through a massive arms buildup. Eisenhower's New Look emphasized high-tech nuclear weapons, stressed air power, and deemphasized troops, bolstering CIA covert operations. Several hundred such operations consisting of political, psychological, and paramilitary methods would be launched in nearly 50 countries.[6] CIA efforts to control foreign governments grew on a grand scale.

In using both the military-industrial complex and the CIA, the federal government had incorporated two fiercely antidemocratic organizations as permanent institutional fixtures. Throughout the nineteenth century and up until the Roosevelt administration, political repression had mostly been a cooperative venture between Congress and the presidents. The appearance of federal agencies serving the president's antidemocratic goals set what remained of internal democracy on a path toward inevitable decay. From the cold war on, Congress became more of a bystander while the executive branch used the military-industrial complex and the CIA to lead the charge against democracy. The cold war was a watershed event, defining world events as in permanent crisis, a definition that allowed presidents to believe they could employ force without legal restraint. The president had eclipsed Congress in deciding when and how to wage war: "beginning with the Korean War in 1950 and again the large-scale commitment to U.S. troops to Vietnam in July 1965, Congress surrendered its formal role in authorizing the declaration of war."[7]

Internal democracy continued to erode as the government increasingly conducted operations in secret. The CIA had so much freedom to engage in covert operations without accountability that only key White House officials knew of them. Many presidents used the CIA to promote antidemocratic agendas, seizing and controlling overseas territories. This entailed subverting existing governments and replacing them with rulers answerable to the United States. Such policies, over many decades, led to U.S. support of dictators, exposing the myth of America as democracy's champion. Greece was an early example in 1947. With the rationale that American intervention was needed to halt Soviet aggression, the United States participated in what was essentially a civil war, siding with antidemocratic forces and establishing a military dictatorship, a pattern that was later repeated around the world. Promoting democracy was simply not the goal. When in 1948, the

Peruvian and Venezuelan militaries overthrew their democratic governments, the United States quickly recognized the new dictatorships. The CIA had become the international counterpart to the political police function of the FBI. Both sought to suppress progressive political movements in the name of fighting Communism. The CIA encouraged and supported antidemocratic forces, which subverted and replaced existing regimes and provided social support for dictatorships. The CIA's role in toppling Mohammed Mossadegh's government in Iran provides an important illustration. A primary goal was to delegitimize the regime; this involved bribing journalists; editors; preachers; and other respected, popular leaders, to create suspicion of Mossadegh. Attacks against respected Iranians were staged, depicted as having been launched by Mossadegh. The CIA recruited Iranians to construct an elaborate campaign to generate a groundswell of social opposition to Mossadegh. With segments of the military and police on the agency's payroll, it was only a matter of time before the regime would fall. Social chaos ensued, and after a brief battle between Mossadegh's loyalists and CIA-controlled troops, he surrendered. As with other CIA coups, an alternative ruler—in this case, the Shah—was selected to replace him. The CIA had overthrown a government, which had dared to act as a democracy and invoke nationalism, which proved unacceptable to Western oil interests.

A similar fate befell Guatemala's President Jacobo Arbenz, who attempted to reform Guatemala's economy, which had been largely controlled by three American companies. He attempted to nationalize privately owned foreign businesses and sought to initiate land redistribution, the root of Guatemalan inequality. He passed the Agrarian Reform Law, which threatened foreign interests, especially those of the United Fruit Company. Passage paved the way for a massive redistribution of land, including land under United Fruit's control. Guatemalans welcomed the plan as a means of achieving economic democracy. But United Fruit saw it would negatively affect its bottom line, viewing it as evidence of Communist infiltration of the Guatemalan government. American policy makers agreed, concluding that such Communist-inspired reforms would spread throughout Latin America. The United States supported United Fruit, agreeing with the CIA's depiction of Arbenz as a Marxist sympathizer. But Arbenz wasn't associated with any Communist plot to take over Latin America and had no military, economic, or diplomatic relations with the Soviet Union. Nonetheless, in December 1953, the agency made preparations to overthrow him with tactics similar to those used in Iran: massive doses of propaganda, violence intended to destabilize the regime, and the orchestration of CIA-sponsored attacks designed to mimic a social uprising. The CIA financed and mobilized support from segments of Guatemalan society opposed to Arbenz's reforms. The United States embarked on an international campaign to discredit the regime, preventing it from obtaining external support. The threat of Communist influence was used to rationalize taking military action. Eventually, all that held the government together was support from the military. Seeking to bolster his weak security forces, Arbenz then struck a deal with Czech arms dealers, playing right into the American argument that Moscow controlled Arbenz. The Alfhlem arms shipment was approved by the Soviet Union, seeming to prove a Guatemalan-Communist link, all the reason the United States needed to overthrow the regime. Air strikes convinced many Guatemalans that a popular uprising was poised to overthrow the government. As in Iran, the CIA subverted democracy, replacing an elected leader with one the United States had handpicked. Many Guatemalans thought a revolution was being led by Carlos Castillo Armas, and that he had significant support from the Army. But soon, Guatemala was transformed from a democracy to a military dictatorship. Its new military junta would serve well the economic interests of foreign companies like United Fruit. Armas was a compliant servant, undoing Arbenz's land reforms and jailing officials from his regime; such repression couldn't have succeeded without the CIA's full support.

The agency also tried to prevent democratic governments from forming. Such was the case with Vietnam. When the French left, the United States saw an opportunity to engage in nation building, in which America could support an independent Vietnam. The United States wasn't prepared to accept the Geneva Accords, which contained a timetable for free elections to create a unified Vietnam; it sought instead to make Vietnam's division permanent. Secretary of State John Foster Dulles believed that if the Vietnamese people were allowed to vote and unify Vietnam, it would eventually be lost to China, allowing the Communist threat to spread throughout Asia. So Dulles enlisted a counterinsurgency specialist, who would recruit Vietnamese to do the bidding of the United States in South Vietnam. The CIA supported Ngo Dinh Diem as South Vietnam's new prime minister, but his fate illustrates what happens when a dictator no longer serves U.S. interests. Out of touch with the Vietnamese people, uninterested in government, and lacking popular support, he would eventually prove unacceptable; decisions were made to remove him through assassination.

Whenever a nation chose to go democratic without the baggage of anti-Communism, the United States painted such choices as Communist-inspired and attempted to overthrow the government. Anti-Communist governments were supported so long as they prevented mass democracy from taking hold. Such was the situation with Fulgenico Batista in Cuba and Rafael Trujillo in the Dominican Republic. Batista had proven a reliable U.S. ally and trading partner; nonetheless, by the early 1950s, a mass-based movement was developing, eroding support for his dictatorship. Batista began making key policy decisions without Washington's advice, overconfident that he could stem the tide of nationalist appeals. As Fidel Castro's popularity rose and Batista proved incapable of stopping the guerrilla war, the Eisenhower administration sought an alternative leader. Soon, he was forced to flee, and the United States faced a ruler in Castro who was serious about political reforms and political and economic independence. The United States learned that dictatorships can be counted on only up to a point and are not immune from nationalist revolts seeking to create conditions that promote democracy.

A similar lesson would be learned from the Dominican Republic. For most of his 30 years as dictator, Trujillo had America's full support. But after Batista fell, he stepped up oppression. His regime became isolated as a rising tide of nationalism swept Latin America and the Caribbean. In a desperate attempt, Trujillo sought to overthrow these governments inspired by nationalism. This backfired, further isolating him. American policy makers realized that his removal was necessary; they needed to prevent the emergence of another Castro-style leader. The brutal nature of Trujillo's rule convinced the Eisenhower administration that even authoritarian governments need to manufacture legitimacy by making limited reforms. Rule by brute force alone couldn't ensure longevity.

The role of the CIA in overthrowing governments expresses American authoritarianism—its belief in a right to intervene in other nations' political affairs—even when prohibited by international law, such as the charter of the Organization of the American States, which the United States had signed. The Kennedy administration's diverse assassination attempts and schemes for toppling Castro, including the use of the Mafia, underscores America's willingness to ignore international law. Its greatest failure was the Bay of Pigs affair. Using recruited Cubans as the main landing force with American air support, the United States mounted a two-pronged attack: the troops would establish a beach front, fight their way inland, and enlist further support from the Cuban populace, which was expected to rise up and support the coup. Simultaneously, American warplanes would knock out the Cuban Air Force. But the troops got bogged down in the Bay of Pigs, and American planes were unable to take out much of Castro's Air Force. Still, the Kennedy administration and the CIA obsessed over removing Castro. Prior to the Kennedy presidency, the Eisenhower administration had already employed the CIA in numerous covert operations. "Ike had undertaken 170 major covert operations in eight years. The Kennedys had launched 163 major covert operations in less than three."[8] Despite public declarations supporting global democracy, these presidents had elaborate plans underway to destroy it, with anti-Communism as the rationale.

Chile was another country that had long been in the CIA's crosshairs. The Kennedy administration developed with the CIA a "political warfare program," funding efforts to support Eduardo Frei, a pro-American alternative to Salvador Allende. Funding was provided to groups opposed to the Allende presidency, in particular, the Roman Catholic Church and certain trade unions. The agency pumped up resistance in the Chilean military high command and the national police. Such efforts paid off with Frei's victory, but it wouldn't last. Frei couldn't run again since the Chilean constitution limited the presidency to a single six-year term. Allende again loomed as a threat. Once he was reelected, the CIA developed a "two-track approach" to overthrow him. One track specified political tactics, pressure on the Chilean economy, ceaseless propaganda, and distorted foreign policy statements by officials. Track two would be a military coup. The Nixon administration and the CIA couldn't tolerate democracy in Chile, which would exclude the interests of American corporations, such as telecommunications giant ITT, which had major business interests in Chile, including the nation's telephone system. At an ITT board meeting, chairman Harold Geneen proposed to board member and former CIA head John McCone to provide $1 million to support a coalition against Allende.[9] With Nixon's approval, the CIA recruited personnel in Chile to implement both tracks. Foreign reporters were paid to create negative stories in the international press, including an overwhelmingly anti-Allende cover story in *Time* Magazine.[10] With Henry Kissinger as the go-between, the president and the CIA's David Atlee Philipps coordinated the Chile task force. Kissinger went so far as to say that the United States need not "stand by and watch a country go Communist due to the irresponsibility of its people."[11] When it was clear that Allende's election would be ratified, the CIA team waged a campaign to destabilize the economy, which led to social unrest, thus, according to CIA director Helms, justifying a coup. Meanwhile, Allende was nationalizing mine operations and capping profits of foreign companies, intensifying American resistance. In a bold move, the government essentially took over an ITT-controlled company. The CIA enlisted the support of senior Chilean military officers, providing them with weapons and funding to overthrow the regime; but it was unsuccessful. The Chilean people rallied in defense of their government. Allende's election was assured and ratified by the congress. This only intensified the resolve of the administration and the CIA; they saw ratification as proof that Chile would soon become a base for the spread of Communism throughout Latin America. Behind the scenes, millions of dollars were funneled to covert operations, intended to unhinge the regime. As in the past, the CIA used propaganda to develop opposition, especially within the military. The United States withdrew economic support and funding through the World Bank and the Inter-American Development Bank. It bolstered ties to high-ranking military officials and increased financial support. But a CIA-staged military coup was unsuccessful, thwarted by General Carlos Pratt, who strongly believed in the Chilean constitution and supported Allende's government. Events spurred by CIA support of anti-Allende forces quickly led to Pratt's resignation. Allende handpicked Pratt's replacement, none other than Augusto Pinochet, no friend of Allende or democracy. "Pinochet was in Panama and while in Panama, talked with more junior officers he knew from days at the School of the Americas, and was told the United States will support a coup against Allende with whatever means necessary when the time comes."[12] Pinochet soon spearheaded a military coup, attacking the presidential palace on September 11, 1973. His 17-year dictatorship was marked by a notorious human rights record, including the mass disappearance, torture, and killing of thousands of Chileans.

The CIA's determination to topple foreign regimes, even after multiple failures, illustrates the gulf between the official myth of America as a beacon of democracy and the foreign policy reality. U.S. policy makers viewed attempts at democratic governance in Iran, Guatemala, Chile, Greece, and Italy as obstacles to its empire-building mission; it replaced democracies it overthrew with police states. In Iran, the Shah maintained control with Savak, a political police force, until his ouster by the Iranian Islamic Revolution in 1979. In Guatemala, a police state was led by Colonel Carlos Castillo Armas, who quickly abolished unions, reversed land reform laws, banned political parties, and arrested individuals considered leftists. So-called subversive literature was banned, including works by Dostoyevsky and Victor Hugo.[13] After the overthrow of Allende, Pinochet's police state crushed Chilean democracy, abolishing labor groups, banning parties, putting Congress into indefinite recess, firing hundreds of professors, and prohibiting the appeal of decisions handed down by military courts, not to mention the arrests of tens of thousands of people, many of whom who were never seen again.[14]

While the United States created police states elsewhere, a parallel development was occurring at home. An examination of American politics during the 1950s and 1960s reveals increased political repression, preconditions that lay the foundation for an evolving American police state. Many of these factors continued earlier historical trends, while some exhibited more extreme forms of repression. Communism was depicted as an insidious global menace that manifested the qualities of otherness that threatened American conformity. The reaction was to once again use legal means to eliminate independent thought. The Internal Security Act of 1950 enacted anticipatory repressive sanctions, such as granting license to accuse individuals with suspect associations of involvement in conspiracies to overthrow the government and targeting organizations that the government doesn't even identify as anti-Communist. This provision charges the attorney general and his Subversive Activities Control Board to act as thought police. Individuals who harbor subversive thoughts can be blacklisted and deprived of employment. Organizations and individuals can be ostracized based on guilt by association; groups can be economically sanctioned. The act gives government a blank check to define a state of emergency and take police state actions. It gives the attorney general the power to detain anyone believed to be engaged in some form of conspiracy, espionage, or sabotage. Absent is any semblance of procedural due process. In one provision, the government gives itself the authority to take actions against a broader group of aliens or those believed to be possible "fellow travelers" with Communists. It also allows the government to deny entry to those identified as Enemy Aliens. In one of its most frightening provisions, naturalized citizens can be stripped of citizenship due to guilt by association.

Many of the act's provisions bear a striking similarity to those the Bush administration adopted after 9/11. Replace the references to Communism with terrorism, and the result is very similar to the Patriot Act, if less comprehensive. The Internal Security Act was, for its time, one of the most comprehensive forms of legal repression; still, it was supplemented with the Magnusson Act, which authorized the president to protect infrastructure from actions meant to undermine the economy. The Internal Security Act and the Patriot Act also are similar because both were hurried through the legislative process, and in both, presidents expressed their belief that they are the sole authorities in determining acceptable American thoughts and behaviors. With congressional assistance, the Truman and Eisenhower administrations implemented a number of acts increasing political repression, in part responding to the Korean War and espionage cases like the Rosenbergs, which justified further repression. Federal agencies followed suit. In 1951, the State Department decided it wouldn't issue passports to individuals if it concluded that they might be Communists or that their travel outside the United States might be harmful. In 1953, the CIA, with the cooperation of postal officials, began examining first the outsides of envelopes sent between the United States and the Soviet Union, then their contents. The mail of American citizens was being intercepted and read. The Eisenhower administration used the legal means provided by the Smith Act as the starting point and worked with Congress to pass the Communist Control Act, which effectively outlawed the Communist Party (CP). It also assumed that organizations described as following in the CP's footsteps were automatically guilty; placed outside the law; devoid of all legal protections, in particular, the right of association. Invoking and accusing an organization as either Communist or more dubious, Communist-affiliated, was enough to warrant legal persecution. This had major implications in the 1950s when it wasn't uncommon for unions to be tagged with the Communist label, automatically excluding members from many federal government positions.

The intent of the congressional hearings launched by Senator Joseph McCarthy and conducted through HUAC and the Senate Internal Security Committee was to foster a social climate of fear and paranoia in which one's thoughts and actions came under continued surveillance, not just from government but throughout society. Any idea, association, or organization was suspect, no matter how local. Hoover and members of Congress were particularly concerned about Communism in the schools. In one two-year period, investigations led to the dismissal of hundreds of teachers. HUAC acquired a well-deserved reputation as a fanatical agent in pursuit of Communists. The committee had virtually unlimited power to dictate acceptable and unacceptable modes of thought. It had the power to destroy lives, on the premise that political and social otherness posed a danger to America. With televised hearings and reports, HUAC sought to instill mass conformity, making those who had to appear follow the familiar procedure: repentance, confession, and betrayal. The royal treatment was given to personalities who agreed to "name names." It turned into prime-time television when well-known Hollywood entertainers did so, serving to legitimize the committee, while those who refused to testify were "tarred and feathered" as Fifth Amendment Communists.

This national climate of political repression was possible because federal measures were often duplicated on the state and local levels. Laws preventing so-called subversives from being employed by the states passed in more than half of them.[15] Maryland, Florida, Georgia, New Hampshire, Ohio, Pennsylvania, Washington, Alabama, Louisiana, Michigan, and Mississippi also passed laws establishing loyalty programs, banning subversive organizations and prohibiting subversive individuals from seeking public office. Many states instituted loyalty oaths, which were supposed to prove one's unquestioning submission to governmental authority. They became potential barriers to employment, as prerequisites for getting hired.[16] "The swearing of loyalty oaths was also required to obtain permits to fish in New York City reservoirs, to become a public accountant in New York State, to sell insurance or pianos in Washington, D.C., to obtain unemployment compensation in Ohio, to box, wrestle, barber or sell junk in Indiana, to be licensed as a pharmacist in Texas or to become a veterinarian in the state of Washington."[17] On the state and local levels, legislative committees were established to investigate activities they identified as un-American, socializing the public to accept only the official truth and banning a wide range of ideas, books, artworks, and speeches.

Oppression works well when a few examples are made, functioning to keep the masses in line. Those who dared challenge HUAC, such as the Hollywood Ten, were ostracized and blacklisted. Red Channels identified those in radio and TV who had suspect or subversive affiliations. Hollywood was quick to conform, producing films that were overtly anti-Communist or purely "safe" entertainment, such as musicals, which had their heyday in the 1950s. Such fear spread to other media; in print, there was an unwillingness to question government's right to label whomever it wished as Communist or subversive. Publishers acquiesced when the government portrayed well-known writers this way. "Little Brown stopped publishing the works of CP member Howard Fast while Paul Robeson, perhaps the most prominent black American before and during World War II, was omitted from Who's Who in America."[18] Academic research on Communist nations such as China was sparse. More chilling was the number of educators dismissed, due to their possible political affiliations. Even colleges and universities acted as thought police, dismissing faculty with questionable political inclinations. Professional organizations, such as the National Education Association and the Association of American Universities, which should have been on the frontline protecting academic freedom, chose instead to accept the position that Communist Party members shouldn't be employed as educators.

Political repression becomes legal repression when the courts determine that there are legitimate legal grounds for denying people their constitutional rights. Such was the situation in cases where the Supreme Court supported the government's right to criminalize speech. In so doing, the nation headed down the slippery slope of eventually oppressing most viewpoints except for the one dictated by government. Supreme Court rulings in the early 1950s illustrate a court that was not above politics. *Dennis v. United States* began with a federal grand jury indictment in New York of the Communist Party leadership under the notorious Smith Act. The charge was conspiring to overthrow the government through the use of force. The basis for the criminal trial and subsequent rulings by the Court of Appeals and Supreme Court was the idea that Communism itself is dangerous. In the criminal and appeals trials, instructions to the jury revealed the assumption that a belief in Communism is equated with engaging in the violent overthrow of government; thus, the defendants, by definition, advocated violent acts. As the case worked its way up the legal ladder, the defendants were also charged with violating the Smith Act. In the Supreme Court's 6-2 decision, the justices referred to the Smith Act with the mistaken assumption that Dennis's speech was criminal because advocating Communism was the same as advocating violence. Thus, all Communist-style speeches and writings represent a clear and present danger. The court's ruling and the concurring opinions of Justices Frankfurter and Jackson stated that the making or writing of a Communist speech amounted to a conspiracy to commit violence and therefore was unprotected. During the criminal trial, the courts chose to ignore the defendants' definitions of Communism. Although Justice Frankfurter supported eliminating legal protections for Communist speech, he was well aware that this ruling would risk eliminating ideas other than those advanced by the defendants. Justice Jackson admitted that his belief that Communism was a clear and present danger was consistent with the official government position that Communism was "a well-organized nationwide conspiracy." But Justices Black and Douglas recognized that the ruling posed a danger to speech, and they took issue with the way the other justices interpreted Communism. They knew all too well what it meant to censor materials defined as Marxist/Leninist, widely available in America's public libraries. Douglas proclaimed that in criminalizing this kind of speech and conduct, "we enter territory dangerous to the liberties of every citizen." He took issue with the political prejudices of the other justices, defending diverse views and free speech as the best remedy to ideas that Americans might find threatening. Justice Black, like Douglas, understood that the ruling was a product of the times; his opinion expressed the idea that rulings can be the product of manufactured fear. He understood that the references of other justices to a clear and present danger amounted to the suppression of free speech. Other objections can be raised. For example, there should be a higher burden of proof than the government's mere allegation that such speech poses a danger. Even if this burden is met, there are other options besides limiting speech. If ever there was a weakness in the court's ruling, it appears in its use of the term "advocacy." Putting aside the difficulties of actually proving advocacy of the government's violent overthrow, the fact remains that the defendants' speech was suppressed because it expressed a particular viewpoint. The court decided to make such speech a form of criminal conduct.

The *Dennis* ruling had a ripple effect. Soon, hundreds of Communist Party leaders and members were arrested, and many were convicted. In case after case, the pattern was the same, the government had legal authority to act against persons charged with having a viewpoint it found unacceptable, or they had to prove loyalty to governmental authority without question. More loyalty oaths appeared as a condition for all types of occupations, and the courts upheld them. Members of the Communist Party in *Harisades v. Shaughnesay* were accorded the same status as noncitizens who could lose their legal standing and be deported. Since the courts had provided the legal means to act against the Communist Party, membership was sharply reduced; the party was transformed into an underground organization. The government's consistent strategy of attacking the party on all fronts forced it to divert attention from its primary role of criticizing U.S. foreign policy to the courtroom. Critics who dared advocate a slowdown in the arms race within a broader peace movement also were considered un-American, since such criticism questioned militarism, one of the mainstays of anti-Communism.

Loyalty and security programs were among the most powerful ways to promote official truths and squelch opposing viewpoints. They invaded the privacy of Americans, punishing those who didn't fit into the preconceived model of citizenship, which required hard-line anti-Communism. In addition to eliminating all novel and progressive ideas, this official truth visibly impacted American culture, engendering the political apathy of a "Silent Generation." On college campuses, a dullness of mind expressed itself as "don't sign, don't join." Throughout the 1950s, the FBI stepped up activities expanding its records and files on ordinary Americans. Its intelligence-gathering program, Cominfil, would target Communist organizations and use suspected Communist affiliations as a pretext to investigate any political organization, ensuring that political movements and the ideas associated with them did not challenge policy making in the executive branch, especially foreign policy decisions. Under Hoover, the FBI used anti-Communism to pursue a broad surveillance program against ideas and organizations that might question official policy. From the 1940s to the 1960s, the FBI used wiretaps, conducted surveillance of personal mail, and acquired detailed information on the records of political organizations. It provided supporting evidence to justify political repression and to identify the political opposition mobilizing against government policy. Most of all, the FBI was concerned with opposition to foreign policy initiatives taken by the executive branch. With no accountability to anyone other than the president, the FBI's activities began to exhibit early characteristics found in police states, assuming the role of the president's personal mind-control agency, assisting him in the quest to concentrate power.

Despite these developments, presidents up until the Nixon administration had not been able to fully concentrate most state power in their hands. The judiciary was still somewhat independent, and Supreme Court decisions still had the potential to give presidents reasons to pause in their quest for power, at least domestically. Slowly, the Supreme Court began stemming the tide of excessive anti-Communism, beginning with the *Yates* decision, which called into question legal justification for the Smith Act; the Court began making it more difficult to use the Smith Act to rationalize prosecutions of Communists. It went further in *Scales v. United States*, carefully distinguishing between advocating action stemming from speech to an individual having knowledge of illegal advocacy; previous rulings had conveniently overlooked the distinction. In another decision, the court overturned an important part of the loyalty program in *Elfbrandt v. Russell*, in effect, determining unconstitutional an Arizona law requiring state employees to swear that they weren't members of organizations that advanced government's violent overthrow. The court was careful in its ruling to distinguish between membership and whether or not an individual had specific intent to commit acts of violence against government. The result was a blanket elimination of a number of loyalty programs established during the late 1940s and 1950s.

Perhaps the delay in the formation of a permanent police state was the result, ultimately, of the self-destructive tendency of extremist politics, which may have emerged in response to McCarthyism. In 1954, McCarthy had broad popular support for his anti-Communist crusade, but that would change once he began investigating loyalty practices in the military. Questions were raised within the Eisenhower administration about McCarthy's tactics after well-known journalist Edward R. Murrow produced a powerful documentary on him. After the Army hearings, McCarthy's demands for access to privileged decisions within the executive branch brought the confrontation to a head. Republicans and Democrats began to denounce him, leading to his censure. Others opposed him on the grounds that he had gone too far. A broad coalition of groups called his methods into question. Another sign that McCarthyism was on the wane was the November 1954 congressional elections. The Republican Party's Red baiting had resulted in a political backlash at the polls. Democrats gained control of both the House and Senate. Stalin died in 1953, and the Soviet Union's new leadership appeared less confrontational. The Korean War ended with the signing of an armistice. Two years later, Eisenhower met with Russian, French, and British leaders in Geneva, an obvious sign of Western and Eastern cooperation.

At both the federal and state levels, legal repression seemed to be declining. Loyalty programs were losing their strength, and there was an increasing outcry over their arbitrary application. Attorney General Brownell highlighted the need to make more reasoned assessments of who was and wasn't loyal. The rejection of guilt by association was especially significant. The government also changed its response to political dissent. The physical confinement of dissenters, an obvious police state measure, was no longer seen as desirable; and by 1956, the government had found other uses for detention camps that the Internal Security Act had authorized. In *Cole v. Young* in 1956, the Supreme Court reversed a loyalty-based firing. Progressive political movements reappeared: in particular, the civil rights movement.

It is significant that the civil rights movement, which began and grew with a commitment to nonviolence was confronted by government-sponsored violence. As the movement grew, it stressed nonviolence, staging direct action-style demonstrations, such as the February 1960 protest, when black college students in Greensboro, North Carolina, sat at the whites-only section lunch counter in the Woolworth Department Store. Their return every day inspired as many as 50,000 blacks and some whites in 15 other states to participate in similar demonstrations, causing many segregated lunch counters to begin serving blacks. They challenged segregation. This also was the goal of the Freedom Riders of CORE (Congress of Racial Equality), who were greeted with violence, assaulted in South Carolina, and whose bus was set ablaze in Alabama. Hoover's FBI did little to prevent or confront these attacks. Justice Department officials refused to investigate. Actions taken by then-Attorney General Robert Kennedy resulted in the arrest of Freedom Riders in Jackson, Mississippi. The infamous 1963 march in Birmingham was televised, and national and international audiences viewed broadcast images of thousands of blacks marching peacefully who were met with water hoses, tear gas, attack dogs, and clubbing by police. Despite impassioned pleas by blacks in Mississippi, who testified to Congress that civil rights workers and volunteers needed protection from daily violence, neither President Johnson nor Attorney General Kennedy did anything to stop it. Such inaction resulted in the 1964 murders of three civil rights workers. Eventually, the passage of civil rights laws in 1957, 1960, and 1964 proved that a nonviolent mass movement could reshape policy.

Behind the scenes, the federal government conducted specialized intelligence gathering to suppress democratic movements. Such efforts would later influence the CIA's post-9/11 role in forming the police state policies of the Bush administration that it started in the 1950s, using thought control experiments, extensive research programs, and torture to break down an individual's sense of self, employing sensory deprivation to cause the victim to feel that they were causing their own suffering. In 1963, the agency codified psychological torture with the Kubark Counter-intelligence Interrogation manual. With the assistance of Yale psychologist Irving L. Janis, the CIA began using drugs and electroshock treatments to conduct thought control experiments.[19] The goal of Operation Bluebird, under CIA head Roscoe Hillenkoetter, was mind alteration, and LSD was used. In 1952, under Project Artichoke, mind alteration efforts made use of more conventional psychological techniques.

With MKULTRA, a program that emphasized mind-altering techniques with the goal of dehumanizing subjects, the CIA created a culture supportive of mind control. Between 1953 and 1963, the CIA spent $25 million in funding for human experiments carried out by

nearly 200 researchers at hospitals and universities.[20] These researchers were recruited to serve the federal government's perceived right to
dehumanize others and inflict pain and suffering. An early pioneer of
psychological torture was McGill University's Dr. Donald Hebb, whose
research and findings that sensory deprivation can quickly destroy a
subject's sense of self became noteworthy for its eventual application to
prisoners at Guantanamo Bay and Abu Ghraib. The CIA also became
interested in the research of his colleague, Dr. D. Ewen Cameron,
which focused on sensory overload, using a constant stream of messages to elicit fear and terror in combination with mind-altering drugs,
revealing that it was possible to advance to a more accelerated, dangerous form of sensory manipulation. Cameron's techniques included
prolonged drug-induced coma, electroshock treatment multiple times a
day for a month, and the repetition of taped messages like "my mother
hates me." The Kubark Counter-intelligence Interrogation manual
adapted these techniques so that sensory deprivation would lead to
psychological breakdown; it would begin with hooding and sleep
deprivation. Once disorientation took hold, verbal abuse would break
down resistance to questioning. Physical pain supplemented psychological pain. Victims were put into uncomfortable positions for periods
of time; they became convinced that their resistance caused their suffering. CIA agents dehumanized their subjects not only overseas but
in the United States, where operations included paying prostitutes to
sneak LSD into clients' drinks, administering hallucinogens to children
at a safe house, and the use of behavior modification techniques with
prisoners. "For 'terminal experiments'—those that were pushed to possibly fatal limits—agents trolled Europe for dubious defectors or double
agents deemed expendable."[21]

In the early 1960s, during the Kennedy administration, the Office
of Public Safety (OPS), a branch of the U.S. anti-Communist program,
exported torture techniques, part of a much larger foreign policy agenda
to prop up brutal police states in Asia and Latin America. The OPS was
a cover with which to school local police officials in torture techniques.
One of the most notorious examples was the agency's establishment of
a counter-terror program in South Vietnam in 1965; its units unleashed
assassinations, abductions, and abuse designed to destroy the Viet Cong
(VC) political leadership. The CIA drove the formation of Provincial
Interrogation Centers, run by field operatives that implemented torture
against persons suspected of working for the VC. Under the torture and
murder program codenamed Phoenix, the CIA set up shop in Saigon,
using the latest intelligence-gathering methods to target and round up

essential members of the VC for interrogation and assassination. As the program expanded, so did its brutality. Paramilitary units worked with the CIA's provincial centers to capture suspected VC cadres. The standard procedure that the South Vietnamese adopted with CIA assistance amounted to a short interrogation, including torture, followed by execution.

The CIA's involvement in the Phoenix program demonstrates a determination to develop torture into an exact science; it also provided the agency with a national network of places to interrogate and torture an endless number of test subjects, ensuring that the CIA was establishing police states. For example, in Iran, after the shah was put into power, the CIA helped create and train the Savak, a secret police force. The agency also supported the brutal police state of Ferdinand Marcos in the Philippines, providing training and manuals. Under Project X, counterinsurgency materials were disseminated, including a manual called "Handling of Sources," a euphemism for dealing with persons in custody. With Project X, the CIA went way beyond Kubark, supporting a broad array of actions to suppress dissident voices or movements and keep dictatorships in power. Similarly, the CIA's Human Resource Exploitation Training Manual in 1983 was used to teach Honduran police officials and military officers the latest means of torturing and intimidating those who dared challenge the status quo. Project X-style methods were taught from 1966 to 1976 at the U.S. Army School of the Americas in Panama, which later moved to Fort Bening, Georgia, where it was renamed Western Hemisphere Institute for Security Cooperation (WHISC or WHINSEC). Its more than 60,000 graduates included some of Latin America's most infamous torturers, mass murderers, and dictators, including Argentina's Robert Viola and Leopoldo Galdieri; Panama's Manual Noriega and Omar Torrijos; Peru's Juan Velasco Alvarado; Ecuador's Guillermo Rodriguez; members of the Grupo Colina death squad, serving Fujimori's Peru; and officers in the notorious Battalion 3–16 in Honduras, which ran the death squads. Another graduate, Colonel Byron Lima Estrada, was tried and found guilty of murdering Bishop Juan Gerardi for exposing the atrocities of Guatemela's D-2 military intelligence unit, headed by Estrada. This unit embarked on an anti-insurgency campaign, destroying hundreds of Mayan villages and killing tens of thousands. Robert D'Aubuisson, another graduate, led El Salvador's death squads, responsible for murdering dissident Oscar Romero. In Chile, Augusto Pinochet's secret police included many graduates. In the early 1990s, the CIA supplied WHISC with training manuals; activities defined as subversive included criticizing the government and military, engaging in political protest, and participating in civic activities. Individuals and organizations that dared advocate going on strike or that made accusations of police brutality were identified as potential subversives. The manuals identify democratic threats as emerging from universities, youth and student groups, labor unions, political parties, and community organizations that were targeted for infiltration. The agency's Honduras Human Resources Exploitation Training Manual of 1983 describes another standard CIA approach in which the victim's physical environment is designed to be so unbearable as to make the victim turn inward, breaking down his resistance and resulting in self-punishment. Features found in the 1983 handbook, such as sensory deprivation, isolation, manipulation of one's sense of time, and threats of pain or injections come from the earlier 1963 Kubark manual, illustrating the CIA's consistent use of torture techniques. During the civil war in Honduras in the 1970s, the CIA sided against democratic forces, training Honduran soldiers in the United States who were then assigned to a special unit acting as a national political police force and a death squad.

The *New York Times* publication of articles on the CIA's torture manuals and its association with the Honduran military junta was met with an international outcry and calls for congressional reforms. However, despite passage by the UN General Assembly of the Landmark Convention Against Torture in 1984, the CIA continued using the same methods in Latin America. President Reagan sent the Convention Against Torture to Congress for ratification with a total of 19 reservations, delaying passage for six years. The administration couldn't accept its definition of torture. To placate international support, the State Department developed this narrow definition: "the intentional infliction or threatened infliction of severe physical pain or suffering, the administration...of mind-altering substances...the threat of imminent death...or other procedures calculated to disrupt profoundly the senses or personality."[22] Left out were the psychological torture methods contained in the CIA manuals, reduction of sensory stimuli, self-infliction of pain, and physical disorientation. The State Department's efforts created a backdoor approach to rationalizing torture, allowing the United States to escape compliance with the UN Convention and international law. Essentially, the United States only agreed to accept prohibitions against physical torture, allowing the CIA to continue employing psychological torture beyond the reach of international law.

This example demonstrates either a lack of understanding of international law by the executive branch or a callous disregard for it. When the Clinton administration finally approved the UN Convention Against Torture, it accepted the Reagan administration's narrow definition. But, in the early 1990s, the military put in writing clear prohibitions against torture in the 1992 field manual, FM34–52 on Intelligence Interrogation, which cited the Geneva Conventions regarding treatment of captured soldiers and civilians, prohibiting any physical or mental torture. But loopholes persisted. There were no calls to reform or denounce the torture techniques in CIA training manuals. This tolerance created an atmosphere conducive to the CIA's eventual extension of this kind of torture, especially after 9/11.

Ironically, both the promise of, and elimination of, mass democracy in America began in the 1960s. Rising expectations after President Kennedy's election contributed to a surge of optimism and hope for a better America. Following the Cuban Revolution, it seemed that it might be possible to develop a viable alternative to cold war foreign policy. Castro visited the United States and met with policy makers in hopes of establishing peaceful coexistence. Repressive regimes were overthrown in South Korea and Turkey. The civil rights movement gathered momentum, and other movements focused on education, civil liberties, and international peace; and women's rights grew into a broader coalition known as the New Left. From Harvard to Berkeley, student activism grew with demands to have a say in campus decisions and New Left journals appeared. The peace movement, which had begun as early as 1957, gained popularity, focused on slowing the arms race, and eventual disarmament. Students mobilized against the witch hunting of HUAC that continued through the early 1960s and organized against efforts to censor campus speakers. The New Left, which protested the Vietnam War, sexism, and racism, was primarily composed not of revolutionaries but of determined, active interest groups. Unlike its predecessors, the movement lacked a coherent critique of capitalism and sought to work through the mainstream power structure. Student activism took off with the Free Speech Movement, which grew into a nationwide movement for student rights, especially the right of free speech on college campuses.

Meanwhile, struggles developed within organizations: for example, over the Progressive Labor Party's role in the SDS; its ties to the Black Panther party; and the move toward more radical action. The government targeted not just extremist groups, such as the Weather Underground, but it used illegal means to repress individuals or groups identified as "radical." When mass movements took direct action to promote their causes, the U.S. government implemented surveillance, violence, and legal repression.

Feminism was growing in popularity, due in part to various historical factors, such as the large numbers of women who entered the workforce during World War II. For the first time, women were employed as bus drivers, lumberjacks, truck drivers, lifeguards, and barbers. Since they were urgently needed, they were able to attain better wages and working conditions. In industries where women were directly involved in manufacturing armaments, the federal government endorsed the principle of equal pay for equal work. Women who were black, older, married, or who had been excluded from the workforce, were now allowed to participate. But for women who continued to work after the war, there were no supporting social services, such as help in furthering their education or with health or child care. Married women with children couldn't move up the promotional ladder. With the enormous growth in the advertising industry promoting mass consumption, homemaking became an activity to "sell." Housewives struggled over gender identity, partly a result of ideas expressed in Simone de Beauvoir's *The Second Sex* and Betty Friedan's *The Feminine Mystique*, which defined gender politics. de Beauvoir established the idea of sex identity as resulting from cultural differences, determining why one sex has primarily an active, positive role in the world and why the other has a negative or inferior role. A man's sense of self was socially determined in a positive manner, further defined by his relationship to women. The implication was that a distinct female identity was impossible in a male-centered culture, due to social roles imposed on women: marriage, motherhood, and homemaking. Friedan viewed this emphasis as a backlash against the World War II phenomenon of women in the workforce. The emphasis on women's roles as homemakers would prevent them from entering the workplace and from developing separate identities and fulfilling individual potentials and talents. The mystique was the "problem with no name," the resignation and anxiety felt by women who lacked the freedom to choose who they were. Contemporary feminism also emerged from the Kennedy Commission and the state commissions, which led to the formation of the National Organization of Women. In the early 1960s, there was a close association between the emerging women's movement and civil rights. The Civil Rights Act of 1964, particularly Title VII, was used to promote gender equality, too.

Feminism as a progressive movement reached its most creative stage in the early 1970s, when feminism was equated with liberation. Radical feminism grew out of the civil rights movement; it considered the cause of women's oppression to be patriarchal gender relations, and it sought to challenge and overthrow patriarchy. Disenchanted with reformist organizations like NOW, some radical feminist organizations were decentralized, working to change the thinking of women in "consciousness-raising" groups, which brought together intellectuals, workers, and middle class women. These sessions allowed early radical feminists to develop a political ideology based on common experiences with male supremacy. Groups like the Red Stockings viewed men's oppression of women as ongoing and deliberate, and they held individual men responsible for their oppression. For radical feminists, social institutions perpetuated a sex-role system. Both radical and mainstream feminists focused on legal reforms, including Title VII and Title IX in the education amendments of 1972, which forbade discrimination in education, as well as the important but ultimately unsuccessful effort to pass the Equal Rights Amendment. The feminist movement was changing cultural attitudes and laws in the areas of rape, health, and reproductive issues. Throughout the 1960s and 1970s, feminism fostered public expression of ideas, enriching democracy and enhancing the possibility that America could become a more free, accepting society.

But a backlash developed against the advancement of ideas that could potentially alter social relations. The government undertook clandestine political repression to undercut other movements comprising the New Left. As in the past, the motive was fear of mass democracy. The justification during the Kennedy, Johnson, and Nixon administrations was the resurrection of the Communist "straw man." Hoover's FBI began implementing Cointelpro, waging a campaign to destroy the Socialist Left and spreading to other organizations. This was undertaken in spite of the fact that by the early 1960s, the American Communist Party had, at most, a few thousand members. Still, the CP and other leftist groups were fanatically pursued. In Cointelpro-CP, the party was the target of surveillance, FBI infiltration, and attempts to destroy it from within. A campaign of disinformation created bogus counter-organizations, which attacked the CP. The FBI's "Operation Hoodwink" manufactured conflict between the party and organized crime, one of more than 1,000 anti-CP actions it took between the 1950s and 1970s. The Kennedy administration approved the FBI's Cointelpro operations against the Socialist Workers Party, to defeat its candidates running for posts as local as those on the Denver School Board.[23] Cointelpro initiatives aimed to prevent SWP candidates from winning or even running for public office and targeted Socialist Workers Party (SWP) candidates, such as Judy White, who was running for New York State governor; FBI agents in New York helped develop an atmosphere that led to the passage of legislation prohibiting individuals under 30 years of age from campaigning for the governorship. Other Cointelpro measures intended to disorganize the SWP included the creation of antagonisms with other organizations, such as the Mobilization to End the War in Vietnam, with which the SWP was forming an alliance. By burglarizing SWP offices and copying thousands of pages of its documents, the FBI's Cointelpro program was designed to disrupt and ultimately destroy the organization.[24]

These programs were the tip of the iceberg. Cointelpro represented a broad frontal assault on democratic movements to silence democratic opposition; it targeted the civil rights movement, the New Left, the Puerto Rican independence movement, and the American Indian movement. Cointelpro undertook political police style initiatives. Attorney General Robert Kennedy was not at all concerned over FBI wiretapping requests; he was a proponent of wiretapping, and as soon as he took office, became a staunch supporter of its use and eventual legalization. He didn't question the legality of secret wiretaps, essentially giving the FBI a free hand in using them. The usual justification was suspicion of a possible Communist link; thus, Kennedy approved wiretaps on newspaper reporters that the FBI alleged had such ties. Reasons given for wiretapping and bugging homes and offices often were vague; political organizations and notable civil rights leaders, such as Malcolm X, were routine targets. Other federal agencies weren't informed of these actions, especially the more secret instances of bugging known as "black bag jobs," which occurred without the Justice Department's knowledge. Kennedy gave the FBI the green light to proceed with arbitrary secret surveillance and spying on organizations that had broken no laws and were nonviolent. The Communist label on an organization or one's association with such an organization was all the justification needed, and surveillance continued even if no link could be found. This was notably the case with the ongoing wiretapping and bugging of Martin Luther King, Jr. The diversity of viewpoints within the Civil Rights movement and others was unacceptable to the FBI and the federal government, even in the face of evidence that these groups posed no national security threat. The only motive for such tactics is authoritarianism designed to end democracy. Once in place, such methods proceeded with unstoppable momentum, for example, the fateful decision by the FBI to gather information about Martin Luther King, Jr., so as to discredit him as a national civil rights leader. Until his assassination in 1968, the FBI waged an all-out campaign to destroy his reputation, going so far as to insinuate to King that he should take his own life. Cointelpro extended its reach into other civil rights organizations, too. The more direct and confrontational an organization's challenge to racism was, the more persistent were the FBI's efforts to destroy it. The FBI monitored meetings of the Student Nonviolent Coordinating Committee and wiretapped leaders' phones. The next step was infiltration, to gather and use information on an organization's inner workings to discredit it.

There is evidence that Cointelpro actions against civil rights organizations were part of an agenda to prevent these movements from questioning the institutional foundations of racism in America. The most striking example was when Cointelpro focused on destroying the Black Panther Party (BP). Key goals for the party were combating police persecution of African Americans and building within African American communities an array of social services. Armed Black Panthers represented a visible display of solidarity and a willingness to fight police brutality. Most of all, the Black Panthers were determined to establish social programs that benefited the community; they offered free breakfasts to children, free health care, and community education and antidrug programs. Another cause for the FBI's concern was the broad reach of the party's organizing efforts toward bringing into the movement elements not often recruited, such as ex-convicts, members and former members of street gangs, prostitutes, and the poor, as well as its strategy to reach out to, and form alliances with, other movements such as the Student Nonviolent Coordinating Committee (SNCC). The FBI quickly responded by releasing false statements about each to the media. It successfully targeted a group's leadership by alleging dubious violations of the law and by manufacturing evidence that a member of the organization was, in fact, a turncoat, working for the FBI itself. The FBI launched a Cointelpro operation designed to drive a wedge between the Panthers and a rival group, the United Slaves, creating a series of inflammatory cartoons and letters, successfully inciting violence between them. It disseminated the idea that the Black Panthers were anti-Semitic. After the organization passed an anti-Zionist resolution, the FBI sent anonymous letters to the Jewish Defense League hoping that it would strike against the Black Panthers. In the late 1960s, the FBI targeted an up-and-coming member of the Black Panthers, Fred Hampton, who was skilled in organizing and forming alliances. Cointelpro operative Roy Mitchell was working with William O'Neal, an FBI plant, who managed to become Hampton's bodyguard. O'Neal supplied the FBI with a floor plan of Hampton's apartment. Under the pretext of a raid to search for weapons, the FBI stormed the apartment, firing point blank at Hampton, who was comatose from a large dose of Secobarbital, which O'Neal had given him in a glass of Kool-Aid.

Four days later, a similar incident took place. This time, another FBI infiltrator, Melvin Smith, who had also become a member of BP Security, gave the FBI a floor plan. The target was Los Angeles Panther leader Elmer Pratt, who survived the attack. These incidents, and continued raids on BP offices in cities throughout the United States, as well as arrests on a broad range of charges, including traffic violations, the illegal use of sound equipment, or possession of stolen goods, constituted a national effort to destroy the Black Panther party, which Hoover called "the greatest threat to the internal security of the country." Vice President Agnew said that the Black Panthers were "a completely irresponsible, anarchistic group of criminals." Within the Justice Department, Jerris Leonard, the agency head of the Civil Rights Division, called the Panthers "a bunch of hoodlums" and went on to say "we've got to get them."

Attorney General John Mitchell put in place a "special Panther unit" to coordinate law enforcement efforts; federal and state authorities worked to disorganize the Panthers through persecution and prosecution of the leadership, such as in the three trials of Huey Newton, starting in 1967. The trials caused major disruption within the organization as did the prosecution of Black Panther chairman Bobby Seal, who was charged with seven other defendants in the Chicago conspiracy trial, even though he had little contact with the other defendants and had left Chicago before the riot broke out. Other Black Panther leaders were brought to trial in May 1971 in what became known as the "Panther 21." Even though they were found not guilty, many of the defendants were jailed for more than two years, unable to make the $100,000 bail bond. By the late 1960s, the Panthers were forced to devote most of their time and energy to avoiding jail, and by the early 1970s, the party had been severely weakened. FBI and police harassment caused the organization to literally fall apart.

The government was willing to go after any organization that questioned the use of state power and exercised constitutionally granted rights and liberties. Starting in the 1960s, such policies lay the groundwork for a police state. The FBI had enacted measures against organizations considered neither a threat to national security nor suspected of having Communist leanings, such as the American Civil Liberties Union (ACLU), toward which the FBI has had a longstanding hostility. For half a century, the Bureau has employed a broad array of tactics against ACLU offices at all levels, including informants, wiretaps, file searches, checks on accounts, monitoring of meetings, and surveillance and harassment of its members.[25] Such scrutiny was motivated by the ACLU's criticisms of the FBI. Likewise, the American Friends Service Committee, a Quaker pacifist organization, was another nonsubversive organization subjected to FBI surveillance, targeted for its persistent criticism of the militarism so much a part of U.S. foreign policy. Individuals are targeted when they dare exercise their right of free association and question government policy. Dr. Quentin Young, chief of medicine at Cook County Hospital in Chicago, was placed under FBI surveillance for almost 30 years. Why? He was politically active in causes ranging from civil rights and liberties to the antiwar movement, enough to put him under surveillance and label him a national security threat. When Thomas Emerson, a professor at Yale Law School, an expert on the first amendment and a staunch FBI critic, questioned the validity of the government's loyalty program, Hoover targeted him, and he was subpoenaed by congressional antisubversive committees.[26] Unsatisfied with Emerson's testimony, the FBI embarked on a surveillance campaign on his friends and associates. Although no evidence of subversive ties was found, the FBI manufactured a connection between Emerson and Communist organizations, placing him on a notorious list of individuals who would be subject to "custodial detention" in a national emergency.

An important trend that emerged from Cointelpro was the FBI's targeting of political organizations viewed as threatening the expansion of state power in U.S. foreign policy. The antiwar movement, for example, was seen as challenging the potential extension of territorial controls around China through control of Vietnam. The Cointelpro program aimed at the antiwar movement was intended to stifle democratic dissent. In partnership with Presidents Johnson and Nixon, the FBI regarded the movement, which routinely questioned justifications for the military-industrial complex, as directly challenging an executive branch that viewed its war powers as unlimited. Johnson and Nixon were not the first presidents to believe that their wartime powers allowed them to act outside of constitutional limits. In many ways, Lincoln began the trend of presidents exercising emergency powers during wartime so that constitutional protections were discarded. He was the first president to declare martial law, seize property, arrest people without warrants, try civilians using military tribunals, and shut down newspapers. When Lincoln acted outside the Constitution, suspending habeas corpus, he claimed that a president, a single person, has the authority to represent the entire government in wartime. Similar actions were taken in service of empire building in the administrations of McKinley and Roosevelt. They asserted the president's right to unilateral use of military force in foreign policy, further expanding presidential power, while diminishing Congress's role. With FDR and Truman, this trend expands. Subsequent administrations further developed what we know as the imperial presidency, in which the chief executive becomes increasingly determined to maintain his power through political repression. Johnson's view throughout the course of the U.S. intervention in Vietnam was that only he could decide American foreign policy initiatives; he and later presidents expressed their authoritarianism by concentrating power through the manipulation of foreign policy opportunities. When Johnson manufactured the attacks on U.S. destroyers in the Gulf of Tonkin in 1964, Congress acquiesced in artificial state of emergency, unwilling to question the president's authority. When Congress ratified the Gulf of Tonkin Resolution, it gave Johnson complete authority to wage war in Vietnam.

A mass-based, antiwar movement emerged during the Johnson administration, partly as a reaction to the oppressive political atmosphere of the 1950s and partly developing from the nuclear disarmament demonstrations of that decade. At first, such demonstrations were small, attracting publicity due to support from such figures as Linus Pauling and Albert Einstein. The movement's goal was to pressure policy makers to ease tensions with the Soviet Union. Activists pointed to tangible evidence that changes were underway, as demonstrated by Krushchev's denunciation of the crimes of the Stalin era. By the early 1960s, an increasing number of Americans feared the implications of the overkill strategy and Mutually Assured Destruction. A grassroots peace movement was gathering support from middle class professionals, such as the Womens Strike for Peace and Physicians for Social Responsibility. It questioned the government's manufacturing of official truth so as to make Americans conform to and accept its policies. Resistance to cultural conformity was also articulated in the art and literature of the Beat generation. Others in the movement described the madness of the military–industrial complex, expressing concerns that democracy was being eroded by the production and reproduction of militarism. After the Gulf of Tonkin Resolution, the peace movement focused on Vietnam. As the war escalated, Johnson and his advisors reasoned that massive bombing would force the Vietnamese to negotiate; instead, it had the opposite effect. Johnson continually increased troop levels while the media, with few restrictions, covered the war, fostering public questioning. The peace movement was becoming an antiwar movement. The "teach-in," a key tool of the movement, spread to hundreds of campuses. Confrontations developed between Johnson and the movement. It began to preoccupy American politics. As the war dragged on, Johnson became increasingly defensive, behaving like a president who was not a fan of democracy; he believed in an abstract right of dissent but not in exercising that right. Like the presidents who followed him, Johnson behaved as though he was above the Constitution and the rule of law, a belief strengthened by his conviction that the antiwar movement had close ties to global Communism.

Early in the 1960s, Johnson had begun to use the FBI to monitor the movement's activities and gather intelligence about it. In April 1965, Johnson asked Hoover to look into allegations of the movement's connections with Communists, which served to justify extending surveillance to other New Left dissenters like the SDS, which was subjected to extensive wiretapping. By this time, Johnson and Hoover were of one mind: that the antiwar movement and the Left, in general, had Communist ties. The surveillance continued, despite the absence of supporting evidence. The FBI focused on the teach-ins, developing intelligence reports from informants, and distributing them to military intelligence and government agencies.[27] Suspicions deepened to the point where the president was receiving reports on the activities of members of Congress, individuals at universities and in the media, even those who had done no more than send an antiwar letter to the White House. The U.S. government employed repressive measures: one law that had been quickly passed essentially prohibited Capitol Hill protests, a joint effort by Congress and President Johnson to eliminate signs of public discontent over the conduct of the war. The effect was an assault on the democratic right to dissent, a law designed to punish speech, targeting individuals for standing on the Capitol steps, peacefully listening to speeches or reading names of dead American soldiers.[28] The director of the Selective Service issued a directive to draft boards that persons who interfered with military recruitment would be subject to the draft. Students who defied militarism by sending back their draft cards found that their student deferments had been suspended because, according to new guidelines, they were now deemed eligible for induction into the armed forces.

It was not enough to target groups that engaged in civil disobedience, political repression was used to make examples to deter others from doing so. Attorney General Ramsey Clark targeted well-known leaders of the anti-draft coalition, including William Sloan Coffin, Yale University's chaplain and author, and pediatrician Benjamin

Spock. The government sought to eliminate all actions that didn't support the administration's view of the war. The eventual political trials of Coffin and Spock had another goal: to remove from public view all persons and ideas associated with political dissent. In the trial, the government's position was to pursue all persons expressing political dissent, as though they were part of a vast conspiracy. The government could, therefore, invoke national security concerns and act without legal restraint. Lawful demonstrations could be turned into criminal actions. The government's position was that dissenters were an internal enemy of the United States. Political dissent was portrayed as dangerous and violent. Legislation outlawing riots defined a riot as an act of violence or the threat of such an act by individuals in a group of three or more. Any number of acts identified as civil disobedience could be defined as illegal when the government asserts that a demonstration has the potential for violence. The legislation also prohibited the use of any mode of interstate commerce, such as mailing, telephoning or traveling with the goal of organizing or attending a so-called riot so that any normal correspondence or phone call could be considered a riot. In 1968, the term became a catch-all excuse to enact legal means to punish dissenters. Congress used the loose definition to stop campus protests, allowing colleges to deny financial aid to those identified as having caused unrest or rioting on college grounds. With student protests and demonstrations identified as riots, and under the cloak of national security, Congress passed the Omnibus Crime Control and Safe Streets Act in June 1968, making it legal for the government to wiretap and engage in surveillance against anyone who committed acts that threatened law and order. According to this bill, students who participated in meaningful dissent had participated in a riot. Threats to the social order are now in the eye of the beholder—in this case, the government and the president—who could make this determination and order surveillance without a court order for 48 hours. The bill allowed the president to act with total discretion in the name of national security to gather any and all information against domestic and foreign threats and to act to prevent them.

Political repression of the 1960s was largely made possible by the close partnership between the Johnson administration, the FBI, and even the Justice Department. With the approval of Attorney General Katzenbach, the FBI was allowed to engage in surveillance of student activist groups, such as the SDS and SNCC. The Johnson administration shared complicity with the FBI in a campaign to ruin the reputation of Martin Luther King, Jr. Johnson and Hoover agreed to step up actions against the SDS, part of an overall strategy to eliminate the New Left as political opposition. As of 1966, the FBI began to implement the Cointelpro program against the New Left; the program increased in scale in response to unrest at Columbia University in the spring of 1968. In targeting the youth movement, in particular, the antiwar segment and the SDS, Cointelpro employed misinformation campaigns and the dissemination of inflammatory materials to members and even their relatives.[29] Such tactics were effective against the SDS, given its hierarchical structure, creating disunity and in-fighting. Hoover justified the FBI's actions with the same rationale he had used to go after other organizations, the supposed Communist connection. FBI tactics to disorganize the SDS in the late 1960s had been preceded by infiltration as early as 1965. Investigations and documentation of SDS activities followed. By 1967, SDS membership was on an upswing, forging alliances with antiwar organizations, such as the Spring Mobilization Against the War and the War Resisters League. The FBI was alarmed by the spread of demonstrations against the war and campus military recruiting as well as the publicizing and protesting of university research funded by the defense establishment. The SDS was placed on the FBI's Key Agitator's Index. SDS and antiwar leaders were described as un-American for engaging in civil disobedience. The FBI developed a campaign of disinformation, portraying the SDS as having reactionary views, using specially trained black agents to infiltrate it, and then leak information to the press, alleging that it was racist. This depiction required the complicity of reporters at major newspapers, such as Ron Koziol of the *Chicago Tribune,* who worked with the FBI to put together and publish a news feature highlighting internal strife within the SDS. Another strategy used legal means to attack SDS leadership; activists were arrested on trumped-up charges and served with subpoenas. Tom Hayden, a prominent leader, was targeted through HUAC, which subpoenaed him and other New Left members.

Fear of mass democracy became so pervasive within the federal government that the FBI's antidemocratic functions had begun to be supplemented with those of the CIA. Originally intended to function as an international political police to suppress democracies overseas, the agency acquired a new role during the 1960s. When Johnson first approached CIA Director Richard Helms, he was reminded that the CIA was not supposed to engage in surveillance of Americans. Johnson retorted, "I'm quite aware of that. What I want you to do is to pursue this matter, and to do what is necessary to track down foreign Communists who are behind this intolerable interference in our domestic affairs."[30]

Thus, another element was added to the evolving American police state: a supersecret intelligence gathering and counterintelligence agency. The CIA's domestic surveillance program, Operation Chaos, embodied a police state mentality, regarding everyone as a suspect and potential political subversive. One goal was to compile a list of potential and actual subversives; another made no distinction between legitimate threats and U.S. citizens expressing their right to civil disobedience. "The agency compiled a computer index of 300,000 names of American people and organizations, and extensive files on 7,200 citizens. It began working in secret with police departments all over America. Unable to draw a clear distinction between the far left and the mainstream opposition to the war, it spied on every major organization in the peace movement."[31] Operation Chaos had had some forerunners. With Project MERRIMAC in February 1967, the CIA hired numerous staff to monitor or infiltrate antiwar groups, under the pretext of protecting CIA facilities and personnel from disruptions. On its own, and without presidential approval, the CIA began to independently conduct intelligence gathering and surveillance of domestic dissident organizations. Another CIA program, Project Resistance, conducted intelligence gathering and surveillance in anticipation of future actions by dissident organizations. Both fed information to Operation Chaos, with the justification that such measures were needed against the antiwar movement's Communist ties. With Operation Chaos, the police state mindset is already in place; everyone is viewed as a suspect with no right to privacy. The pattern is set, in which the government coordinates supersecret agencies that operate without accountability, providing them a license to target anyone and any organization because they participated in dissent. This authoritarianism extended beyond the actions of the CIA and FBI to the NSA, which created special lists of dissenters and other citizens who might participate in civil disobedience.

Other parts of government joined in a concerted effort to put down dissident groups. Army Intelligence embarked on a plan to commence large-scale domestic surveillance, including preparations to use troops to put down domestic unrest, another indicator of the government's willingness to use force against expressions of civil disobedience. It targeted a broad cross section of organizations from the ACLU to the NAACP to Women's Strike for Peace. Like their civilian counterparts, Army Intelligence collected extensive files on hundreds of thousands of protesters. Its operatives infiltrated the antiwar movement, partnering with other intelligence gatherers, sharing information with local police. This pattern evolved throughout the 1960s: antidemocratic agencies aimed to suppress diverse views through surveillance, infiltration, disinformation, legal repression, and force.

Since political diversity was the enemy, it's no coincidence that groups, such as the American Indian Movement, longstanding victims of political oppression, were also targeted by Cointelpro. By the late 1960s, Indian activism in the movement called AIM surged to protest racism and neglect of Indian lands and resources. The Nixon administration began to take AIM seriously after dissidents seized the Bureau of Indian Affairs national headquarters to draw national attention to the "trail of broken treaties." AIM leaders were targeted; the FBI compiled extensive files. The agency even planned to go so far as to kill selected AIM leaders, such as Russell Means, who had been arrested on fabricated charges. Local police had placed a gun in his cell, taunting him to attempt to escape so as to justify shooting him. The FBI and local police used provocation as an excuse to use violence. Such was the case with the movement's leaders and followers who sought justice for Ojlala Wesley, who had been murdered by a white man. When the offender, Donald Schmitz, was charged with second-degree manslaughter, AIM leader Dennis Banks arranged to meet with State Attorney Hobart Gates to change the charge to murder. Banks mobilized support, enlisting followers to demonstrate in front of the county courthouse; they were confronted by a combination of local police, county deputies, and FBI outfitted with riot gear. The prosecutor refused to upgrade the charge. When AIM representatives refused to leave, police attempted to remove them. An escalation ensued: police attacked the crowd with clubs and tear gas. Declassified documents reveal how the FBI participated in raising tensions, creating justifications to use violence against AIM.[32]

Another often-used tactic was divide and conquer. A rival group headed by Dick Wilson, the leader of the OGLALA Sioux Tribal Authority sought to ban AIM activities on Pine Ridge Reservation. Wilson received grant monies from the Bureau of Indian Affairs to set up what became the Guardians of the Oglala Nation Goons. While the BIA was instructed to provide money and personnel to establish the group, they refused to intervene when tribal members sought help against oppression from Wilson's Goons. Wilson had established a cozy relationship with the federal government; he ruled without outside interference. He became the obstacle to AIM's efforts to initiate land reform on reservations. The Indians sought to remove Wilson by exercising their right of impeachment, but the federal government sent in law enforcement officials to protect him. Tribal leaders and AIM leaders who agreed to meet at Wounded Knee to issue a set of demands were met by a powerful alliance of Wilson's goons and federal law enforcement officers. The military also sent in high-ranking officers, who answered to the White House. Wilson and the federal government were intent on using force, and AIM paid a heavy price: 2 dead and 14 wounded. The violence at Wounded Knee was the outcome of the extensive surveillance and compilation of files on AIM members. Using these files, the federal government arrested many who had been involved with protests and participation in the Wounded Knee incident. The government-backed perpetrators never faced charges.

On all levels, in the 1960s, the government resisted and fought against the expression of mass democracy. Even the Red Squads reappeared, bringing police state practices to the local level, to undermine and eliminate grassroots, mass-based movements. To the Red Squads, there are no differences between criminal and political behavior. Dissent became a political crime in which the suspects or activists are investigated and subjected to surveillance, while efforts are made to dismantle organizational structures. The proliferation of police countersubversive units provided additional evidence for this merging of the criminal with the political. In many locales, they were incorporated within urban police forces. Designed to gather intelligence to produce evidence of political crimes, they were on the lookout for ideas, essentially thought crimes against the state. Police forces in many communities began consistently photographing demonstrations and marches. Innocent organizations were monitored and infiltrated. Their existence was deemed a threat, and all members were suspects. This facilitated the charge of guilt by association. Once an identification was made, files were created and surveillance began, often including wiretapping and the use of bugging devices. Red Squads worked with the FBI's full support and cooperation. They relied heavily on informants enlisted from the ranks of police departments, who operated as thought police, gathering information which they interpreted as subversive. Once a dossier was created, the activities of the person in question were added. The mere possibility that Red Squads could target individuals or organizations and create files on them had a chilling effect. People thought twice about expressing an opinion or performing an action that could draw attention. The act of gathering intelligence amounted to confirmation that the groups in question were a menace, guilty of the abstract charge of subversion, justifying repression of the political other. Senator John McClellan, who chaired the permanent Subcommittee on Investigations of the Senate Committee on Government Operations, concluded that dissent among Americans was incited by Communists: "The police witnesses set the tone for the hearing by their proudly submitted list of names, identifications of leaders and members of target groups, wiretap logs, photographs, informers' reports, dossiers, minutes of meetings, flyers and pamphlets, as well as literature and publications distributed by local groups under surveillance obtained through confidential sources or raids."[33] The federal-local partnership in pursuit of subversives extended to college campuses. Using surveillance and well-placed police informers inside student organizations helped lend credence to government allegations that student radicals had an extremist agenda. Committee hearings were held to prove that the purpose of student activism was to commit criminal acts. Local police developed programs geared toward preventing social unrest through the Law Enforcement Assistance Administration which lumped together legitimate civil disobedience with criminal actions. With the program's significant economic incentives, such thinking became commonplace. Local police units were all too willing to disregard procedural due process.

The equating of political dissent with criminality was also promulgated through the Law Enforcement Intelligence Unit (LEIU). Developed as an independent intelligence gathering unit within the Los Angeles Police Department, it also put down political dissent and gathered data against individuals under suspicion. LEIU conducted intensive surveillance of political dissidents, blurring the line between political and criminal actions: in meetings and conferences, there were panels devoted to dealing with, and prosecuting, subversives. They rejected citizen's legitimate rights to participate in progressive causes, viewing themselves as defenders of the status quo. National LEIU chairman Thomas F. Fitzpatrick publicly connected the Communists with organized crime, making dissent criminal and eliminating any semblance of political participation as a legal right. The LEIU acted on this alleged association, supplying state and federal officials with extensive files on persons engaged in political activities and promoting a crusade against a stereotype of the "radical agitator." This served as a pretext to use violence against political dissent. The Army began teaching riot control to police officers at local and state levels. Protesting and demonstrating now fell into the category of civil disturbances justifying the use of force.

In the 1960s and 1970s, the CIA began working with police departments to subvert democracy in the United States, despite clear provisions in its charter, prohibiting domestic surveillance and intelligence gathering. The CIA got around this provision by using police as its surrogate, becoming deeply involved in training police officers to perform counterintelligence actions, and use various weapons. It provided a broad range of supporting materials, such as "explosives, recorders, transmitters, explosive-detection kits, safes for storage of sensitive material, photographic equipment, lighting equipment, microphones, radio-equipped cars, forged identification cards and polygraphs."[34] This CIA-police partnership was symbiotic—the federal agency provided resources, such as radio cars and drivers while local officers provided intelligence on local antiwar demonstrations.[35]

Many Red Squad initiatives occurred in cities with large numbers of political organizations, such as Chicago, home to the Students for a Democratic Society and the location of the police riot at the 1968 Democratic Convention. The mission of its Red Squad developed by the Daley administration was to go after any form of unrest through surveillance and prosecution. By the 1970s, its mission had expanded from antiwar and New Left activists to any individual or group deemed a national security threat. These Red Squads targeted not only political organizations but any organization seen as potentially questioning the policies of city government and the police, including the Parent Teacher Association, Save the Children Federation, the American Jewish Congress, and the League of Women Voters among many others, which were placed under surveillance.[36] Overt techniques by the Red Squads included finding out who was active in an organization. Once personal data was gathered, the next step was to either prevent or break up public meetings by denying permits. Covert tactics included the use of undercover agents and civilian informers. Surveillance extended to emerging grassroots organizations, including civic or neighborhood block associations. All group activities were monitored. Even Chicago-area high schools and colleges were targeted. The ever-watchful eye of the Red Squads was extended through active collaboration with local media, especially newspapers, which operated as a kind of propaganda arm writing articles critical of those who questioned the activities of the Red Squads.

New York City was another center of Red Squad activity with its broad spectrum of political organizations. The New York Red Squads or Bureau of Special Services (BOSS) operated as a separate political police force. Members were recruited from the New York City Police Department and were trained outside of standard police procedures, with emphasis on undercover surveillance of political organizations.

BOSS members functioned under a cloak of secrecy, tracking various political organizations. The monitoring and compilation of dossiers was undertaken without evidence of threats of violence by the organizations in question. BOSS repressed democracy, first by conducting surveillance and then by carefully documenting public events. Reports were provided to the federal government; they included lists of individuals who had engaged in activities that authorities saw as a threat, and many were then blacklisted. During the 1960s, New York City's Red Squads had shifted from insuring crowd control and orderly demonstrations to the covert gathering of intelligence to intimidate and destroy organizations from within. Police functioned as informers, gathering information and providing evidence of political crimes. The next step was a political trial, which served to warn those who took political participation seriously.

Such trials led to the decimation of the Black Panther Party. BOSS infiltrators leveled 30 counts against individual defendants involved in two plots, one allegedly involving plans to dynamite police stations and the Queens Board of Education and to shoot escaping police; and the other, known as the Easter plot, allegedly to blow up a police station, the New Haven railroad, department stores, and flowers at the Bronx Botanical Garden.[37] The purpose of this political trial was to muzzle a political organization and to criminalize holding a political perspective, sending a public message that the Black Panthers had no legitimate viewpoints. Political trials provide government with a cost-effective means to regulate dissent, but the outcome was not guaranteed. The legal proceeding was infused with the political prejudices of the intelligence gatherers. In seeking a guilty plea, the government faced an uphill battle, given the lack of tangible proof that the defendants intended to commit a criminal act and the lack of evidence other than the defendants' political views. The testimony of key infiltrators was contradictory and inconclusive. But despite the not guilty verdict, the government achieved an important goal. The prosecution, jail time and energies devoted to their defense ended any hope of reestablishing the Black Panthers as a viable political organization. In this sense, the government won.

The trend with Red Squads and other tools of political repression is an ebb and flow. Red Squads appear and grow to be followed by temporary backlashes, the result of a failure of police state measures to fully take hold. That failure comes out of resistance to police state measures, not only from political movements, but from other segments in society. Perhaps the most important reason why police state practices did not, at this time, become permanent, was the failure on the part of police and the government to establish a permanent state of emergency. Also, in the 1970s, unlike the 1920s and 1950s, there were as yet no clear connections being drawn between internal and external threats. Without political hysteria supporting the politics of extremism, government officials lacked justifications to enact full-scale police state-style measures, such as suspending basic civil liberties. The courts came to the assistance of individuals and organizations that had been victimized by Red Squads. Lawsuits filed against police and local officials in cases such as *Holmes v. Church* shined a light on the extent of surveillance that police departments conducted against dissidents; this resulted in public disclosures and measures ensuring that such practices would not be repeated. In Los Angeles State Court, the surveillance of an environmental organization by the police department was found to violate the group's civil liberties. Guidelines were put in place to prevent police surveillance of nonviolent political activism. These were positive developments, but there remained a struggle between advocates of greater control over Red Squads and entrenched resistance to such controls from police departments, many of which remained susceptible to authoritarian inclinations. In 1976, a request from a Memphis resident to inspect his intelligence files resulted in the burning of files that had been collected by the local Red Squad.[38] Apparently, the Red Squads had much to hide, as was later revealed when more documents were discovered. Unearthed in those documents was evidence of a systemic assault on a host of groups, including the ACLU, several biker gangs, the Memphis Sanitation Workers Union and PUSH, as well as the use of a broad range of illegal methods, including the use of bank records, phone company data, photos and other data to conduct surveillance and target them.[39] The lawsuit against the Memphis Police Department led to an injunction to halt covert intelligence-gathering on organizations. The ruling equated such methods with a First Amendment violation and the Mayor and the Police Department were prohibited from engaging in a number of clandestine practices.

Police departments and local officials persisted in engaging in cover-ups when publicly confronted with Red Squad activities. This was the case faced by attorneys who sued to disclose the actions of the Seattle Red Squad, which like the Memphis Police Department, attempted to quickly destroy all of its files. When organizations such as the American Friends Service Committee, the ACLU and the National Lawyers Guild learned that some of the files still existed, they formed a coalition on government spying and filed suit to obtain the documents.

To their surprise, they learned that nearly 200 individuals and organizations and numerous plaintiff groups were still being targeted.[40] Such revelations led to a groundswell of support, which led to the passage of a law that prohibited the use of covert operations to gather intelligence on domestic organizations exercising their constitutional right to political association. The law also prevented police from gathering secret information on any specific political, religious, or civic organization unless there was a legitimate suspicion that they were engaged in criminal activity. Despite resistance from police departments and local officials, civil libertarians prevailed. Litigation in Chicago produced an agreement that police departments could not obtain data on an organization's political actions without evidence of criminal intent.

There was a clear backlash against the Red Squad policies that used to quell political dissent on the local level. But police state methods continued on the federal level. During the Nixon administration, the federal government would go through a kind of dress rehearsal for a police state. In the twentieth century, successive administrations supported various antidemocratic agencies, and no president has ever attempted to rein in or dismantle them. Instead, presidents have enlisted these agencies in an assault on democracy through political repression of social movements. Presidents enter into a partnership with these antidemocratic agencies, in the ongoing effort to expand power at the expense of democracy at home and overseas. Mass movements were regarded as a threat to the "imperial presidency." The ideology was to maintain order at all costs; social control was the ultimate goal. During the Johnson administration, the concentration and coordination of surveillance accelerated so as to better monitor all forms of dissent. A Justice Department Inter-Divisional Information Unit was created to better coordinate all the intelligence that federal agencies were gathering.[41] The Johnson and Nixon administrations targeted some of the same groups, but the Nixon administration was prepared to go further in getting other federal agencies to target political dissent.

CHAPTER 4

Absolute Power at the Expense of Democracy

Once in office, Nixon expanded the apparatus of agencies involved in political repression, a move that would culminate in Watergate, the quintessential illustration of his administration's efforts to eliminate legal constitutional principles. Watergate was a historic first: an administration sought to undermine the electoral process, and in effect, fix an election. The only police state element that Watergate lacked but which was present with 9/11 was an external-internal crisis. Nixon was, in part, hampered by mass movements and an unpopular Vietnam War, while George W. Bush was not; unlike Nixon, the Bush administration had successfully manufactured a threat in Saddam Hussein. Nixon endeavored to eliminate mass-based democracy inside and outside government; by the time Bush took office in 2000, there was not much democracy left to speak of. The Nixon administration helped lay the groundwork for the Bush police state by confronting the broad-based political movements that America hadn't seen since the Great Depression. Nixon was deeply suspicious of diverse viewpoints and those who questioned his authority. His governing style was paranoid, and he exhibited ongoing concerns over whether his associates were friends or "enemies." Nixon's closest advisors regarded opponents of Nixon's policies, especially student demonstrators, as enemies. The administration used the FBI, the CIA, and the IRS to accelerate measures against political dissent.

The Johnson administration had established an important prerequisite for the political repression that would characterize the Nixon administration: subverting legal political participation. Piecemeal police state practices, such as the Mitchell Doctrine, after Attorney General John Mitchell, weren't terribly different from those of the post-9/11 era. The Mitchell Doctrine granted the president inherent power to launch electronic surveillance without a court order in situations identified as important to national security; it stated that the president alone had the authority to make this determination. This radically redefined constitutional authority away from the courts and Congress. Now the executive branch had a free hand to engage in surveillance. This would have dire implications as the administration conducted surveillance inside and outside government. Communications of targeted individuals, including reporters, were recorded through "Kissinger taps." The Kennedy, Roosevelt, and Johnson administrations had all engaged in wiretapping using the FBI. But during the Nixon administration, surveillance was not entirely outsourced; the executive branch developed its own secret unit of intelligence gatherers, "the Plumbers," who sought to control information that might damage the Nixon White House to eliminate diversity of thought. Their tactics aimed at destroying perceived opposition—this was the case with Daniel Ellsberg and investigative reporter Jack Anderson, who was subjected to CIA surveillance, phone tapping, an IRS audit, and general monitoring. The Plumbers' aim was to undermine the electoral process; they sought to smear Democrats by digging up scandalous tidbits with the help of the IRS and the Secret Service. Such actions were supplemented by the Watergate burglars, who broke into the Democratic National Committee offices. National security was the official justification for the break-in, a rationalization traditionally used by administrations engaging in illegal, unconstitutional acts. The White House tape of March 1973 recorded Nixon remarking to Dean that the break-in of Ellsberg's psychiatrist's office could be justified on the basis of national security. The perception that enemies were everywhere set in motion a campaign of illegal break-ins in an effort to gather evidence against them. The administration also embarked on a campaign against mass-based political movements, having decided that democratic expression exhibited by the antiwar and civil rights movements and general campus unrest should be diminished in favor of law and order. These actions were geared toward producing order but not law. Ultimately, the Nixon administration used political repression to diminish political movements so much that the formation of a police state was a matter of time and historic opportunity. It also attempted to eliminate procedural democracy through clandestine measures used against the Democratic Party. This step was without historical precedent.

The "Restless Youth Report" was submitted by CIA Director Helms to Kissinger with the goal of tying student and peace movements to foreign influences. John Ehrlichman was assigned to use the federal government's intelligence gatherers to investigate foreign support for student unrest. Ehrlichman and the president were dissatisfied with the lack of evidence so White House staffer Tom Huston was assigned the task of developing a detailed research report with support from the CIA, FBI, and NSA, connecting campus and domestic unrest to radical foreign movements. The response from the CIA also was not encouraging; it outlined only a peripheral Communist association. But the FBI produced a more positive assessment, describing foreign intelligence services in the United States as attracting American youths and indicating that new international movements on the horizon would soon solidify connections between Communists and domestic unrest. The report did not conclusively prove there were ties; it speculated about future possibilities, imitating the posture of previous administrations that all movements overseas, including nationalist movements, threatened U.S. expansion. But these reports didn't uncover the evidence the White House needed to crush democratic opposition. Plans were developed for intelligence agencies to work with the White House to confront political dissent. The formation of the Interagency Committee on Intelligence revealed a bureaucratic push to invent more radical means than those used by the FBI to quell mass democratic movements. Assembled and promoted by Huston, the ICI recommendations included a broader mission for the NSA to use telecommunications to engage in surveillance on individuals and organizations who posed a threat to national security. It advocated broader surveillance of the mails and extensive use of infiltrators to spy on political organizations. Hoover didn't object to these methods, but he feared a backlash like the one that had occurred in the 1920s over his excessive tactics during the Palmer Raids. He also was concerned that the ICI proposal would block access to the White House, which he had enjoyed for over three decades. Nixon, not wanting to offend and isolate Hoover, withdrew his support for the plan. Nonetheless, it was a historic first in advocating that the government implement a political police structure, clearly violating many constitutional provisions. Previous forms of political repression had set the stage, leading the administration to believe that such a plan was achievable; Nixon said so before the Church Committee. Its unrestrained approach in dealing with diverse political perspectives foreshadowed developments in the Bush administration. It didn't matter whether or not dissent was legal; the view was that no limits should be placed on political repression. Both the FBI and the White House had much to gain at the expense of democracy.

The FBI's leadership position among antidemocratic federal agencies was made public in 1971 when FBI files were stolen from a field office in Media, Pennsylvania. They contained information on the agency's strategy to neutralize the New Left, the more militant segments of the civil rights movement, and the antiwar movement. FBI activities and surveillance were meant not just to monitor political dissent but to eventually act against politically active persons and organizations who, the agency believed, had the potential to participate in activities that could undermine the status quo. The FBI presumed that the government's political enemies were political "others," subversives conspiring to overthrow the government, even when there was little actual evidence to support this: "not a single prosecution for planning or advocating such activity resulted from the over 500,000 subversive investigations carried out from 1960 to 1974. A General Accounting Office study of almost 1,000 FBI domestic intelligence investigations carried out in 1974 estimated that of the total 17,528 such investigations in 1974, only 1.3% led to prosecutions and convictions for violations of any laws and that advance knowledge of any activity—legal or illegal—was obtained in only 2 percent of the cases."[1]

That the Justice Department would use the secret Internal Security Division (ISD) to judge political crimes—even those not yet committed—reveals an obsession to eliminate perceived civil disobedience. Assisting the ISD, the FBI investigated suspect individuals and organizations, acting against individuals who practiced alternative lifestyles, such as those who lived in communes. The FBI put itself in the position of judging which ideas or organizations had the right to exist. But the full extent of its paranoia only becomes clear when one looks at the individuals who found themselves under surveillance, such as participants in Black History Week programs at the Smithsonian and students protesting school cafeteria menus.[2] Such surveillance always involved the creation of extensive files and dossiers in order to identify the enemy. It created a chilling atmosphere. People feared publicly expressing their thoughts, even Senators and conservatives. That members of Congress feared their phones were bugged points to how much surveillance had become a reality for government officials. Given the right set of circumstances, surveillance like this is intended to lead to the seizure and control of persons identified as posing a national security threat. The FBI also created lists of people who would be subject to immediate arrest in a national crisis. First known as the Security Index and later the Administrative Index (ADEX), this list would enable the president to arrest and detain people without due process. Containing political and nonpolitical offenders alike, ADEX listed individuals and/ or organizations that could influence others and, according to the FBI, threaten national security, implying that the FBI had the necessary knowledge to determine what constituted a national security threat.

During the Nixon administration, the CIA worked with the White House to subvert procedural democracy, another historic first. The CIA supplied the fake identities of the Plumbers, who broke into the Watergate Complex, one of many domestic actions that violated the agency's charter. In another violation, the CIA prepared for the White House a psychological profile on White House enemy Daniel Ellsberg. Working with the White House, the CIA attempted to derail the Watergate investigation and cover up the crime; it continued illegally spying on Americans in the Operation Chaos program. Five of the seven Watergate burglars had been employed by the agency. The CIA was especially interested in hiding from prosecutors its assistance to one of the burglars, E. Howard Hunt; it even destroyed evidence. FBI investigators encountered resistance from CIA executive director, William Colby, who directed subordinates to withhold relevant information, specifically denying the CIA's assistance to Hunt. It also withheld evidence that White House staff member John Ehrlichman had requested that the CIA help Hunt. Another Watergate burglar, James McCord, a 22-year CIA veteran, shed light on the White House-CIA connection. In an attempt to unravel the burglary, the FBI sought information from Lee Pennington, McCord's immediate superior at the CIA and a close friend. Sensing that the FBI was about to tie Pennington to McCord and Watergate, Pennington went to McCord's home to destroy documents.

Just three months after the burglary, the administration used the IRS to attack Nixon's political enemies, including those in the Democratic Party. The IRS began its own form of intelligence gathering, collecting the fiscal records of persons and organizations solely on the basis of political perspective. In response to the FBI's request, part of its Cointelpro program, the IRS provided to the agency confidential tax records of leaders of political groups. Now another federal agency had been enlisted in the campaign to diminish democracy. A specialized department, the Special Services Staff, was established to go after political dissenters. It allowed the IRS to selectively persecute and intimidate any person or organization strictly on the basis of their politics, including progressive movements, and a cross section of American society, including Common Cause, the National Council of Churches, the Playboy Foundation, and the New York Review of Books.[3]

The IRS had a history of selective persecution of organizations, working with administrations to silence political opposition through economic sanctions. The Internal Security Act of 1950 provided the IRS with the rationale it needed to investigate tax records and the tax-exempt status of organizations. Partly at the urging of Congress, political repression by the IRS from the 1950s to the 1960s drew upon fear of political outsiders coupled with incentives for those who informed on others. In the 1960s, through Cointelpro, FBI infiltrators joined suspect groups, allowing them to gather financial data, which was then passed on to the IRS. The FBI also obtained financial data from tax returns that the IRS had provided. The IRS was used to realize the administration's intentions as John Dean put it, in the infamous 1971 memo, using "the available federal machinery to screw our political enemies."[4] Eventually, Dean requested that IRS Commissioner Walters have the agency thoroughly investigate persons on his enemy list, including entertainers, members of Congress, economists, and McGovern supporters. Like other intelligence gatherers, the IRS initiated clandestine surveillance through programs like "Operation Leprechaun," created in 1972, in which it recruited agents to use sex and alcohol to obtain tax information through an extensive network of informants. The IRS created intelligence-gathering operations intended to violate the privacy of U.S. citizens and obtain information irrelevant to their tax status. Nonetheless, for all the information gathered, this program failed to meet any objective criteria as to what constituted relevant tax information. The IRS used Operation Sunshine to get informants to obtain information far outside the scope of tax information; most of it concerned sexual activities and personal habits of suspect individuals. IRS agents were now in the position of using information gathered on their private lives to prejudge political inclinations.

Many of the administration's actions went beyond the Constitution. Article 1, Section 8, says that only Congress has the power to authorize domestic use of the military and only to repel an invader; put down armed rebellion; and, if necessary, to execute the laws. The president's authority is limited to deploying troops to protect the United States from an invasion and halt national violence and then only with the approval of state authorities. But during the Nixon administration, the military developed the nation's second largest program of domestic surveillance after the FBI. Its key purpose was to monitor civil disobedience. This was not entirely new: the Army has a history of confronting those who opposed military intervention overseas. Army intelligence during World War I had played a central role in oppressing resistance to U.S. entry into the war, setting up the Domestic Core of Intelligence Police with a surveillance arm, the Military Intelligence Division. But in the 1960s, Army intelligence would create Continental United States Intelligence (CONUS), a massive surveillance program, to gather and store intelligence data on civil rights and antiwar organizations. It consisted of the U.S. Intelligence Command (USAINTC); the Continental Army Command (CONARC); the Counter-intelligence Analysis Branch (CIAB), also a part of the Chief of Staff of Intelligence (OACSI); and finally, the Directorate of Civil Disturbance and Planning (DCDPO), later changed to the Directorate of Military Support (DOMS). The acceleration of Army intelligence coincided with the height of civil rights activism, increasing as the movement shifted focus after Martin Luther King, Jr.'s assassination with the establishment of the DCDPO. Other intelligence bureaus used sophisticated technology to monitor all forms of communication in the United States.

With USAINTC and CONARC, the first step needed to engage in wholesale political repression was in place: technology to gather information on political "others," whom Army Intelligence could characterize as a national security threat. Military intelligence agencies gathered these data as other agencies did, by identifying the menace presented by political outsiders and by using confrontations with outsiders as a lesson to bystanders. Also characteristic of Army intelligence was its creation and maintenance of files on a broad spectrum of individuals and more than 700 organizations. Army Intelligence was on the lookout for signs of political participation, such as groups of people who march and demonstrate, seen as a disturbing indicator of possible future violence. The way to halt political participation, according to this assumption, was to focus on the leaders of mass movements, the "agitators." For Army Intelligence, the FBI, and the CIA, a single incident could serve as the rationale to monitor, act against, and politically repress an entire organization. The USAINTC would fabricate evidence that the leadership had been working on elaborate conspiracies to disrupt American society. One example was the reaction to the assassination of Dr. Martin Luther King, Jr., after which Army Intelligence units implemented surveillance of civil rights organizations, searching for reasons to act against the movement. They searched for sources of political unrest at the Democratic National Party Convention, to which as many as 60 intelligence agents were dispatched; there was a similar presence at Nixon's inauguration. Units concentrated surveillance on gatherings of all kinds, including "a procession of black Olympic stars...a Halloween party for elementary schoolchildren in Washington, D.C., suspected of harboring a local dissident; a demonstration of welfare recipients; a meeting of a sanitation workers' union in Atlanta, Georgia; a Fayetteville, North Carolina church group; a Southern Christian Leadership conference...an anti-war vigil in the chapel of Colorado State University."[5]

While the Nixon administration had not become the fully developed police state that would appear during the Bush administration, both legitimized repression following a major incident. On March 1, 1971, the U.S. Capitol switchboard received a call, warning that the building would blow up in 30 minutes. Thirty-three minutes later, a bomb exploded in the ground floor men's room. Although the bombing pales in comparison to 9/11, both events triggered extensive legal repression on the pretext that they represented actions by political outsiders. Almost 24 hours after the Capitol bombing, the Weather Underground, a splinter group of the SDS, took credit for it, as a response to the invasion of Laos. The government demonstrated its legitimate authority to act against those who use violence, destroying property and endangering human life. But the Nixon administration used the event to rationalize excessive methods. Consider the FBI's arrest of a material witness, antiwar activist Leslie Bacon. Despite what was supposed to be credible testimony from an informant, the FBI would conclude that Bacon knew nothing about the bombing. Her proximity to the Capitol made the FBI initially suspect her involvement in or knowledge of the bombing, and an informant had connected her to it. That was the extent of the evidence against her. Then her legal odyssey began. She attended numerous hearings and appeared before a federal grand jury. With the Organized Crime Control Act of 1970, the prosecutor, Guy Goodwin, had the tool he needed to charge Bacon with what amounted to a political crime, forcing her to renounce her due process rights. The Act forced witnesses to accept immunity during the grand jury only to be indicted later; if witnesses refuse, they can be sent to jail for the 18-month duration of the grand jury or longer if they still refused,[6] placing defendants in a legal catch-22. If he or she testified in the manner that the prosecutor wanted, it amounted to self-incrimination, but defendants would be jailed indefinitely for refusing to testify against themselves. The prosecution was determined to find Bacon somehow responsible, due to her past political associations with a radical group, the Piggy Bank Six, which had bombed the First National Bank of New York. In fact, Bacon had left the group a month before the bombing. Her attorneys knew that, given the provisions of the Organized Crime Control Act, she could be compelled to testify in spite of invoking the Fifth Amendment. She had no choice but to waive her right against self-incrimination. Although she hadn't been charged with a crime, Bacon found herself in custody.

The political nature of the trial becomes evident when one considers that Attorney General Mitchell was the driving force behind Bacon's prosecution. Mitchell had issued the order to indict her on bank conspiracy charges based on her loose association with the Piggy Bank Six. This was despite the fact that even the New York County District Attorney's Office didn't believe that credible evidence linked Bacon to the bank bombing. In September 1971, the U.S. Appeals Court ruled that Bacon had been illegally detained and arrested. Other charges were dropped when the Supreme Court ruled in the *Keith* case that a grand jury witness could not be compelled to provide testimony if the government had gathered evidence through illegal surveillance. The New York County District Attorney's Office had to drop the bank conspiracy charge against Bacon, or it would have to reveal how it had acquired the wiretaps with evidence against her. The political trial of Leslie Bacon underscores the lengths to which the Nixon Justice Department was willing to go to in order to exemplify what could happen to political dissenters. The case proceeded, even though the FBI had found unreliable the one piece of evidence provided by an informant.

Bacon's prosecution indicates how a federal grand jury can be used as a weapon to undermine the right to dissent. The administration had created the federal grand jury in accordance with the goals of the Justice Department's Internal Security Division, which dealt with cases involving essentially political crimes, defined as any thought and related action that questioned administration policies. Robert Mardian, a high-ranking Justice Department official, controlled an intelligence-gathering unit of the White House, the Intelligence Evaluation Committee, with which the ISD monitored activities seen as jeopardizing national security. Led by Goodwin, the ISD operated in many ways outside of normal legal proceedings. Unlike prior grand juries, it didn't investigate to determine if sufficient evidence supported allegations that a law had been violated; instead, it proceeded with an assumption of guilt and gathered evidence to prove it. Political activists were by their nature, guilty; they were targeted primarily through ISD's subpoena power, which forced defendants to admit guilt or face imprisonment for contempt, extending the power of a grand jury to persecute dissidents. Subpoena power equaled guilt by association. This grand jury's reliance on informants also placed it outside the law, violating the constitutional right to confront one's accusers. On the assumption that conspiracy lay behind alleged political crimes, the grand jury could draw in as suspects any persons that a prosecutor chose to subpoena; in one antidraft case, more than 100 witnesses, including parents of draftees, counselors, and doctors, were subpoenaed.[7] Goodwin had made it his life's work to use the legal system to pursue radicals; in his hands, the grand jury undercut political participation. He used a criminal conspiracy charge to subpoena members of Vietnam Veterans Against the War for exercising their right to demonstrate outside a political convention.

Another grand jury maneuver supported government surveillance of the Black Panthers. Eldridge Cleaver was under surveillance and faced prosecution. Numerous individuals and groups publicly defended him in an advertisement in the New York Times. In response, a Philadelphia grand jury subpoenaed his defenders and donors, allegedly to investigate mail fraud.[8] The message that the grand jury sent was clear: any person or group supporting a right to dissent could be prosecuted. The ISD was an unregulated agency that looked with great suspicion upon even nonpolitical activities. Grand juries served two purposes: to silence dissident voices of all kinds and to use the law as a weapon so that the government could, for arbitrary reasons, label anyone a political criminal. The Nixon administration ruled out of fear that Americans were conspiring against it. People who questioned the president's policies or expressed antiwar sentiments could automatically trigger scrutiny and placement on Secret Service lists.

The administration also attempted to achieve thought control by muzzling the press. Units of the IRS, the Justice Department and the Federal Communications Commission were assigned to monitor and undermine the press.[9] Not long after Vice President Agnew publicly attacked the media, the FCC began investigating news coverage. When the administration used the courts to control how reporters used their sources, which amounted to censorship, it won favorable rulings, having argued that it had the right to discover the origins of information for news stories. This effectively made reporters function as government informers, setting a precedent in effectively shutting off information sources. With subpoena powers in hand, the government argued to the Supreme Court in *U.S. v. Caldwell* that a reporter must reveal sources to a grand jury when asked. The case had the desired chilling effect. Those who refused to disclose their sources faced jail time. Despite the administration's loss in the Pentagon Papers case, it issued subpoenas for all of the publishers' businesses records, including every bank check written in a given period.[10] It didn't take long for such actions to have a cumulative effect, resulting in a press far less critical of the Nixon administration. At first, the press didn't pay much attention to the Watergate break-in. When the Washington Post began its coverage, the White House relentlessly attacked it. The historical development of an American police state was not completely linear. It grew over time in waves, advancing and receding. While the measures taken by the Nixon administration represented an advance toward a police state, other events—in particular, the Watergate scandal and the unfavorable course and outcome of the Vietnam War—slowed it down.

By the 1960s, the United States faced a developing world rebelling against colonialism and dictatorial rule. Revolts occurred against colonial regimes in Africa while there were nationalist-inspired revolutions in China and Cuba. Vietnamese Communists fought to liberate Vietnam from the French to unite the country. During the Kennedy, Johnson, and Nixon administrations, the United States accelerated support of various puppet governments in Saigon; meanwhile, increasing troop levels began having negative consequences, such as an upsurge of anti-Americanism in Western Europe and the developing world. Escalating costs for the war strained the U.S. economy and weakened the dollar's strength abroad. The United States also bore the burden of the costly arms race with the Soviet Union. Pressure mounted to limit the use of strategic nuclear weapons, improving United States-Soviet relations so as to isolate China. Nonetheless, both superpowers were committed to achieving a technological breakthrough, leading to a first-strike capability. As the war dragged on, America's ability to impose its will on the internal affairs of other nations began to be questioned. Despite sending over 500,000 troops and dropping 7 million tons of ordnance, no progress was being made toward victory. It became increasingly clear to the media and many Americans that after the 1968 Tet Offensive, the war couldn't be won. Nixon had pledged that upon assuming office, he would withdraw from Vietnam. Yet, despite the massive troop withdrawal, he continued the bombing, even extending the war into Cambodia. The 1970 invasion generated the greatest opposition to the war, with peace rallies attracting hundreds of thousands.

Ironically, the administration's political repression reinforced the credibility of the antiwar movement and helped shape public opinion against the war. Congress attempted to reassert its authority over foreign policy with the Fulbright Hearings, threats to cut off funding for the war and passage of the War Powers Act in 1972 requiring that presidents explain their actions within 30 days of committing troops to a foreign war. After that, such actions required congressional approval. The last time the president had consulted with Congress over war-making was in 1964, when Johnson submitted the Gulf of Tonkin Resolution. The eventual exit of the United States from Vietnam showed that American empire building could be checked, even defeated by a nationalist revolution.

But while Congress reasserted its oversight power by investigating Watergate and holding the Church Committee Hearings, the result of these actions would be primarily cosmetic. The hearings failed to recognize that the administration's actions were part of a larger historical pattern of political repression and an assault on democracy. Congress failed to connect domestic political repression and the elimination of democratic movements overseas. The Church Committee report included no references to the extension of the Vietnam War and the bombing of Cambodia. The most glaring omission was the failure to understand that the underlying causes of Watergate were structural, not simply the result of the personalities involved. Nixon was able to conduct such a broad assault on democracy because of the existence of institutions—the FBI, CIA, Army Intelligence, and even local police departments—which, by their very nature, functioned in a manner hostile to democracy. They viewed political dissent as tantamount to committing political crimes. The televised hearings emphasized particular esoteric aspects of the break-in, such as mistakes made by Watergate burglars and favors done for Nixon pals, while ignoring the extensive use of Cointelpro against the civil rights and antiwar movements and how government used political dissent to rationalize assaults on democracy. Without political movements, little stands in the way of government's natural tendency to expand its power, supporting increasingly authoritarian policies. The Nixon administration had accomplished extensive political repression against mass movements by the time the Watergate scandal had unfolded. By the mid-1970s, the political movements of the previous decade were being worn down by political repression. With a few exceptions, by the 1980s and 1990s, mass-based political movements were no longer a visible presence in the streets.

But while progressive mass-based movements declined, movements of a different kind had begun to fill the political vacuum, eventually facilitating, not opposing, the formation of a police state. In post-Watergate America, right-wing movements would form an enduring political alliance with policy makers. Two principles paved the way: staunch anti-Communism and cultural traditionalism. Anti-Communism, the backbone of U.S. foreign policy, was used to crush global nationalist movements. It was a moral crusade, providing an added bonus: the facade of an America that supported democracy. The Right promoted moral traditionalism to an extreme, against all diverse viewpoints, making one ideal standard of conduct for society. As the right grew throughout the 1970s and 1980s, its agenda demonized a broad range of policies and ideas that advanced democracy; it condemned behaviors from premarital sex and birth control to homosexuality and sex education in the schools and opposed all efforts toward racial and gender equality. Well into the 1990s, the Right would align itself with government so long as policy makers resisted initiatives that narrowed class, racial, or gender differences. The right feared democracy and any government expansion of people's freedoms.

The roots of the political right go back decades. With anti-Communism among the oldest right-wing concepts, the movement had confined itself to projecting influence in foreign policy. Anti-Communism surged during McCarthyism, while the Right also mobilized against the Civil Rights Movement. In 1954, the Supreme Court decision *Brown v. Board of Education* galvanized the racist Right. Fighting back with legal repression, Citizens Councils organized, eventually forming alliances with the Ku Klux Klan to halt efforts to integrate the South, passing laws supporting segregation. As the civil rights movement grew, the councils disappeared, but a larger strategy was now unfolding by the Right to attack any progressive policy; by the early 1980s, it would translate into the acquisition of significant political power. This strategy had its roots in the 1930s during the passage of the New Deal. Right-wing movements criticized government's growth, especially its provision of social services, the New Deal, and passage of civil rights legislation, all associated with the Democratic Party.

Although political repression originated from both parties, the Right had greater access to Republicans. Progressive movements targeted the Democratic Party. During Barry Goldwater's presidential campaign in 1964, the Right began broadening its demographic base, appealing to Southern voters disturbed about civil rights, staunch anti-Communists, and opponents of New Deal programs. Despite Goldwater's defeat, the Right continued organizing to raise funds to support like-minded candidates. This grassroots alternative to left-wing organizations proved valuable. Campaign volunteers had been trained in organizing; on college campuses, the Young Americans for Freedom formed alliances with evangelical Christians. In 1968, anti-Communists, anti-civil rights groups, the John Birch Society, and the Liberty Lobby all supported George Wallace. Nixon was the beneficiary of this pushback against civil rights. His campaign made numerous negative references to welfare, affirmative action, and street crimes, not-so-subtle references to African Americans. By the 1970s, having developed into a powerful grassroots organization, the Right had created a cultural climate and a political agenda that fostered political repression.

By the eighties, the "New Right" replaced the "New Left" as the social foundation of American politics. Political repression of the New Left allowed the right to fill the political vacuum. Front and center were the moral traditionalists of the evangelical Christian Right. This new coalition agreed on basic principles: militarism, traditionalism, and libertarianism. It helped put Nixon in office and supported his conduct in Vietnam and support of global dictatorships. The remaining mass-based democratic movements, such as feminism, further mobilized the right wing against the Equal Rights Amendment, abortion, and gay rights. Grassroots groups opposed school textbooks and curriculums that taught Darwin's theory of evolution. Ironically, even Nixon supported the ERA's guarantee of equal protection for women. Its defeat demonstrated how right-wing movements contributed to political extremism. Phyllis Schlafly joined with ERA's congressional opponents, and Anita Bryant helped organize against it. The political perversity of right-wing movements is that they distort democracy's meaning. Right-wing movements claim to represent the masses, but they serve the interests of elites. The ERA was a legal reform that would have benefited all women, yet it was twisted to be depicted as a measure against all women. The same applies to how such groups portrayed gay rights, civil rights, and abortion. The right to choose how one lives frightens members of right-wing movements, threatening the authoritarian mindset.

The Church Committee Hearings, a noble effort, investigated executive power and the relationship of the executive branch to intelligence agencies. Their findings implied that other branches of government, especially Congress, had enabled the executive branch to assume powers that were nearly dictatorial; presidents used intelligence agencies without legal restraint, developing relationships defined by ambiguous laws with no effective limits on presidential authority. The Committee also identified institutional breakdown: officials within the executive branch were instructed to violate the law, while in covert actions at home and overseas, intelligence agencies clearly subverted democracy. These actions mostly took place without Congress's full consent, and a broad range of national security initiatives had no congressional oversight. The pattern the committee identified was that national security was used broadly to rationalize political repression. The executive branch used the cloak of national security or the threat of subversion to act as an autonomous, decision-making body outside legal guidelines and constitutional principles. The hearings determined that the concentration of power in the executive branch and its partnership with intelligence agencies worked to eliminate mass-based democratic movements and that a clear pattern existed of covert actions designed to intimidate, disrupt, and destroy political organizations engaged in lawful activities, protected by the Constitution. Surveillance and intelligence gathering extended to citizens who were nonpolitical but dared to question or adopt a lifestyle at odds with the administration's policies or narrow ideology.

In exposing the administration's disregard for law and the Constitution, which was implemented through federal agencies, the committee's findings seemed to promise that what had been a steady march toward a police state would be halted. It made more than 180 detailed recommendations, intended to prevent future abuses of presidential authority and intelligence gathering. Congress passed bills regulating how presidents wage wars, prohibiting warrantless surveillance by the executive branch, even limiting the FBI director's term of office. Congress also created permanent committees in charge of overseeing the intelligence community. The Church Committee and Congress understood the effects of the unrestrained, unaccountable concentration of power; they also understood what happens when institutions rationalize political repression. The committee criticized the FBI's role in violating constitutional protections afforded to organizations and its suppression of diverse viewpoints essential to democracy in the name of fighting subversives. According to the committee, when federal domestic and foreign intelligence-gathering institutions lack clear legal guidelines, they will arbitrarily monitor the activities of all Americans, whether or not they pose a national security danger. The committee also found that in abiding by the wishes of the executive branch without legal restraints, foreign and domestic intelligence gatherers violate the rights of U.S. citizens and principles of international law. So a central theme was the establishment of clear legal guidelines, spelling out what intelligence gatherers can and cannot do. But the committee did not adopt the proposal that would have subjected intelligence agencies to legal guidelines determined by Congress, which would have defined their function and clearly limited their authority.

The most significant reform emerging from the hearings was the passage of the 1978 Foreign Intelligence Surveillance Act, which would ultimately figure prominently in the emergence of the American police state. FISA appeared to address the lack of legal guidelines on when to engage in surveillance. In principle, the purpose of the FISA court was to prohibit presidents from acting as the final interpreter of what is legal and constitutional. The FISA court removed the Nixonian claim that presidents decide what is legal and can appeal to any inherent authority they believe they possess. It would eliminate open-ended political repression in the form of covert operations justified by references to subversion or national security. Under the FISA court, requests to gather intelligence and conduct surveillance would only be granted if they could be proven necessary to deal with espionage or terrorism. According to the provisions establishing the court, warrantless surveillance of U.S. citizens was legal only as a temporary measure, suspending the constitutional requirement for a warrant. An emergency provision in FISA made it possible to conduct surveillance prior to obtaining a warrant. If Congress issued a declaration of war, warrantless searches would become legal for a period of not more than 15 days.

With that provision, Congress had done something it had never before done; it gave the federal government legal authority to conduct surveillance without a warrant. Over time, the FISA court began operating as a paper tiger, since the laws make no mention of how to prevent or punish violations. Ironically, it would not be long before incoming administrations would come to use the FISA court to rubberstamp political repression. Administrations would strongly resent having to go to a FISA court to conduct surveillance, a clear indication of just how concentrated power was becoming in the executive branch. The government was willing to ignore the FISA court in times of crisis, since it still felt it had a license to sidestep law in favor of covert operations, essentially eliminating procedural democracy. Even when the government played by FISA's rules, the court had the effect of essentially making illegal actions legal by rubberstamping requests to engage in secret surveillance. Finally, according to the FISA law, any consultation that Congress had with presidents amounted to no more than the submission of information instead of a genuine check on presidential power.

For all the reforms the Church Committee made on the federal level, it failed to address the role that local police forces still played as political police, gathering evidence to build cases—through wiretapping, bugging, harassment, even infiltration—against participants in lawful and peaceful association. Local police authorities cooperated across local and state boundaries.[11] Right-wing political organizations were not subjected to the same kind of infiltration and surveillance as those on the Left, so a political double standard emerged. In fact, right-wing organizations formed alliances with local police officials to gather intelligence on left-wing organizations. In New Hampshire, pro-nuclear forces partnered with state police who infiltrated a pro-nuclear group.[12] Local police and right-wing groups worked together to suppress those who sought alternatives to the status quo. In 1968, the New York Red Squad considered forming an alliance with Edgar C. Bundy, who led the Church League of America, a far right-wing organization with extensive files on so-called subversives. Bundy was already working with the Chicago police to share files on subversives in a cozy arrangement that the police found extremely beneficial.[13]

For all the reforms that came out of the Church Committee Hearings, resistance from right-wing political movements and local Red Squads reversed many of them while repression and surveillance of progressive organizations persisted on the local level. In the 1980s, the Christian Right undertook nationwide violent attacks on abortion clinics, using bombings, arson, vandalism, death threats, and assaults on clinic workers to shut down clinics. Right-wing violence and hatred extended to various minorities, especially homosexuals. Pop singer Anita Bryant led the opposition to reverse Miami-Dade County's local antidiscrimination ordinances, and her "Save Our Children" campaign attempted to pass a California state initiative to ban homosexuals from teaching in the school system. Antiabortion forces successfully prevented federal funds from being used to pay for abortions of poor women. In 1979, the Federal Protection Act was passed, an expansive bill with many provisions, further restricting access to abortion and limiting gay rights, weakening sex discrimination laws, and providing tax relief for stay-at-home mothers.

On the surface, it had seemed that Church Committee revelations, coupled with the defeat in Vietnam, could shift U.S. foreign policy away from supporting dictators and crushing nationalist-democratic movements. Instead, there was little real change, despite the committee's well-documented narrative of all the dictatorships that the CIA helped install after overthrowing governments. While the Ford administration and Congress were fully aware of how Pinochet came to power in Chile, the administration decided to continue the policies of its predecessor, eliminating any chance for democracy there. The rationale was the age-old argument that Communism must be stopped.

Although the Church Committee had established that Chile posed no danger to national security, the Allende government was overthrown because it represented a threat to U.S. corporate interests. Despite his military dictatorship and humans rights abuses, Pinochet remained in office with American support, as did other unsavory leaders, such as the Shah of Iran and Indonesia's President Suharto. These leaders were necessary to maintain U.S. control of key third world areas.

The Church Committee findings produced a temporary hesitation in U.S. foreign policy. There was an understanding on the part of some government officials of the need for alternatives to global hegemony. Significantly, the committee made a clear statement as to the implications of the increasing growth of executive power inside and outside the United States; Church even compared the "imperial presidency" to the domination that Caesar sought in ancient Rome, warning of similarly dire consequences.[14] There was a temporary pushback against the excessive concentration of power within the White House and its exercise through foreign policy. The Cooper-Church Amendment made it clear that U.S. troops could not be sent to Cambodia without Congressional approval, giving Congress the means to limit Nixon's extension of the war into Cambodia. In Cambodia, U.S. support shifted from Prince Norodom Sihanouk to the successor who deposed him. Congress also sought to limit presidential prerogatives in foreign policy by repealing the Gulf of Tonkin resolution. Then, in 1973, there was the Case-Church amendment, which prohibited troops from reentry into Southeast Asia without congressional authorization. Such assertions of congressional oversight were, however, short lived.

From the Ford administration on, a pattern emerges in which the executive branch fights any attempt to limit presidential prerogatives, whether they involve support for dictators who serve as regional foils to the Communist menace or excluding Congress from questioning where the president is sending troops. Such prerogatives reveal authoritarian thinking on the global stage, which explains why, even after Saigon fell, President Ford was emphatic that the administration not change the direction of its foreign policy, still determined to prove that the United States hadn't weakened its global position. That also was the point of the American response to the Cambodian takeover of the SS Mayaguez. Reassertion of America's global dominance unfolded in an exaggerated crisis in which Congress fell in line, fully supporting what the president dictated and joining in celebrating a quick victory. Such behavior helped expand presidential power, demonstrating how Congress enabled presidents to operate with greater secrecy, violating the principle of checks and balances. The Church Committee had been clear about the consequences when the executive branch has unlimited freedom to overthrow foreign governments, such as Chile, Iran, Guatemala, the Congo, and others, or to conduct assassinations of foreign rulers. It recognized that such actions were antidemocratic and subverted constitutional principles. Exposure of such actions through the release of the committee's findings did not, however, result in any fundamental foreign policy change. In the summer of 1975, the Ford administration promised continued support for right-wing dictator Suharto during his visit to Washington. There was an understanding that the Indonesian military, using weapons supplied by the United States, would have a free hand in carrying out the brutal campaign to end the East Timor Independence Movement. One day after Suharto's meeting with Ford, Indonesia invaded East Timor, beginning a 25-year occupation that many have characterized as genocidal. Even though Congress asserted its foreign policy authority and cut arms shipments to Indonesia, relations were quietly reestablished behind closed doors.

The Carter presidency, which resulted from Watergate, the end of the Vietnam War, and the Church Committee Hearings, provided some interesting twists in American foreign policy. Carter came to office claiming that he would reform foreign policy, emphasizing basic human rights principles and rejecting interventionist policies. He understood the shortcomings of blind support for dictators and was keenly aware that most oppressive regimes would eventually generate opposition, leading to their overthrow. He understood that the most excessive forms of political oppression, which violate human rights, undercut the legitimacy of regimes that practice it; he also supported human rights because failure to do so would undercut the support of reliable allies. This explains why the administration withdrew support for Somoza in Nicaragua and the Shah of Iran, seeming to depart from its predecessors' cold war anti-Communism, declaring on many occasions that far too much emphasis was placed on fear of Communists and that too much support had been given to oppressive right-wing dictatorships. He had reason to believe that there was broad support for this position. As a result of the Church Committee findings, Congress had passed legislation aimed at making it difficult for countries with human rights violations to receive U.S. support. The International Security Assistance and Arms Export Control Act stated that the United States sought to comply with global human rights standards, and that it would not provide aid to any nation whose government had a consistent record of human rights abuses. The goal of Carter's Presidential Review

Memorandum I was to redirect foreign policy in Latin America toward a greater emphasis on human rights. Carter instructed Secretary of State Cyrus Vance to enlist the Services Assistant Secretaries, in particular, Deputy Secretary of State Warren Christopher, to establish the Interagency Group on Human Rights and Foreign Assistance to formulate a general human rights policy.

But problems emerged in the selective application of Carter's human rights agenda. The administration was willing to cut ties to Nicaragua and Iran because those regimes were already becoming destabilized, due to pressure from mass-based movements. But support for other dictatorships continued, such as in the Philippines and Indonesia, whose invasion of East Timor was resulting in a genocidal war. No human rights concerns were raised when American arms were shipped to support dictatorships fighting left-wing guerrilla groups. In choosing between essential overseas interests or human rights, the former always wins; that was the case with Carter's 1980 request to Congress for millions of dollars to support the military junta fighting a peasant uprising in El Salvador. Even more striking was Carter's request for economic aid to the Marcos dictatorship in the Philippines, which was carrying out an extensive campaign to suppress procedural democracy. Half of the opposition candidates in the 1978 National Assembly elections were imprisoned, some were tortured, and there were many civilian murders; nevertheless, Carter asked Congress to send Marcos $300 million in military aid.[15] The consistent ominous element of the Carter administration's foreign policy was the gulf between its official pronouncements of a softening of anti-Communist policy and the policy decisions it made regarding the Soviet Union.

Even prior to U.S. involvement in Afghanistan, the Carter administration continued to provide extensive economic support for the military industrial complex. Its first budget increased military spending to an unprecedented level with a ten billion dollar increase over previous allocations. Over the next five years, the administration allocated a total of a trillion dollars in military spending. It is no coincidence that given such expenditures, the administration would return to cold war policies directed at the Soviet Union. Early administration pronouncements had seemed to back away from the idea that the US must soundly defeat the Soviet Union and shortly after the inauguration, Carter ordered America's nuclear weapons removed from South Korea, expecting the Soviets to respond with a gesture of their own, but they did not. This prompted some in the administration, such as Zbigniew Brzezinski, to advocate a tougher stance, pressuring the administration to abandon what they viewed as accommodations to the Soviet Union. Members of the "Committee on the Present Danger" stepped up criticism of U.S. foreign policy as a "cult of appeasement," and events seemed to confirm their view. In 1979, the Russians supplied Cuba with jet fighters, troops ,and a submarine pen. Carter concluded that the Soviet Union was violating the 1962 Cuban Missile Crisis Agreement. Brezhnev denied that the weapons and troops were offensive, thus there was no violation. The superpowers failed to come to terms over the proposed SALT II talks, which would have limited the numbers of missiles and bombers each country could develop. Senate hawks and some administration officials strongly advocated developing high-tech nuclear weapons and SALT II faced stiff opposition in the Senate. Although SALT II was eventually signed, it didn't address the kinds of weapons the US and the Soviet Union could build. It was now possible to construct deadlier nuclear weapons. With mounting pressure, Carter threw his support behind development of intercontinental MX missiles; in December 1979, he and the NATO ministers issued a warning to the Soviet Union that unless it removed its nuclear stock piles from Eastern Europe, NATO would deploy Cruise and Pershing missiles starting in 1983.

The Soviet Union's December 1979 invasion of Afghanistan best illustrates the complete deterioration of U.S.-Soviet relations; at the same time, more than any other actions it undertook, the Carter administration's policies toward Afghanistan would contribute to the eventual formation of an American police state. The Soviet invasion so shocked Carter that he remarked that "the implications of the Soviet invasion of Afghanistan could pose the most serious threat to world peace since the second World War." All diplomatic and arms treaties between the United States and the Soviet Union were suspended, grain sales were stopped, the United States boycotted the 1980 Olympic games in Moscow, and Carter insisted that the Senate postpone indefinitely the SALT II treaty ratification. Carter now wholeheartedly embraced the hard-line cold war position of previous administrations, convinced that Afghanistan was part of the Soviet Union's grand strategy for global domination. He began implementing policies that were clearly contrary to what he had had in mind upon taking office. Now, like its predecessors, the administration gave lip service to abstract democratic ideals, while acting in ways that were clearly antidemocratic. It also began to directly confront the Soviet Union, making Afghanistan the focus of cold war politics. After coming to power following an April 1978 coup, the pro-Soviet government of Afghanistan was threatened by a Muslim uprising. The Soviet Union felt threatened on two fronts: by Muslims at home, whom they feared would rise up in rebellion and in Afghanistan.

Carter administration policy makers also encountered troubling developments in Iran. The Shah, who had been put back in power by the CIA, represented America's clear support for dictators; he became a visible target for anti-American sentiment. Many Iranians believed that the Shah remained in power only because of the large sums of money received from the United States, much of which was spent on maintaining the military and Savak, Iran's brutal military police. Carter saw the Shah as representing American interests in the Middle East but failed to recognize the extent to which hostility was brewing among Iranians. When Ayatollah Khomeini returned from exile, instructions were issued to his followers that they should foster conditions, including mass demonstrations, that would end in the Shah's expulsion. When the Shah finally left for what he termed an extended vacation, Khomeini was greeted by hundreds of thousands of supporters as Iran's de facto ruler. The Iranian Revolution, was, in essence a mass revolt against the Shah's police state. If Iranians shared a single belief, it was that so long as the Shah was alive, the CIA would, as it had previously, attempt another coup. The fedayeen and the mullahs could not have been clearer in showing that their anti-Americanism was linked to their hatred of the Shah. While the Shah underwent cancer treatments in New York, outraged Iranian students who wanted the Shah returned to be brought to trial seized control of the US embassy in Teheran, taking 66 Americans hostage.

By the end of the Carter administration, Afghanistan and Iran had assumed important roles as the settings where American foreign policies against Communism and Islamic fundamentalism eventually contributed to the formation of an American police state. Such steps unfolded explicitly as the Reagan administration dealt with these two enemies. With grassroots support from right-wing organizations, Reaganism chipped away at some remaining institutional supports for American democracy. In foreign policy, the Committee on the Present Danger led the rallying cry of militarism in service of anti-Communism. At the same time, 36 freshmen senators were elected, among them Richard Cheney of Wyoming and Newt Gingrich of Georgia; the new senators were not only staunch anti-Communists, but they also sought to destroy the social welfare state. Attacking big government became one of Reaganism's mainstays, portraying the New Deal and Great Society programs as ineffective and not cost-effective. The goal was to diminish the federal government's role as a social services provider. While the secular right focused on this issue, the religious right acted as extremist foot soldiers, fomenting hatred to exclude those who didn't reflect the views of white, male, Protestant evangelicals. Funding was provided by the corporate coffers of individuals like Joseph Coors and Richard Mellon-Scaife, heir to the Carnegie-Mellon family fortune. They worked with Paul Weyrich, who in turn, doled out money to sympathetic members of Congress running for reelection. The emphasis was on measures that would further erode democracy by dismantling the social welfare state. While Reagan was elected with huge support from the religious right, his primary concern was corporatism. Through supply-side economics, a trickle-down theory, cutting taxes for those at the top was to encourage employers and investors to generate more capital which they would then invest. The net effect would be to stimulate greater business activity, hiking personal incomes and providing greater tax revenue. The other side of Reaganomics was a massive increase in military spending – more than a trillion dollars during Reagan's first term. To fund such increases, the administration cut social welfare spending. In his first year, Reagan successfully proposed $144 billion in cuts to social programs and increased military spending by $180 billion, while pushing through tax cuts of $190 billion, mostly to benefit the wealthy.[16] The goal was to starve social programs and polarize the population, defining politics as "whose side are you on?" Reducing social programs and redistributing monies to the upper classes and the military industrial complex benefited the privileged few. As income disparities grew, those at the top accumulated more wealth while the incomes of those at the lower rungs of the economic ladder declined. "in 1980, the chief executive officers (ceos) of corporations made 40 times as much in salary as the average factory worker, by 1989, they were making 93 times as much."[17] The economic disparities resonated across America.

For all the official pronouncements about the benefits of Reaganomics, most of the economic growth it produced was in low-paying service jobs without benefits. Labor unions became a shadow of what they had been, desperately struggling to obtain higher wages and benefits and relying on strikes as a last resort. The "whose side are you on question" became especially relevant when Reagan took an aggressive stand against the Professional Air Controllers Organization, which threatened to strike for better pay and benefits. Reagan gave the union 48 hours to call off the strike, return to work, or be fired. Although 38 percent of the strikers returned to work before the deadline, and the government enlisted the services of military contractors, Reagan fired 11,000 air traffic controllers, signaling that the federal government would not tolerate strikes. Unions became increasingly hesitant to strike. Labor unions were less able to act as a proponent for democratic reforms and less able to provide better-paying jobs with benefits while employers had a freer hand to exploit workers or fire them. With declining union membership came a dramatic rise in unemployment: in 1982, unemployment averaged 9.7 percent, the highest since the Great Depression.

Several mass movements appeared in the early 1980s in response to Reagan's military budget and the buildup of nuclear weapons. The administration's anti-Communism was supposed to reassert American power overseas, compensating for the defeats of the Vietnam War and the Iran hostage crisis. Reagan combated Communism through militarism, advocating development of the B-1 bomber and obtaining congressional approval for a new B-2 bomber, cruise missiles, the MX missile, and a 600-ship Navy. During his two terms, total military spending reached nearly $2 trillion.[18] In response, in June 1982, nearly a million people protested the arms race in New York City. Large demonstrations took place in other cities. Hundreds of municipalities passed resolutions in support of halting the arms race. A Harris poll found that 79 percent of Americans advocated a nuclear freeze agreement with the USSR.[19]

The administration was more concerned over dissent regarding its Latin American policies. The FBI implemented extensive surveillance over individuals and organizations who challenged American intervention in Latin America, particularly the Committee in Solidarity with the People of El Salvador (CISPES). A federal agency again collaborated with local police and right-wing groups. Dissent did not entirely disappear, but it couldn't reshape government policy or halt the development toward a police state; even large-scale protests against the arms race did not slow military allocations. Despite protests against U.S. involvement in Latin America, the administration remained undeterred. Government actions against democracy were focused overseas in support of authoritarian regimes, while the administration claimed that the goal was to support democracy.

The Reagan Doctrine, a key element of a foreign policy designed to halt democracy in the name of anti-Communism, included a novel justification—a splitting of hairs—over the distinction between authoritarian and totalitarian regimes. This idea, both naive and ultimately false, was based on the argument that authoritarian right-wing dictatorships in partnership with the United States have the potential to become democratic states, while totalitarian regimes are permanent dictatorships hostile to the United States. Thus, the administration justified support for authoritarian governments as essentially supporting democracy and acting as a bulwark against Communist expansion. This reassertion of militarism further eroded what remained of procedural democracy in the United States, especially through military and covert operations that violated the Constitution. The Reagan Doctrine supported oppressive right-wing military dictatorships in Guatemala, Afghanistan, Cambodia, Mozambique, Angola, and El Salvador.

The doctrine also supported El Salvador's military junta, locked in a brutal civil war. Unconcerned about extensive human rights abuses through the widespread use of death squads, whose members included graduates of the notorious School of the Americas, the United States contributed billions of dollars of military hardware to El Salvador to eliminate the guerrilla army. Such was the arrogance of American empire building, expressing a right to intervene anywhere, to put in place a government of its choosing. The strange distinction made between authoritarian and totalitarian regimes first advanced by Georgetown University Professor Jean Kirkpatrick was designed to justify American support for military dictatorships. The administration had rejected any reference to human rights standards as a basis for foreign policy initiatives. Early in the administration, restrictions were lifted on exports and military aid to countries like Chile, South Korea, and Argentina.[20]

In many ways, the Iran-contra scandal was a culmination of the steady concentration of power within the executive branch and the propensity of intelligence agencies to rule above the law. It began when the Sandinistas forced the U.S.-backed dictator Somoza into exile. Administration officials believed that Nicaragua could become another Cuba, providing the Soviet Union with a foothold to promote revolution throughout Latin America, although Soviet involvement in Latin America was minimal. There was evidence that the administration had greatly exaggerated support given to rebels in El Salvador and how many Cuban personnel were in Nicaragua. Nonetheless, from 1981 on, large sums of economic and military assistance flowed into El Salvador. CIA covert aid was funneled to Nicaraguan fighters called "Contras," who were fighting the Sandinista government. In 1982, the administration's support for them was exposed, and Congress learned of Contras in Guatemala, whom the CIA had supported and trained. Congress resisted Reagan's request for additional monies to support

Contras, or "freedom fighters." The House of Representatives unanimously passed the Boland Amendment, prohibiting economic and military aid to the Contras; the president signed it but chose to ignore it. Thus, the administration acted outside its authority as previous administrations had, going outside the law to pursue antidemocratic policies. It followed its predecessors in attempting to avoid accountability for actions that would be legally unacceptable to Congress, using intelligence agencies, such as the NSC, which formed an alliance with drug dealers and enlisted the support of Manuel Noriega, Panama's drug-dealing dictator.

When Congress learned of the secret mining of Nicaragua's harbor, it passed a second Boland Amendment, prohibiting military support to the Contras. The NSC then became the go-between as the administration sent aid to the Contras with the assistance of NSC director Robert McFarland and his assistant Oliver North. Prior to the passage of the second amendment, they created a secret fund of millions of dollars with help from the Saudi government to support the Contras. They believed they were above the law, convinced of the special status of NSC operations. The other key player was Iran, for the administration had committed itself to reshaping Middle East politics through involvement in Lebanon. A small force of so-called peacekeepers had been taken hostage, setting the stage for the Iranian part of the scandal. Admiral John Poindexter, McFarland's replacement, began to put in motion a secret arms deal through Iran, while North was working on using profits from arms sales to Iran to assist the Contras. The administration intended to make a direct arms-for-hostages exchange. Things came to a head when an American cargo plane carrying arms to the Contras was shot down over Nicaragua. When news broke that the administration was trading arms for hostages; the president admitted as much, resulting in Poindexter's resignation and the relief of North's duties. A special review board, headed by former Senator John Tower, led to the appointment of an independent special prosecutor, Lawrence Walsh, and the House of Representatives launched its own investigation. But, in a now-familiar pattern of executive branch covert operations, administration officials worked to insulate the president, repeating what had taken place during Watergate, except that in Nixon's case, the participants had not as effectively covered their tracks. Iran-Contra investigators were unable to clearly connect the White House to the actions of subordinates. Using the cover of plausible deniability, Poindexter convinced investigators that he had approved of diverting funds to the Contras without seeking presidential approval. The independent prosecutor concluded that the president had knowingly created circumstances that would allow the crimes that others committed to go forward, thus helping to cover them up.[21] Walsh reached other disturbing conclusions, namely that the president does not have to express a direct command to go outside the law; all that needs to be expressed are vague references and wishes; others then execute the details. Such operations remain covert; are carried out without consultation with Congress; and, most disturbing, go unpunished. The Constitution should be the most important legal document determining the conduct of presidents, but the Reagan administration continued a trend in which presidents decided what was or was not constitutional.

Meanwhile, protests continued against policies in El Salvador, Nicaragua, and South Africa's regime as well as the domestic policies that redistributed wealth upward and cut social spending. Progressive organizations sought to pressure the administration to halt the arms race, stay out of Latin America, and prevent a roll-back on issues such as abortion, but their overall impact was minimal, largely because they lacked direct access to key policy makers. This contrasted with the Right, which had direct access to the executive branch, in large part, a result of Cointelpro's successful persecution of the Left. Right-wing groups were shaping policy in an antidemocratic direction, spreading the idea that Contras were Latin America's anti-Communist freedom fighters, overlooking the inconvenient fact that the Contras were working to overthrow a government by using a paramilitary force, creating a reign of terror and murdering civilians. Right-wing insiders had lobbied the Reagan administration and Congress to support a militaristic foreign policy and exorbitant military spending, while supporting covert operations by intelligence agencies. They issued public statements through various media outlets, decrying those who appeared to be soft on Communism.

During Reagan's 1980 presidential campaign, the Committee of Santa Fe, a group of well-funded anti-Communist activists, developed a key piece of the administration's foreign policy. The New-InterAmerican Policy for the 80s, a guidebook on how to stop Communism in Latin America, contained the standard references to how Communism subverted national governments and established links to Moscow. The policy implications were clear: overthrow any government identified as Communist through covert operations. In the first Reagan term, the president's assistant, Faith Ryan Whittlesey, assembled an Outreach Working Group on Central America, in which a who's who of right-wing groups attended White House briefings;

they included Jerry Falwell and his Moral Majority, Pat Robertson's Freedom Council, the Neo-conservative Institute on Religion, and the Young Americans for Freedom. The administration even offered its direct assistance. Whittlesey involved these organizations in fundraising and in directives assisting the Contras. Behind some of the clandestine operations was the World Anti-Communist League, which had established ties to neo-Nazis and to future leaders of Latin American death squads. Its U.S. chapter was led by former Major General John Senglarb, who had connections in many parts of the world, including Latin America, often acting as a mediator in the administration's covert operations. Only after the infamous helicopter crash of September 1980 did the media and the American public hear about the secret missions of these Contra suppliers. Since the Boland Amendment prohibited sending money or supplies to such organizations, the administration was illegally supplying these groups. Money flowed in from paramilitary mercenary organizations, such as the Soldier of Fortune, the Air Commando Association, and Civilian Military Assistance and the religious right, including Pat Robertson's Christian Broadcasting Network and secular groups, including the American Security Council, Citizens for America, and the Council for InterAmerican Security. Even the cultlike Reverend Sun Myung Moon's Unification Church sent money.

Despite all this evidence, the Iran-Contra hearings avoided exploring the covert role that these right-wing leaders and organizations played. As it had during the Watergate inquiry, Congress ultimately failed to rein in executive power and the resulting constitutional violations. The failure of post-Watergate and Iran-Contra reforms resulted in Congress enabling the executive branch to further concentrate and extend its power in conducting foreign policy; in particular, it failed to address the extent to which funding of a secret mercenary army acting without any regulation committed war crimes. In overlooking and failing to punish the Contras' actions, Congress allowed this mercenary army to act in similar ways to Blackwater, the mercenary army that would, under the Bush administration, later be deployed in Iraq—in both cases, raising the issue that their actions violated the rights of civilians during wartime. In using mercenaries, these administrations overlooked the principles of international law in the Geneva Conventions and exhibited a trait common to police states.

U.S. mercenaries continued to wage war against civilians in Latin America. In El Salvador, the administration supported the country's Arena Party, headed by Roberto D'Aubisson, a graduate of the School of the Americas and a leader of death squads implicated in the plot to assassinate Archbishop Romero. He was known to have participated in many murders, including a mass killing in the village of El Mazote, that left over 900 men, women, and children dead. The School of the Americas, renamed the Western Hemisphere Institute for Security Cooperation, provides another example of an American government-supported institution used to crush democracy throughout Latin America. WHISC was responsible for training many Latin American dictators including Argentina's Roberto Viola, Panama's Manuel Noriega, Peru's Juan Velasco Alvarado, and Ecuador's Guillermo Rodriguez, as well as the notorious leader of the Grupo Colina death squad in Fujimori's Peru and those who ran the Battalion 3–16 in Honduras. Two other graduates were Guatemalan dictator Efrain Rios Montt and Guatemalan chief of Army intelligence, General Manuel Antonio Callejis, who was responsible for the murder of political activists; Montt famously remarked that he ruled according to the principle of "beans for the obedient; bullets for the rest."

In 1992, a CIA training manual for WHISC was leaked to media. With details on torture techniques, intimidation, and using false imprisonment and extortion, it was a blueprint on how to diminish democratic practices and identify threats, including any individual or organization that voiced discontent toward the military or government. Once identified, these so-called enemies would be targeted if they had circulated petitions, urged youth to avoid the draft, participated in strikes, or made accusations of police brutality. Such persons were "guerrillas" and would become targets of surveillance, imprisonment, and torture. The manual described how to infiltrate student groups, labor unions, political parties, and community organizations, noting that governments should make full use of spies, who it said could be recruited with threats of imprisonment or possible execution of family and friends. U.S. support of WHISC indicates how behind-the-scenes policies undercut democracy, without regard to rule of law. Failure to investigate WHISC's role in Latin America during the Iran-Contra investigation is one of many instances where Congress paid only lip service to supporting democracy. The end result was that prosecution against a state determined to step outside the law and the Constitution proved ineffective. Most of the 11 who were convicted got plea bargains, small fines, or community service; Pointdexter's and North's convictions were reversed on appeal; and just before one short sentence would have begun for Weinberger, President George H Bush pardoned him and the others.[22]

From Watergate to Iran-Contra, officials who violate the law and the Constitution have received, at best, a weak response from the courts.

Both Congress and the courts were fast losing any willingness to defend procedural democracy and the U.S. Constitution, a trend that would lead directly to the police state of the Bush administration. Clear examples of lawbreaking by the executive branch were investigated only along very narrow lines by Congress and the courts so as to avoid confrontation with the executive branch. At least after Watergate, Congress attempted to roll back some of the president's increasing powers. No such effort was undertaken in the Iran-Contra aftermath, revealing tacit acceptance that one branch of government could act outside the law. There was no political will, as there had been, during the Church Committee Hearings, to investigate the role of intelligence agencies in implementing the Reagan administration's Latin American policies. Congress wasn't just turning a blind eye; it was becoming complicit in failing to respond to the emerging police state.

More evidence was demonstrated by increasing American involvement in Afghanistan. The Carter administration had set the stage for the Reagan administration's more aggressive commitment to Afghanistan, by signing off, at Brzezinski's urging, on CIA covert actions to supply Afghan forces with money and supplies. During the Reagan administration, the concern that Russia would take advantage of the Iranian Revolution to increase the Soviet presence in the Middle East intensified U.S. involvement in Afghanistan. It worked to draw the Soviet Union further into Afghanistan, well aware of the increasing strength of the muhjaddin guerrillas. White House and CIA policy makers were correct: a Soviet-backed government was being challenged by a mass-based uprising. The administration correctly believed that the Soviet Union was about to experience its own "Vietnam," that a Soviet commitment of troops to Afghanistan would turn into a drawn-out war without victory. Policy makers also accurately interpreted a Soviet withdrawal as contributing to its demise as a rival superpower. Soviet commitments to Afghanistan accelerated its eventual economic collapse, already severely strained by the arms race. With the removal of the Soviet Union as America's chief rival for control of global affairs, an ideological justification for militarism in service of empire building also was removed.

In the 1970s, even before the collapse of the Soviet Union, terrorism was replacing the Communist menace. Confrontation with this new enemy would convince policy makers that the United States could finally overcome its "Vietnam Syndrome." As the world's only remaining superpower, the United States could overlook setbacks, such as the loss of the Shah to the Islamic Revolution. But to defeat the Soviet Union in Afghanistan, the United States would make a Faustian bargain, which, according to the CIA, would result in "blowback." Consider how CIA director Casey, who had a close relationship with President Reagan, confronted Soviet Communism by associating the CIA with Saudi intelligence and Pakistani intelligence services, headed by General Mohammed Zia Ul-Haq. It is a classic example of how the head of a federal agency in charge of intelligence gathering can act on his own initiative to instigate a global crusade based on a simplistic view of world affairs. Although Reagan tacitly approved Casey's anti-Communist mission in Afghanistan, he had a free hand to work out the particulars. Under Casey, the CIA began to follow the lead of Zia Ul-Haq's religious and political agenda in Afghanistan. An important symptom of the internal decay of procedural democracy in America is the role that opportunism played in its entanglement in Afghanistan, an opportunism that functioned in secret, resulting from individuals' arbitrary self-serving motives: Representative Charlie Wilson and CIA agent Gust Avrakotos helped the muhjaddin win the war, through the use of secret funds from the "Black budget" of the CIA and the Pentagon. As the ranking member of the Defense Appropriations Subcommittee, Wilson had the opportunity to request virtually any amount for special projects. "Earmarks," the monies Wilson had access to, were used to support General Mohammed Zia ul-Haq, supplementing CIA monies that armed Afghan guerrillas. The Saudis provided matching funds while Pakistan operated as a safe haven for training guerrillas and a base where they could be supplied with weapons and advisors for staging military operations. From the outset, General Zia insisted that Pakistan's intelligence service, the ISA, had to distribute the weapons guerrillas used. In agreeing to do so, the CIA made what proved to be a crucial error. Oblivious as to the long-term consequences, Wilson's partner, CIA agent Avrakotos, provided Afghan fighters with a weapon that would ultimately decide the war's outcome: the American-manufactured Stinger shoulder-fired missile. They were used with deadly accuracy against the Soviet Union's most effective weapon, the MI-24 Hind helicopter, finally leading Prime Minister Gorbachev to conclude that he should pull out of Afghanistan. Not long after, the United States would face the blowback of that Soviet defeat. But in the immediate aftermath, the Reagan administration, the CIA, and the American media interpreted the exit of the Soviet Union as a triumph of good over evil, of a "people's army" that defeated a mighty Soviet aggressor.

Even during the Afghan war, there were troubling indications about the future of American participation in the region. It was the largest covert action the United States had taken since World War II, given the combination of Pakistani recruiting, Saudi Arabian money, and American political and military support, totaling more than $2 billion. During the war, Osama bin-Laden, who had inherited an estimated $300 million from his father's construction business, left his life of wealth and privilege to dedicate himself to fighting Communism. At the time of the Soviet occupation of Afghanistan, bin-Laden was recruited by the CIA to assist in financing what he considered a holy war. As a result, bin-Laden and his supporters received CIA training in shipping money, using dummy companies, building explosives, using coded messages, avoiding detection, and hiding out in safe places. Bin-Laden also received support from the Saudi government and assistance from Pakistan to train recruits, drawn by his charismatic appeal, to join the muhjaddin army. With the Soviet Union's departure, Afghanistan was essentially at war with itself, with various factions vying for control. Pakistan and the United States sided with one of the more extreme fundamentalist factions, the Taliban. With the 1991 U.S. invasion of Kuwait, under the pretext of halting Saddam Hussein, the focus was no longer the Soviet Union; the United States was the new global threat for Islamic fundamentalists.

From the end of the Afghan war in the early 1990s to the administration of George W. Bush, policy makers had one overriding goal: that the United States can and should control world affairs. But to do so, another enemy, terrorism—in many ways, an American creation—had to be eliminated. After the 1993 attack on the Twin Towers, the U.S. government expressed a willingness to discard procedural democracy and with it, rule of law, because it failed to understand the motives behind terrorist attacks. The United States began to adopt authoritarian policies, eliminating a host of the remaining freedoms Americans still had. The first failure that policy makers made, back in 1970, was not taking into account what motivated Bin-Laden and al Qaeda. When Bin- Laden committed himself to being a holy warrior, he put in place a well-organized conscription program in association with an important Muslim Brotherhood leader, Abdullah Azzam. They recruited followers through the Makab al-Khidamat (MAK-services office) throughout the Arab world, making the case that Muslims should fight in Afghanistan. Bin-Laden used his family fortune to train new recruits and set up training facilities; the base, or al Qaeda, was set up to maintain contact with Muslim followers in many countries, through high-tech devices, faxes, satellite telephones, and the Internet. The United States also overlooked the organization's main goal to overthrow what it viewed as corrupt, heretical governments in Muslim nations, to replace them with the rule of Islamic law. Afghan veterans returned to their countries, some having been radicalized with a determination to topple what they now regarded as Western-shaped governments. Muhjaddin veterans fomented unrest in Somalia, Bosnia, Kosovo, and Chechnya, flush with the victory over the Soviet Union. Bin Laden returned to Saudi Arabia more militant, with the intention to challenge what he considered its infidel government. The Saudi government took him seriously, stripping his citizenship and deporting him. Having established himself and a large number of followers in Khartoum, Sudan, bin Laden used his monies to build roads, build infrastructure, and provide jobs for unemployed muhjaddin while setting up training camps. To promote good relations with the United States, the Sudanese government asked him to leave. Upon returning to Afghanistan, he formed an alliance with the Taliban, which had grown from a group of displaced Afghans in Pakistani refugee camps into an effective, fighting force. They embarked on a takeover of territory, culminating in the capture and control of Kabul. Bin Laden supplied the Taliban regime with people, arms, and money to fight their bitter rival, the Northern alliance. In exchange, the Taliban provided him with a safe haven, from which he continued to build training camps.

From the early 1990s on, a pattern emerged: Bin Laden and al Qaeda were working toward staging attacks wherever the United States had committed troops. The American invasion of Kuwait angered Bin Laden, and he staged attacks to accelerate its departure; in October 1993, al Qaeda killed 18 U.S. military personnel stationed in Somalia as part of Operation Restore Hope. Later that year, al Qaeda operatives in Kenya attacked the U.S. embassy in Nairobi, payback for American participation in Operation Restore Hope. As of December 1999, a terrorist cell with al Qaeda connections was uncovered as part of a plot to initiate attacks inside the United States. An Algerian, Ahmed Ressan, was arrested at the U.S.-Canadian border with 100 pounds of bomb-making material. He confessed that he intended to set off a bomb at Los Angeles International Airport on New Year's Day and admitted that he had received terrorist training at al Qaeda's camps in Afghanistan. On January 3, 2000, al Qaeda members trained in Afghanistan attempted to stage an attack against a U.S. destroyer, using a small boat packed with explosives. The overloaded boat sank, and the attack never happened.

Then, in October 2000, a similar attack on the USS Cole succeeded, killing 17 crew members and injuring 40. Several participants had been trained at one of Bin Laden's camps. The two leaders who planned the attack had also planned the East African embassy bombing. Then there was the 1993 car bombing of the Twin Towers in New York.

So, in the name of supporting groups in Afghanistan that would do the bidding of the United States and push back the Communist threat, the United States removed one enemy only to create another. In a post-Soviet world, U.S. foreign policy was still characterized by the need to eliminate former allies who had become troublesome dictators and were no longer reliable. Toward the end of 1989, George H Bush took steps to eliminate a prime source of trouble in Central America, Panamanian strongman Manuel Noriega, who had outlived his usefulness. The Reagan administration, with the assistance of the CIA, had supported Noriega's regime with economic and military aid; in turn, Noriega had assisted the Contras. But given the geopolitical importance of the Panama Canal and concern over U.S. economic interests, the Bush administration was alarmed over what would happen if Noriega gained control over this vital asset. With Operation Just Cause, Bush ordered 24,000 paratroopers to overthrow him. In 1992, he was convicted of cocaine trafficking, money laundering, and racketeering and sentenced to 40 years in prison. Next on the list for removal was Saddam Hussein, a staunch American ally against Iran, who had received American money and weapons. The Reagan administration had looked the other way when Hussein used chemical weapons against Iran and authorized their use against the Kurds. Such tolerance would fall by the wayside when Hussein made the fateful decision to invade Kuwait. His conquest of Kuwait would seriously threaten Western oil interests. Once again, in working to maintain its empire and safeguard its oil interests, the United States assumed it had the right to wage war against a nation and its civilians. The attack, lasting over a month, involved the bombing of Kuwait, Baghdad, and other Iraqi cities, destroying the power grid and creating massive food shortages, disease outbreaks, and major breakdowns in the health-care system.[23] Having forced Hussein's retreat, the United States did not order troops to advance into Baghdad. Bush was following a UN mandate as well as a congressional resolution, which stressed the liberation of Kuwait only to cause Hussein's retreat. The administration didn't grasp that U.S. intervention served to further ignite the anger and resentment of Muslims, outraged by the permanent American military bases in Saudi Arabia, the site of one of Islam's holiest shrines. And as the Taliban regime forged an alliance with Bin Laden, permitting it to establish terrorist training camps, the United States continued diplomatic relations with it, mainly because of plans by U.S. company Unocal to build a $2 billion pipeline through Afghanistan; "for that reason, Unocal was eager to see a government in Kabul—any kind of government— that could pacify the country."[24] So once again, in the name of empire building, to which a steady flow of oil was key, the United States found itself in an alliance with some of the most oppressive antidemocratic regimes in the world.

While the Reagan administration had accelerated democracy's demise with the dismantling of the social welfare state, the upward redistribution of wealth, and stepped-up militarism, the Bush administration that followed it pursued a mixed domestic policy agenda. Unlike Reagan, Bush was not as connected to the evangelical Christian Right. Right-wing activists were, for the most, absent from influencing policies, such as Bush's domestic war on drugs or the invasion of Panama. Bush would eventually alienate the secular Right when he violated his "no new taxes" pledge and signed a 1990 civil rights bill making it easier for individuals to seek redress for allegations of racial discrimination against employers. Bush's decision not to advance into Iraq to overthrow Saddam Hussein and what some saw as his administration's restraint and accommodation toward the Soviet Union on nuclear weapons issues, following its collapse, further alienated the Right. On domestic issues, the Bush administration was moderate; it didn't automatically resist funding social programs, and it demonstrated greater interest in achieving higher education standards. Congressional progressives managed to nearly double funding for Head Start. The administration didn't resist the Americans with Disabilities Act, and the Clean Air Act also was passed. On the other hand, Bush vetoed the Family and Medical Leave legislation and a civil rights bill and nominated Clarence Thomas to the Supreme Court. The administration's inaction following the acquittal of police officers in the Rodney King verdict helped fuel the rioting, looting, and burning in Los Angeles. The sense that Bush was "out of touch" was underscored by the administration's biggest domestic failure—its inability to anticipate and confront a serious economic downturn.

The evangelical Christian Right still maintained a viable presence within the Republican party, emphasizing antiabortion and antigay rights issues. Nearly half of the delegates at the 1992 Republican Party convention were born-again Christians, and the party platform advocated a constitutional ban on abortion, positions against civil rights, and support for school prayer and home schooling. The religious Right also achieved some electoral success at state and local levels, partly prompted by unease over the country's direction. Social unrest stemmed from numerous acts of violence through Operation Rescue, which in the early 1990s was responsible for killing seven, including doctors working at abortion clinics, and militaristic attacks by right-wing groups, such as the Aryan Brotherhood. In 1995, right-wing extremists Timothy McVeigh and Terry Nichols blew up the federal building in Oklahoma City, killing 168 people. At the time, it was the country's worst domestic terrorist attack.

CHAPTER 5

A Police State

In many ways, the Clinton administration's foreign policy initiatives helped lay the groundwork for those implemented during the administration of George W. Bush. For both, efforts to combat terrorism marked the beginning of a transformation into a police state.

Clinton's domestic policies were somewhat transitional, featuring corporate initiatives as well as some support for social programs, protecting Medicare and Social Security from proposed cuts and making a half-hearted, unsuccessful effort to reform health care. Small victories included removal of the "gag rule," which prohibited doctors from providing abortion counseling in federally funded clinics and an executive order, allowing for the use of fetal cells in federally supported medical research. Clinton signed a modified version of the Family and Medical Leave Act and initiated a ban on the sale of certain semiautomatic assault weapons. Congress and the president agreed on the "Motor-Voter Law," allowing citizens to register to vote when applying for a driver's license. A national service program was established, providing federal assistance to pay for college in exchange for community service. But overall, such measures were largely ineffective. The assault weapons ban left millions of weapons unaffected, the motor vehicle law did not significantly expand registration, and the community service provision was not widely implemented.

Better insight as to the true direction of the Clinton administration can be learned from its corporatist initiatives. Clinton was a "New Democrat," not associated with "tax-and-spend" policies. That meant working to reduce the federal deficit so as to maintain a balanced budget. In striving to reach his goals of not increasing taxes on the upper class while maintaining high levels of military spending, Clinton took aim at programs that impacted the poor, children, and the elderly, opposing congressional proposals to repair schools and extend health insurance to uninsured children. Military spending continued to rise, conveniently dovetailing with the administration's foreign policy priorities. Clinton supported and signed the Crime Bill of 1996, which stressed punishment instead of rehabilitation and expanded the death penalty as punishment for a broader range of offenses. The bill was part of a larger administration agenda to fight the so-called war on drugs, which made the United States a world leader in imprisoning its own citizens. Prisons became a leading growth industry, and a disproportionate number of inmates came from poor inner-city neighborhoods, whose inhabitants were convenient outsider groups to identify as a menace to society. Fear of immigrants paid political dividends as the administration viewed the large number of immigrants, especially from Mexico, as responsible for taking jobs from citizens, receiving government health benefits, and leading to increased taxes. To combat this alleged menace, Congress and the president worked to eliminate from legal and illegal immigrants a host of benefits, including food stamps. Other outsiders were the large numbers of political refugees who had escaped from U.S.-backed military juntas in Guatemala and El Salvador. To provide political asylum to them would amount to an admission that the United States had supported regimes engaged in human rights abuses, so they were turned away. Poor families with dependent children also were marginalized by the administration's Personal Responsibility and Work Opportunity Reconciliation Act, which ended Aid to Families with Dependent Children, a federal program dating back to the New Deal. In forging alliances with Republicans who sought social services cuts, Clinton proclaimed, "the era of big government is over."

That era remained in effect, however, for defense contractors and recipients of corporate welfare. As with its predecessors, the Clinton administration championed various foreign policy initiatives through militarism, acting as a global arsenal, selling combat planes to Saudi Arabia and Taiwan, sending weapons to poor countries, and allowing for advanced weapons to be sent to Latin America. Foreign policy actions taken by the administration would foreshadow those taken by the second Bush administration, including waging war in violation of international law standards established during the Nuremberg Trials and the legal prohibition on waging aggressive wars. The Clinton administration claimed to have identified and attacked an "Intelligence headquarters" in Baghdad, resulting in six civilian deaths. This bellicose act was intended to signal that America would bomb at will. Clinton tried to distance the United States from Saddam Hussein, an unreliable dictator. In keeping with actions taken following the first Gulf War, Clinton continued the use of UN weapons inspectors and no-fly zones over Iraq. Such measures set the stage for justifying more excessive initiatives, linking the Clinton administration with the Bush administration that followed; both expressed the need to use force under the pretext that Iraq was not allowing weapons inspectors to search for "weapons of mass destruction." Administration officials, such as Secretary of State Madeline Albright, discussed creating public support in the event that the United States embarked on a bombing campaign against Iraq. When the Clinton administration instead made extensive use of sanctions, it was the Iraqi people, not Hussein, who suffered. Albright later admitted that the sanctions, which prevented some medical supplies from entering Iraq, had resulted in the deaths of hundreds of thousands of Iraqi children.

Events in Somalia further illustrate how the Clinton administration intervened when U.S. interests were at stake. In the 1990s, anti-American sentiment was surfacing, motivated by U.S. support of Israel and anger over American forces in Saudi Arabia. The anger spilled into Somalia in light of the U.S. withdrawal of promised economic aid. In the chaos, groups jockeyed for power, and civil war broke out, further complicated by massive hunger and a lethal drought. The U.S. government's concern was that such events could foster terrorism throughout Africa, reason enough for the administration to dispatch a small force to Somalia. The United States sought to locate a powerful warlord, who had led an attack on tribal elders and who the United States claimed, comprised a terrorist cell. The United States sought to retaliate by sending to Somalia a small attack force. A bloody battle ensued in Mogadishu, in which no distinction could be made between the killing of soldiers and civilians.

Ten days later, in Haiti, the United States took another step to halt democratic rule. U.S. involvement in Haiti dates back decades to its support for the father-son dictatorship of Papa and Baby Doc Duvalier. The Carter administration's actions there related to the protection of U.S. economic interests and its role as a regional base for geopolitical operations. Haitians had a long historic memory of a Western presence in their country; they were particularly angered by the U.S. presence in Somalia and greeted American noncombat soldiers with shouts of "Somalia! Somalia!" as they entered Port-au-Prince to train Haitian police. Tensions were exacerbated when democratically elected President Jean Bertrand Aristide was forced from office by a U.S.-funded coalition of military and secret police. Not long after, in an attempt to quell the resulting outcry, the United States then tried to persuade Aristide to return to power as long as he didn't interfere with the power and privileges enjoyed by the military and local police. Aristide refused, so the military and police remained in control.

But different circumstances arise when American interests are not directly involved. In 1994, the Rwandan genocide lasted for 100 days, and an estimated 800,000 were killed, approximately 70 percent of the minority Tutsi population; UN peacekeepers were prohibited from intervening. The United States took the lead in discouraging intervention, calling for remaining peacekeepers to leave Rwanda, which only gave the perpetrators a freer hand. In Bosnia, both the Bush senior and Clinton administrations did little, other than maintain an arms embargo, to further weaken the ill-equipped Muslims; the small number of UN peacekeepers in Bosnia could do little to halt the mass killing of some 200,000 Muslims from 1992–1995. On the other hand, because it served U.S. interests, a country like Indonesia could receive economic and military aid, even though it was well known that it had killed as many as 200,000 out of a population of 700,000 during the East Timor invasion. The U.S. government's sale of deadly weapons to the Suharto regime made the genocide possible, crushing the East Timor independence movement. During the Clinton administration, the United States attained the dubious distinction of being the global leader in the sale of weapons used to promote civil unrest and warfare. In addition to refusing to sign the international agreement abolishing land mines, the United States also refused to establish an International War Crimes Court, further evidence of U.S. resistance to the promotion of peace and cooperation.

The so-called war on terrorism would end what remained of democracy in America. The scope and scale of political repression against progressive mass-based movements had diminished, largely because it had been so effective from the 1960s to 1970s. Whenever small-scale political protests appeared, for example, with CISPES' peaceful activism against U.S. policies in Latin America in the 1980s, the FBI began conducting surveillance, gathering intelligence and sharing it with other agencies, including the Department of Justice, the Defense Intelligence Agency, and even the Secret Service. As in the past, the net was cast broadly to include all organizations—such as Oxfam America, the Southern Christian Leadership Coalition, the ACLU, and the Catholic Conference—that had ever associated with CISPES. No distinctions were made between the activities of CISPES and other organizations, and 178 additional investigations of other groups and individuals were launched. The surveillance of CISPES and like-minded organizations demonstrates a shift in ideological emphasis from the Communist menace to terrorism: the FBI's purpose was to tie the organization to international terrorist conspiracies. As it had done with Communists previously, the FBI viewed CISPES members as political outsiders despite the fact that CISPES was homegrown, and its main objective was halting military aid to the El Salvadoran junta through peaceful protests. As it had done in the past, the FBI was making the patently illegal predetermination that this organization would, at some point in the future, commit a political crime, thus subjecting it to surveillance in the present. According to this rationale, the FBI had the right to act as a court of law in determining the guilt of CISPES, even before the organization took any action. But unlike a normal court, the FBI issued a guilty verdict before gathering evidence. When the FBI did gather evidence, it was to bolster its preconceived notions. Rallies and meetings were monitored and infiltrated, thousands of photos were taken, license plate numbers of cars parked near meetings were recorded, telephone company records were obtained, and mailing lists and phone numbers were taken from posters announcing rallies.[1]

In 1984, after the CISPES investigation was launched, legislation was proposed that would criminalize what was described as "support for terrorism."[2] The abstract wording of such laws made it possible to define just about any organization as terrorist or supportive of terrorism. During the 1980s, the U.S. government had articulated a dual menace from Communism and terrorism. But later in the decade, terrorism became the primary threat; consequently, the FBI opened nearly 20,000 investigations of international terrorist activities, many involving individuals who were not directly involved in such activities.[3] At the same time, a reformism had developed in response to FBI surveillance of CISPES. Even though the full extent of this surveillance was uncovered by the Office of Intelligence Policy and Review (the part of the Justice Department that is supposed to monitor intelligence gathering), nothing was done to stop it until a Senate subcommittee investigated, and the Center for Constitutional Rights exposed it. Members of Congress argued that reforms were needed to prevent the FBI from investigating groups that were exercising their right to free speech. But such reforms, like those enacted during the Watergate era, had no lasting effect. This failure on the part of Congress to limit authoritarian measures promoted America's historical drift to a police state. For decades, Congress acted as an enabler, allowing the executive branch to concentrate ever-greater power. Congress and other parts of the federal government also began working together, especially after foreign-inspired acts of terrorism of the 1990s.

The 1993 World Trade Center bombing provided the federal government with the basis to establish measures giving it more authority to act outside the law; it would allow the government to begin operating in a permanent state of emergency, an essential component of a police state. The government was releasing a steady stream of propaganda, manufacturing fear, socializing the population to accept each new encroachment on civil liberties as necessary to combat the terrorists, and stepping up repression. The Clinton administration passed the 1996 Anti-Terrorist Act, which monitors those identified as outsiders, leading to the political prosecution of the LA Eight. As immigrants, the seven Palestinians and one Kenyan were easy targets. The government assumed their guilt by association because they were members of the Popular Front for the Liberation of Palestine; it sought to deport them under the 1952 McCarran-Walter Act, charged with promoting ideas associated with the doctrine of world Communism. Such paranoia demonstrates how those in power see conspiracies where none exist and in the absence of credible evidence. The LA Eight were never charged with crimes or identified as engaging in behavior that might threaten national security.[4]

The incident demonstrates the government's obsession with outsiders, cloaked in expressions of anti-immigrant sentiment. It had ongoing investigations of enemy aliens, described in documents such as the "Alien Terrorists and Undesirables: A Contingency Plan." Immigrants were the first individuals subjected to the Bush administration's post-9/11 policies. Persecution of immigrants is a common theme justifying political repression over the course of U.S. history; they were targeted regardless of their immigration status because they criticized American foreign policy. The implication is that the act of questioning foreign policy is un-American, a common theme for political witch hunting throughout the twentieth century. Identification as a political outsider, especially if an individual has immigrant status, also means not having legal standing with which to exercise free speech or freedom of political association. In 1999, the Supreme Court said as much in its ruling, the implications of which would be felt years later, when two of the LA Eight's defendants were later charged with violating the Patriot Act.

The 1980s Library Awareness Program provides another example of the connection between pre- and post-9/11 repressive initiatives.

Under the program, FBI agents paid a series of visits to public and university libraries in cities throughout the United States, requesting information identifying the readers of various technical journals.[5] The FBI was on a fishing expedition to discover persons harboring thoughts and ideas that did not conform to the status quo. FBI officials sought to make librarians, especially after 9/11, partners as thought police and to be particularly suspicious of persons who appeared to be foreign born.

FBI surveillance extended to a broad range of activities perceived as subversive, including organizations engaged in peaceful acts of civil disobedience, in particular the AIDS Coalition to Unleash Power (ACT-UP). The surveillance of ACT-UP began, in part, because of its "in your face" political tactics, such as marches with thousands of activists near President George H.W. Bush's home in Maine, chanting "Shame" and dramatizing the number of AIDS deaths. Despite the group's obvious advocacy of nonviolence, the FBI maintained constant surveillance on it, partnering with local police. Whether it was monitoring or repressing a domestic group such as ACT-UP or forming alliances with dictators overseas, gathering intelligence and when necessary, overtly using force, political repression was employed to maintain the American empire. The result is that democracy at home and overseas is suppressed. Empires are incompatible with democracy, which has been seen throughout human history. To maintain and expand power, an empire must limit dissent, rolling back democracy; only mass democracy could challenge the authoritarian policies of the U.S. government.

The pattern that continued through the 1990s was that the government, in many ways, sought to evade its responsibility to rule in accordance with rule of law and the Constitution. The executive branch throughout the twentieth century became more uncomfortable with, and resistant to, constitutional restraints placed on the exercise of its authority while Congress began functioning as an enabler, abdicating its responsibility to act in accordance with rule of law and failing to put in place essential legal restraints to control the growth of executive authority. On one hand, Congress was willing to accept and support the secret policy-making partnership that presidents had developed with intelligence agencies; on the other, whenever Congress attempted to place legal limits on presidential power, it did so without sufficient foresight into how presidents could work around such reforms. For example, from the time FISA was enacted as a post-Watergate reform, it made legal whatever actions a president wanted to take in terms of surveillance. This meant that the executive branch could legalize political repression—something it had never been able to do before. FISA typically rubber-stamped requests for surveillance; in addition, Congress allowed the court to act without sufficient oversight. FISA became a tool to concentrate state power in the executive branch, whenever new emergencies were declared.

Propelled by events that triggered shock, confusion, and fear, the Clinton and George W. Bush administrations used the rapid enactment of more extreme emergency measures to continue the march toward a permanent police state. The 1996 Anti-Terrorism Act grew out of previous measures and contained new far-reaching provisions. The 1993 bombing of the World Trade Center and the 1995 bombing of the federal building in Oklahoma City would result in the suspension of civil liberties in favor of security. Clinton administration officials articulated the need to respond quickly in a national emergency. Provisions of the 1996 Anti-Terrorism Act were, in some ways, similar to other actions taken to identify and repress targeted political outsiders, allowing the government to persecute and deport immigrants, to erect prohibitions against groups labeled terrorists, and to give agencies license to gather intelligence in secret with no accountability, all relics of the past that now reappeared. Political repression was again justified through guilt by association in which being a member of a group identified as terrorist is, in and of itself, grounds for removing basic due process rights as well as deportation. The 1996 act was similar to the 1952 McCarren-Walter Act, only now it is terrorist organizations and not Communist or anarchist organizations that are targeted. With specific incidents serving as a trigger, the government presses its case for swift action. In 1984, the Reagan administration had requested that Congress make it a federal crime to raise money to support terrorism, a proposal close to the version adopted in the 1996 Anti-Terrorism Act. Another Reagan administration initiative granted the government a license to identify which groups could be defined as terrorists. The administration of Bush senior had proposed that providing material support constituted a basis for a group to be targeted as terrorist, and contained within the Clinton crime bill were references to measures against those providing material support for terrorism. Congress had previously rejected such measures, but they were finally accepted as part of the 1996 Anti-Terrorism Act. During the first House Judiciary Committee hearing on it, nearly all the witnesses called expressed unequivocal support. After the Oklahoma City bombing, the same rush to pass legislation was evident, with no criticism voiced during Senate hearings. Given that very few members of Congress dared question the act's sweeping provisions, the executive branch seized the moment and pressured legislators to quickly pass it. Congress, afraid of being depicted as weak or not sufficiently concerned for national security, made every effort to get the bill signed by the president by April 19, passing it with lopsided margins after making only minor changes. With its provisions revealing an intent to place legal restraint on democratic practices, making the Constitution in many ways, null and void, the Anti-Terrorism Act demonstrates the further development of police state practices. The act replaces the courts with the government, especially the executive branch, as the final authority to judge what is legal. So, political organizations, even nonpolitical ones, can arbitrarily find themselves without legal or constitutional protections. In the end, the act allows government to outlaw the expression of democratic practices, making it a political crime for citizens and noncitizens to give any kind of support to groups designated as terrorist by the Secretary of State. The intent is clear: to prevent people from engaging in political participation, civil disobedience, or questioning of domestic and foreign policy initiatives. The act makes reference to alien-terrorists and their rivals, once again, political outsiders arbitrarily identified as enemies of the state. As such, these terrorists are to be placed outside the law and confronted with excessive secrecy, denying the accused a right to know the source of information being used against them.

Therefore, to be labeled a terrorist amounted to an automatic denial of access to the court system, especially the right of habeas corpus. The act implies that diverse viewpoints are political crimes against the state, correlating the questioning of government policy with acts of terrorism. The act strives to disorganize groups that were labeled terrorist. Once the label is applied, the federal government can act to crush the organization, alleging that it has committed, or will commit, political crimes. The act criminalizes contributions to such groups "even for its social, political or humanitarian activities, all members of the group are barred from entering the United States and are deportable if they were members prior to entry, even if they have never been involved in illegal activities, and banks must freeze funds of any designated organization and its agents."[6] This means the government can encroach upon and control a host of economic actions, whether or not they are related to terrorism.

The act also allows the government to express prejudice toward persons and groups who fall under parts of immigration law, so that foreign and domestic policy intersect. Persons from nations deemed hostile to U.S. foreign policy objectives now fall under the act's guilt-by-association clause, because they come from a country with terrorist ties. The Anti-Terrorist Act allows the Department of Justice to deport a noncitizen identified as a political outsider or alien terrorist, based on secret evidence. Missing is any semblance of due process in the deportation proceedings, for the act stipulates that the government only need supply a noncitizen with the reasons for the deportation. The summary provided in all likelihood could never make its way to an immigration court, and even if it did, the court does not have sufficient due process procedures in place. The authority of the judge is limited to determining the nature of the summary of charges. Any possible appeal to the court of appeals would not be granted, leaving a noncitizen at the mercy of a special removal proceeding, in which the defendant is assumed guilty and not provided an opportunity to make bail. In addition, the act identifies distinct categories of noncitizens who have no rights, once accused of having any association with a terrorist organization. Individuals in the United States on visas, including student or tourist ones, cannot have hearings about their detention; while lawful resident aliens can have hearings, the government is allowed to use classified information, and the burden of proof rests with the individual.

The Twin Tower and Oklahoma City attacks provided government with a rationalization for moving quickly to enhance its concentration of power against the American people, creating a political climate of extremism. This was especially true with the use of extraordinary renditions during the Clinton and Bush administrations. Renditions had been used to seize a suspect elsewhere and bring him or her to stand trial in a U.S. court, allowing American courts to turn a blind eye as to how the suspect was apprehended. Courts allowed law enforcement officials to supercede another country's law without having to take into account any extradition treaty the country may or may not have with the United States. This history of extraordinary rendition dates back to the 1880s. Until the Clinton administration, these seizures had one thing in common: the suspects would face regular criminal trials in the United States. The sea change that the Clinton administration brought about demonstrates how a novel policy developed from the drive to sidestep procedural due process in the courts and replace it with police state methods. The shift was motivated by the government's seizing of an opportunity to extend state power to deal with the terrorism threat. No longer were seizures justified solely in criminal cases; the Clinton administration's rendition program now allowed the kidnapping of those charged with political offenses. The Clinton administration accelerated the use of extraordinary renditions, the political

roots of which lay with the Reagan administration's seiz
suspects, when the policy still was to have such suspect
U.S. court. But there was an important difference between the Reagan
and Clinton administrations' uses of rendition, for during the Reagan
administration, rendition policy meant a close working partnership
between the United States and a cooperating country in accordance
with international law and for the purpose of returning the suspect
to the United States. Even the CIA, which was to have a pivotal role
in the renditions of the Clinton and Bush administrations, was then
legally required to abide by national and international law. The FBI
was also subject to legal restraints, pertaining to the agency's adherence
to a strict following of international law and respect for a country's
sovereign authority.

A critical step in transforming the use of rendition occurred when
President Bush senior issued NSD-77, which allowed for renditions to
be carried out, taking into account the noncooperation of a foreign
government and other possible circumstances. If a situation presented
itself in which extradition procedures were impractical, the United
States could request a country's help through a secret agreement, putting the suspect on a plane headed either to the United States or a third
country to be tried. That shift in policy was significant: NSD-77 represented a significant transition toward secretive police state procedures
for whatever purpose the government saw fit. Only a few months after
the Oklahoma City bombing and not long after the first Twin Towers
attack, President Clinton took this initiative one step further, initiating Presidential Decision Directive (PDD-39) in June 1995. With this
directive, extraordinary rendition was no longer a policy option; it
became standard policy for dealing with suspected terrorists. With this
policy in place, all legal pretenses were dropped. In essence, seizing
anyone was just a matter of identifying a suspect, for there was no due
process within a U.S. court to challenge the terrorist label. The executive branch had now set itself up as a court of law, making the determination of guilt and sending the suspect elsewhere to be punished.
Such a practice is common in police states. It is also consistent with
the history of political repression in the US in that political outsiders
are designated enemies of the state and therefore have no rights. The
concern over whether or not there are actual terrorists determined to
attack civilians inside and outside US borders is not what motivates the
government to act in all circumstances. A prime indication is the government's neglect of appropriate legal avenues to arrest, interview, try
and imprison such suspects. Instead, in the name of pursuing terrorism,

the government seeks to exert absolute authority over the thoughts and actions of the American people.

Changes that moved the country incrementally toward a full-fledged police state during the Clinton administration and others culminated in the George W. Bush administration, which acted, as its predecessors had, in accordance with the Unitary Executive, a concentration of power within the White House. Clinton expanded presidential power at the expense of Congress when he reinforced the process begun by the Reagan and Bush administrations, requiring executive agencies to allow the White House to review proposed rules before they could go into effect. Clinton's reliance on executive orders allowed him to avoid consulting Congress on a range of issues, including the enforcement of international human rights treaties.[7]

The Clinton-Lewinsky affair had the unintended outcome of removing oversight on the president, for the lengthy investigation by independent counsel Kenneth Starr "convinced Democrats to join Republicans in wanting to get rid of the Ethics in Government Act. Congress allowed the law to expire in 1999, freeing all future presidents from the threat of a prosecutor they could not fire."[8] What remained of congressional oversight over foreign policy was diminished by Clinton's intervention in Somalia. In response to a congressional request to withdraw troops according to the War Powers Resolution, the administration's legal advisors determined that the law wasn't applicable since troops were not involved in sustained combat.[9] The president's free hand to send troops without congressional approval is additional evidence of the continuing expansion of power: Clinton sent troops to Haiti and Bosnia and launched strikes against Iraq, Afghanistan, and Sudan without asking for congressional approval. "Like his predecessors, Clinton refused to acknowledge that the War Powers Resolution restricted his actions as Commander in Chief."[10]

The police state of the George W. Bush administration was finally achieved by two triggers: the 2000 presidential election and 9/11. The first ominous sign was the 2000 election, which, in the final analysis, was not decided by the electorate. Throughout the campaign, Bush didn't say much about terrorism; it wasn't a topic in the debates. The election's outcome would be decided by Florida, which had, like many other states, an error-prone set of voting procedures. Throughout American history, various techniques have been employed to disenfranchise the electorate. The technical problems of hanging, dimpled or pregnant chads aside, most significant was the failure to record the votes of African American and Latino voters and the invalidation of registered African American and Latino voters; thousands were incorrectly excluded due to erroneous placement on felon lists. Such actions resulted in fixing the election in clear partisan terms to favor Bush, the result of a legal strategy coordinated by Bush backers, including former Secretary of State James Baker; Jeb Bush, George's brother and governor of Florida; and the Republican-controlled Florida legislature, which would figure prominently in the election by certifying its outcome. The Gore strategy of seeking a manual recount sent the matter first to Florida Supreme Court. The favorable ruling calling for a manual recount in four disputed counties was unacceptable to the Bush team, which requested that the U.S. Supreme Court review the issues. As the oral arguments were being made, Secretary of State Harris, also cochair of the Florida Bush campaign, halted the recount, certifying that Bush had won Florida by just 537 votes. Gore's attorneys argued before the Supreme Court that the actions of Harris and the Florida legislature clearly violated Florida State law and the state constitution, which they wanted the Florida Supreme Court to look at, using its power of judicial review. At first, the Supreme Court appeared to pass the buck to the Florida court, where the legal wrangling had begun. The Florida Supreme Court's first opinion was to have a statewide recount of the 61,000 contested undervotes. The Bush legal team could not accept this and went back to the Supreme Court to halt it. The Court issued a stay with the five majority votes consisting of justices appointed by Reagan and George H.W. Bush. In another five to four ruling, the U.S. Supreme Court decided the election in favor of Bush, basing the ruling on a question of equal protection, a legal defense often used to protect the rights of minorities. In this strange decision, the Court's majority reasoned that equal protection in this case was meant to protect a possible violation of the basic democratic principal of one person, one vote. What the equal protection ruling achieved was the opposite, for it meant that the Supreme Court had nullified eligible voters from voting or having their votes counted. The antidemocratic nature of this Supreme Court decision was intended to operate only for this particular election. It had no real standing as legal precedent. The Court had, in effect, selected Bush to be the next president.

Once in office, the Bush administration set in motion a chain of events that culminated in a highly developed American police state. Given historical trends toward diminishing democracy and federal agencies' hostility to democracy, the 9/11 attacks provided an opportunity to complete the concentration of power and end what was left of the rule of law. The attacks brought to the surface the radical steps perceived as necessary to combat terrorism in the United States and overseas. These radical measures emerged in part from the shock of being caught unaware; President Bush lacked knowledge and experience in foreign affairs. Many within the administration's inner circle ignored or dismissed the ever-growing threat from al Qaeda, with the exception of Richard Clarke, who had served Democratic and Republican administrations as a counterterrorism expert in the National Security Council. In spite of recent attacks on U.S. national security interests overseas, a cold war mindset lingered among officials, especially Dick Cheney, who would become one of the police state's key architects. The idea that the United States could be attacked by a group waging asymmetric warfare caught Cheney, the quintessential cold war warrior, off guard. This helps to explain how the final version of the police state appeared, as compensation for blindness to the looming threat. The police state quickly emerged in response to the state of emergency that developed after 9/11. For the Bush administration, 9/11 made it necessary to invent novel means to deal with terrorism. The administration's approach would do away with all legal restraints. Standard legal practices in the Constitution were set aside, and it soon became a hollow prop, replaced by the pseudolegality of what were essentially decrees passed by a Congress working quickly and without much questioning. The Constitution in post-9/11 America is now a relic, replaced by other documents that provide the administration with the ability to act without question in a state of permanent emergency.

Some of the roots of these developments lay in the political psychology of various administration officials. Since the 1970s, Vice President Cheney had long been an advocate of expanding presidential power. Less than a week after 9/11, he discussed the extreme methods that were going to be employed in secret, without restraint; on "Meet the Press," he said the administration would "work sort of the Dark Side, if you will." With political extremism the guiding principal, all actions become acceptable. The administration was prepared to break new ground, going to any lengths to deal with terrorism, leading the executive branch to act with a license and a will to dominate, to control the thoughts and actions of citizens and noncitizens. To prevent another 9/11, it would establish extreme forms of repression, such as the pseudolegal decrees of the Patriot Act, in which all Americans are possible enemies of the state. This was the New Paradigm—a radical break—permission to invent repressive measures. Bush communicated as much to Attorney General Ashcroft, warning that it would be Ashcroft himself who would be on the line if such an attack were ever repeated; Ashcroft understood the warning as permission to become more aggressive on every front where national security was concerned. "Shortly after September 11, Bush looked his attorney general John Ashcroft in the eye, according to Ashcroft's memoir, and told him icily, 'Don't ever let this happen again.'"[11] Other officials would be involved, too; acting without regard to legal precedent was now the norm. Ashcroft communicated this to the head of the FBI, stating "that criminal trials were beside the point. All that mattered was stopping the next attack. Due process, it seemed, was too time-consuming."[12]

The White House found another willing, innovative partner in the CIA, with Counterterrorism Chief Cofer Black. The post-9/11 political culture was to break with the past, ignoring legal restraints and international law. Black's proposal was a license to act anywhere and answer only to the White House, involving "the inauguration of secret paramilitary death squads authorized to hunt and kill prime terror suspects anywhere on earth. A week earlier, those deaths would have been classified as illegal assassinations."[13] CIA agents were waging a clandestine war against anyone abstractly defined as a terrorist. Black's proposal was a blank check for the agency to go after those they suspected of terrorism or activities that supported terrorism in as many as 80 countries. A consistent part of the Bush administration's police state is a covert war against civilians inside and outside of the United States. Black's plan included CIA authorization for breaking and entering private property of citizens and tracking communications and financial transactions of those they suspected of being terrorists, even in the United States. In this covert war on civilians, permission to spy within the United States was now granted to the CIA; its awesome and novel authority now included the power to conduct interrogations and detentions. In this climate, all methods were now acceptable, as Black indicated when he addressed the House and Senate Intelligence Committees on September 26, 2002: "All you need to know is that there was a before 9/11 and there was an after 9/11. After 9/11, the gloves come off."[14]

A key aspect of the police state mentality is that all persons are potentially guilty, so their thoughts and actions must be monitored and ultimately controlled. Such was the motivation behind Attorney General Gonzales's request that Congress grant the president authority to wage war against suspected terrorists in the United States and to identify virtually anyone defined as a terrorist. The Bush administration sought assurance that these new powers would remain permanent, since the administration believed that the United States was in a state of permanent emergency. The intention was to implement a key police state feature, that is, to suspend any limitations on the president's use of force in the United States. Thus, with sufficient threats, the federal government was now authorized to deploy the military domestically, raid homes of suspected terrorists even if innocent parties could be affected, shoot hijacked civilian airliners, and establish military checkpoints in cities. It "could also shoot down civilian airliners hijacked by terrorists and set up military checkpoints inside American cities. The Justice Department also said that the executive branch could ignore both fourth amendment protections against illegitimate searches and without court warrants, specific laws passed by Congress prohibiting wiretaps and other surreptitious surveillance of American's communications."[15]

In post-9/11 America, the complete concentration of power in the executive branch, which allowed it to act without consulting Congress, was a key goal of the presidents' advisors, and they sought to terminate laws Congress had passed to curb unrestricted use of presidential powers. Spearheading the effort was Cheney's legal counsel, David Addington, who would join forces with John Yoo, deputy chief in the Justice Department's Office of Legal Counsel. Cheney, Addington, Yoo, and Attorney Generals Ashcroft and Gonzales collectively lacked an understanding of both national security law and the Constitution and shared a willingness to embrace police state methods. Cheney and Addington believed that Vietnam and post-Watergate reforms had significantly weakened the presidency and that especially in foreign policy, the president should be all powerful. The American police state would be accomplished with the realization of a Unitary Executive with absolute power. Bush was in general agreement with his subordinates while the particulars were left up to Cheney and Addington. Cheney shaped the decision-making process, in many instances, acting as copresident, determining which items would be decided by the president, while Addington, whose lack of concern about the Constitution was well known, controlled the paperwork. Addington regarded even the FISA court as obstructing presidential authority. At best, FISA was a means for presidents to formally request a surveillance program. Requests were rarely turned down. But in considering how another attack could enable further growth of presidential power, he remarked, "We're one bomb away from getting rid of that obnoxious [FISA] court."[16] The fact that the Bush administration didn't see the need to send any formal requests for surveillance to the FISA court demonstrates the lengths to which they were willing to go to resist legal compliance. To act in such a manner, according to prerogative, places the actions of the Bush administration outside a legal framework.

There was an Orwellian dimension to the administration's perspective; it chose to disregard law, instead creating decrees to legitimize illegal actions, giving itself permission to act without any semblance of power sharing as required by the Constitution or international law. This political extremism emerged from the pseudolegal guidelines issued from the Office of Legal Counsel (OLC), which resulted in making the executive branch the U.S. government's sole policy-making branch. The president and Congress had delegated to the attorney general the power to legally determine whether or not the laws passed by Congress and executed by the president were legal and consistent with the constitutional authority granted to each branch. The OLC is charged with ensuring that the executive branch responsible for carrying out laws was also bound by law, but after 9/11, that function changed. As the Bush administration began taking actions which violated the Constitution, the OLC provided legal cover. All that stood in the way of the abuses of rights at home and overseas was concern by officials about violating the law and facing the consequences. But once the OLC issued an interpretation, any action becomes legal. After 9/11, the OLC created what were essentially get-out-of-jail free cards,[17] allowing the administration to do anything in the name of fighting terrorism, generating immunity from prosecution. There were no legal restraints on the administration's actions; the OLC had made everything legal.

John Yoo, an ideologue who believed in an imperial presidency on steroids, was the administration's ally in the OLC, who helped create what Cheney and Addington wanted: a branch of government that worked in secret, did what it pleased, and answered to no one. Yoo and Addington created what they believed to be an all-powerful president, who possessed the power to use force at will, actually a military dictatorship. Yoo's September 25, 2001 memorandum, "The President's Constitutional Authority to Conduct Military Operations Against Terrorists and Nations Supporting Them," was a blank check to take military action, including preemptive action, whether or not it related to the 9/11 attacks. According to the memo, citizens of the United States and foreign countries were soon to be regarded as terror suspects. When everyone is a possible terror suspect, the openness of a democratic society is not possible. The American police state further developed as a secret government within a government. This concept is introduced in Yoo's memorandum, where he argues to exclude Congress from interfering with how the president deals with the terrorist threat. A government that operates in secret is a government run by and controlled by a small number of people, who are the true guardians of state secrets. This mini-ruling group called itself "The War Council" and consisted of Yoo, Addington, Flanigan, Gonzales, and Hayes, the Pentagon's general counsel. This group represented the most arrogant form of authoritarianism; they couldn't claim any specialized knowledge on how to deal with terrorism or related issues, yet it functioned as a secret shadow government. This mini-cabal of advisors consulted with select members of Congress as an afterthought, after key decisions were made. For example, on October 25, 2001, Cheney and Addington hosted a top secret White House meeting with Congress's intelligence experts and high-ranking members of the intelligence committees. The purpose was to brief those in attendance about a new police state initiative, designed to target everyone as a potential suspect. This new National Security Agency program would allow the government to listen in on phone calls and various forms of electronic communications without obtaining a warrant. Called the Terrorist Surveillance Program (TSP), this program had no geographic boundaries and lacked the most basic legal requirement, probable cause that criminal acts were being committed. Yoo and Addington's rationale for this program was that warrantless surveillance, like the president's war powers, was simply a matter of presidential prerogative. With this NSA program, the Bush administration had discarded the bare minimum congressional requirement that surveillance required: a formal request to the FISA court. "After 9/11, they and other top officials in the administration dealt with FISA the way they dealt with other laws they didn't like: they blew through them in secret based on flimsy legal opinions that they guarded closely so no one could question the legal basis for the operations."[18]

Secrecy to enact draconian measures thus became an important part of the Bush administration's police state. Ten days after 9/11, the FBI, without justification, began mass arrests of hundreds of foreign Arab and Muslim men in the United States who drove cabs, worked in restaurants, or attended college and had no relation to the attacks.[19] Such wholesale roundups over expired immigration visas would not have taken place in a pre-9/11 America. As in the past, these outsiders were looked upon as an internal threat, and proceedings against them were kept secret. Family members, media, and the public were barred from attending the deportation hearings that followed, and the names of those arrested were never listed on public documents.[20] Additional steps helped further the atmosphere of secrecy: Ashcroft directed that all FOIA requests be rejected even if the information requested was of no concern.[21] The administration sought not so much to keep information from terrorists as it did to keep it from the American public, the media, Congress, good government groups, and even government agencies.[22] Secrecy of all kinds is integral to police states because their activities cannot be legitimized, so the Bush administration began "shutting down the flow of unclassified information to the public. Websites went dark, periodic reports that compiled politically inconvenient information were shut down."[23]

Such secrecy spread to other federal agencies, not only the traditional "secret keepers": the Departments of Defense, Justice, State and the intelligence gatherers; the CIA; FBI; and NSA but also the departments of Agriculture and Health and Human Services as well as the Environmental Protection Agency.[24] In general, the Bush administration had been moving toward making many more actions of government secret, using a multiplier effect known as a derivative classification where documents that include even part of a secret contained in another document must automatically then be classified as secret, too.[25] Ultimately, the Bush administration used secrecy not only to hide information from critical scrutiny but also to deceive, allowing the most authoritarian and destructive policies to escape examination, especially as to their real motives, maintaining and expanding the concentration of power in the White House. Such secrecy serves to expand gross errors in judgment, creating and enforcing political paranoia, an inability to distinguish real from imaginary threats. This was the case with the extensive secrecy surrounding the apprehension of Abu Zubaydah in Pakistan in March 2002. The administration described Zubaydah as an important player in al Qaeda and touted his capture as a major strike against the organization, but investigations by reporter Ron Suskind later revealed that that depiction was completely false, and he was judged mentally incompetent.[26] The administration's obsession with secrecy often echoed Goebbels' big lie, often repeated so that it will be believed sooner or later. Secrecy also separated administration officials from any possible blowback. Extensive secrecy surrounded the conditions of prisoners held at Guantanamo Bay and the horrors to which they were subjected in Abu Ghraib and various secret prisons, a vital part of CIA rendition and torture programs. Initially, secrecy was successful, providing plausible deniability. But eventually, some secrets do see the light of day.

What was left of formal democracy ended very quickly with the passage of the Patriot Act. Congress bears its share of responsibility as a branch of government so gripped by fear that it did not dare challenge presidential prerogatives; it became the quintessential enabler, completing America's final escape from democracy. The Patriot Act expressed the government's mindset that democracy and rule of law are a burden and should be abandoned, and that the country is in a permanent state of emergency. The act's provisions, in many ways, are meant to replace the Constitution. Ashcroft and his subordinates drafted it in less than a week. The few members of Congress who saw it were surprised by the president's and attorney general's insistence that it be quickly approved; and by administration statements, in one case that "Congress would have blood on its hands" if another attack occurred before it was passed.[27] Members of Congress had little time to read and discuss it, with most acknowledging that they had read very little, if any, of the nearly 350-page document.[28] The Democrats were provided with only two copies. The administration knew that pressure could be successfully applied, given its portrayal of America in a state of emergency. Congress knew it had to go along. "Rep. Peter DeFazio (D-Ore) remembers, 'It was a time to be stampeded, and who wanted to be against the USA Patriot Act at a time like that?' "[29] It passed in the House of Representatives, 357–66 and in the Senate, 98–1.

A close examination of the act's titles points to the extent to which it attempted to excessively and permanently concentrate power. It allowed the president to virtually ignore the Constitution, making it possible for the state to engage in social control. It endowed all members of law enforcement with new authority to look for terrorist threats and to protect the population from terrorism, essentially creating new industries that would engage in assessing threats, conducting sophisticated surveillance, sharing data, and developing new computer security tools. The act created an even closer partnership between the executive branch and federal agencies, providing both with new powers that they had hoped to have in a pre-9/11 America. The Patriot Act expanded the definition of terrorism to include attacks to damage or destroy mass transit systems, airplanes and airports, and activities involving the use of chemicals or computers. Significantly, it refers to efforts to commit, or conspire to engage in, a crime of domestic terrorism, or harboring a person who might commit or be about to commit an act of terrorism.

Due process is noticeably absent. Title I expands the president's authority to investigate terrorism and terrorist attacks and confiscate property used in these attacks. Due process is not mentioned in the part that grants the president the authority to freeze assets at the start of, or even prior to an investigation, instead of after it is completed. All property seized can be disposed of according to the president's wishes.

There is no legal requirement to have a court order prior to a seizure, creating the possibility that mistakes may be made and, in most cases, won't be corrected.

Much concern over the Patriot Act pertains to Title II, the granting of enormous power to enhance surveillance authority and information sharing on any form of communication. The new definition of terrorist activities expands what intelligence gatherers can do to investigate persons identified as participating in a conspiracy to commit an act of terrorism or as supporting members of a terrorist organization. All information gathered in such undertakings is deemed relevant. Information sharing is no longer limited to criminal activities but includes grand jury testimony; financial and consumer records, which can be provided to any federal official working in law enforcement; intelligence; immigration; defense; or national security.[30] This sharing of information is so broad that just about any activity could be investigated as terrorist. Standard legal procedures, like the requirement to have a court order, are gone. The federal government determines what is legal. Investigations require simple references to anything bearing a relation to any matter of national security. Information sharing takes place in secret, including how the information was obtained. The executive branch and federal agencies determine and interpret law without contact with the courts, an important police state trait.

Also in Title II, no provision allows for a traditional challenge to the federal government conducting illegal search and seizure, a Fourth Amendment violation, while sneak and peek warrants allow investigators to enter a residence, business, or other location, search, then leave without taking anything and without informing the targeted individual. One of many permanent sections of the Patriot Act, this is most disturbing, especially since such provisions need not pertain to possible terrorist-related activities. Related to this unwarranted intrusion into privacy is another section in Title II, allowing for extensive use of what is known as pen, register, and trap and trace devices. These wiretap and surveillance methods are used to monitor calls made from a specific telephone line. Investigators can also conduct surveillance on Internet user accounts, Internet e-mail addresses, Internet protocol addresses, and cell phone numbers. This provision, too, is a permanent feature of the Patriot Act. One section allows voice messages to be seized, while another permanent provision grants intelligence gatherers, such as the FBI, the right to file a request with a federal judge to obtain all business records of persons who are not U.S. citizens without notifying the individual beforehand. There is no requirement to obtain a search warrant. All the FBI needs to do is state a need to obtain the records as part of an authorized investigation. This extends to the acquisition of records outside the investigation's scope. There are few legal safeguards in the event of an abuse of this provision. Whether or not evidence obtained through this kind of surveillance will be suppressed in court is uncertain. Information obtained from one individual and used against another might not be suppressed, and with information sharing, finding out who actually did the surveillance would be very difficult. Even if the information gathered is never used in a courtroom, the surveillance can remain ongoing. There is little to no congressional oversight, only a general report containing the nature of the investigation, what was obtained, and where the items are stored.

Title III deals with banking, money laundering, international funds transfers, and currency crimes. It demonstrates the extensive control the federal government, especially the executive branch, can exercise over diverse institutions. The inclusion of banks and financial institutions with what are called "special measures" illustrates how far institutions have gone as willing partners with the federal government against this threat of terrorism. The section established extensive controls to monitor any economic transactions by American citizens, including ordinary international business transactions. Often, a set of conditions would set in motion a federal investigation termed a finding, indicating that there may be evidence of criminal or terrorist activities. Part of the problem with the Act in general, and in this instance, is the lack of an objective basis for determining who is a terrorist. Some cases are clear; many are not. A large number have more to do with identifying terrorist organizations according to U.S. foreign policy objectives. When a finding is made for political reasons, "special measures" are put in place, requiring that a bank turn over all records and transactions, including names, addresses, and kinds of transactions; the bank would then be issued a directive stating that it could not allow this kind of account. Surveillance is arbitrary, and investigations target organizations which, according to the government, provide economic support for terrorism. Federal officials now have the authority to investigate the financial structure of nonprofit and nongovernmental organizations, despite indicators that they have no economic ties to terrorist activities. Under Title III, banks become an investigative arm of the government, conducting elaborate tracking and monitoring of customer activity and sharing it with the government.[31] This section also contains general forfeiture and seizure provisions, which can be conducted with no burden of proof on the government, even though the property may not have been used to commit a crime or support terrorist activity. There is no probable cause requirement nor is it necessary for the courts to determine a seizure's legality. Investigations and seizures are conducted in secret; persons or organizations are not informed that they are under investigation. It is revealing to note that even before 9/11, the federal government had extensive and broad authority to use legal means through the federal courts to obtain search warrants and conduct surveillance. Denial by FISA was virtually nonexistent.

Title IV demonstrates how political repression against outsiders becomes extreme in a developing police state. Subtitle B, "Enhanced Immigration Provisions," contains a problematic definition of terrorism and terrorist activity as any act determined to be unlawful. This makes the definition dependent on the definer's political perspective. This "eye of the beholder" definition leads to actions that can be taken against support of terrorist activists, from raising money or having membership in an organization; it includes material support, safe houses, transportation, and training. Justice and State Department guidelines define as a so-called alien anyone who is, in effect, identified as a member of a foreign terrorist organization, tied to a specific political ideology, which espouses terrorism. Aliens are broadly defined as involved in terrorist activity even without organizational affiliations. As was the case with the act's other titles, there is an almost total lack of legal and/or constitutional safeguards: if an alien is determined by a federal official to be a member of a terrorist organization or supporter of terrorism, the person is automatically assumed guilty. There can be no legal defense to this charge. This includes an individual who is a member of an organization and is unaware of its terrorist activities. The burden is on the alien to prove he or she did not know that the organization was associated with terrorism. It is guilt by association. Titles II and III also contain provisions on sharing records. The individual in question is investigated in all areas, including work history, personal associations, and bank records, all of which takes place in the absence of criminal charges; there are no due process procedures in place. Within Title IV, non-U.S. citizens confront new authority given to federal immigration and law enforcement officials to seize and confine aliens residing in the United States.

The act lists seven offenses that would lead not only to seizure and confinement but deportation as well, including engaging in espionage or sabotage, opposition to the government or seeking to overthrow it by force and violence, involvement in a range of conduct qualifying as terrorist activity, or engaging in other activity that endangers national security. Once identified as falling into at least one of these categories, an alien can be detained by the Justice Department for a week before being charged with a criminal offense. If not subject to deportation proceedings, the alien can be held for up to six months, and this can be extended for another six months. The only due process procedure in place under Title IV is an appeal to either the U.S. Supreme Court with any Supreme Court justice or with a circuit judge of the court of appeals in federal district court. This habeas corpus application, which could be limited, faces formidable obstacles to any kind of legal relief. It is highly unlikely that a person charged with being a terrorist will have an impartial hearing. Then there is the technical prohibition in Title IV, which only allows for a six-month grace period to challenge the confinement. Delays and reconfinement could lead to aliens being held indefinitely. If the case were to go to trial, it is not out of the question that the identified alien would be tried before a military tribunal and not in a criminal court. Title IV also includes a provision making foreign students and foreign exchange programs the objects of increased investigation and surveillance. Institutions of higher education are mandated to provide lists of foreign students. Title IV also requires that schools that conduct training in flight, languages, and vocations now report to the federal government. As a result, a number of federal agencies are keeping a watchful eye on the activities of foreign students in the United States.

In the name of investigating terrorism, Title V provides for the comprehensive surveillance of Americans in novel areas. The DNA Analysis Backlog Elimination Act, under which DNA was collected of persons convicted of specific crimes, was broadened to include any crime of violence and any attempt or conspiracy to commit any of the above offenses. The federal government now had the right to obtain a DNA sample of anyone convicted of a conspiracy to commit any act of terrorism. The FBI also has expanded authority to gather vast amounts of personal information, including phone records and financial and consumer reports, in connection with a terrorism investigation. Absent is the need for a court order, which was required before the Patriot Act. There are no First Amendment protections of free speech under this provision, for the FBI is the judge. To acquire financial and consumer records, authorization is just a matter of a formal request by a high-ranking FBI official. As with telephone surveillance, no court order is required. To acquire educational records, there is a low threshold in the court order requirement, a brief statement of probable cause, a description as to the nature of the investigation, and a justification regarding the need to have the documents. Evidence of probable cause is no longer a legal requirement. Other federal agencies besides the FBI, such as the Justice Department, can request from a federal court an ex parte order, a statement of reasons to believe that an educational institution has records essential to an investigation. Upon receiving the order from the court, the institution is required to turn over any relevant files. With these powers, the federal government has the authority to search and seize with little burden of proof; those under investigation have no legal recourse. There are no limits on the scale of the investigation or the information that can be obtained.

Title VI, which provides for victims of terrorism, public safety officers, and their families, lacks controversial provisions. Titles VII–X contain some of the act's most controversial, permanent parts. A recurring theme is a governmental conspiracy to monopolize control and maintain secrecy as the thoughts and actions of Americans are monitored with, at a bare minimum, great suspicion. Another theme is the federal government's association of absolute power with absolute surveillance. Title VII establishes an integrated information-gathering system to coordinate activities on the federal, state, and local levels. Information and misinformation is shared at all levels of government and law enforcement. Such systems generate a tendency to snowball, making more likely the prosecution and persecution of thoughts and actions, which, without this rush to judgment, would not constitute true acts of terrorism.

Title VIII, Strengthening the Criminal Laws Against Terrorism, illustrates the extent to which a broad range of activities are repressed. Section 801, which equates criminal acts to terrorist acts, "criminalizes actions to wreck, derail or disable mass transportation systems, to place biological agents or other destructive substances or devices on a mass transportation system."[32] The line is blurred between criminal and terrorist acts. Section 801 demonstrates how broad the definition of terrorism has become. In the reference to "New Crimes of Domestic Terrorism and of Harboring Terrorism," thoughts and actions are equated with more traditional expressions of speech and assembly; expressing political perspectives is now equated with terrorism: "Domestic terrorism is an act which is dangerous to human life, and which is a crime under federal or state law and which appears to be intended to intimidate or coerce a civilian population, change federal government policy by intimidation and coercion or effect the conduct of a government by mass destruction, assassination or kidnapping and which takes place primarily within the United States."[33] Most striking is the reference to seeking to "change federal government policy by intimidation." Activities that were, at one time, legitimate political dissent now constitute terrorism. Criminal offenses of all kinds are also identified as terrorist activities.

In Title IX, Improved Intelligence, section 901, the act continues to expand permanently information sharing, especially among the CIA, FBI, and other agencies. There is a blank check to use all kinds of methods, including physical searches. Absent are references to standardized procedures, intended to protect the rights of persons subject to physical searches, which can, and have, led to instances of abuse and torture of terrorist suspects. Section 903 makes everyone an agent of the state seeking to spy on and gather intelligence on anyone. Anyone in a position of authority or with dubious motives as an agent of the state can set in motion a federal investigation, based on the most undocumented and flimsy evidence. Employers, acquaintances, and neighbors become the eyes and ears of the state.

Under Title X, Miscellaneous, one subsection describes a new Justice Department Office to Track Complaints, revealing a truly perverse police state practice, the notion that a government that has created extreme forms of repression also will consider complaints. This afterthought to all the other titles is a strange public relations stunt mixed in with a self-serving rationalization for the previous titles. In practical terms, according to the provisions, it is unworkable. There is no institutional mechanism to address civil liberties abuses. Given the act's secrecy, it would be extremely difficult to file a civil suit against the federal government. The reference does not spell out how the special bureau will proceed when complaints are received. There is little Congress can do, since the relevant standing committees are not required to hold hearings.

Through the absence of legal restraints and its granting to government and federal agencies the ability to target anyone, the act grants a license to engage in police state practices. The idea is that government's purpose in civil society is to control thought and action and that U.S. and non-U.S. citizens are subject to surveillance, considered enemies of the state. Under the act, intelligence gatherers and federal law enforcement officials do not have the burden of proof; government grants itself the right to monitor telephones, Internet service providers, and network administrators without a court order. All the government needs to act is a belief that intelligence gathering is relevant; the Fourth Amendment requirement for probable cause is gone. The courts are sidelined, unable to determine whether or not the intelligence gathering is legal. Under the Patriot Act, the government can even acquire blank warrants without having to identify who and for what purpose it is being issued. The act eliminates the higher standard of probable cause: only a reasonable cause is needed for a search warrant. It also provides greater latitude to conduct secret searches and seizures, another violation of due process procedural safeguards. The sneak-and-peek provision clearly violates the legal requirement to knock and announce to carry out a search warrant.

The Patriot Act demonstrates how a police state can result from a government's hasty response to an emergency. It gives the federal government the power to imprison indefinitely those targeted due to their status as immigrants and noncitizens without probable cause. U.S. citizens also become enemies of the state if they practice what had been a right to political association. Political activity is now identified as a political crime. The Patriot Act allows the government unlimited access to books; records; and documents from any source, public and private, without needing to show evidence of criminal activity, whether in residences or offices. Other provisions give the federal government the right to require public libraries to reveal who is using computers and what books are checked out, while video stores tell the government which titles were purchased and rented. To supplement this surveillance of peoples' thoughts, the Patriot Act makes use of National Security letters, which force "electronic communication service providers" to turn over any information on anyone, including the specific content of their communications. As with other provisions of the act, there is no burden to prove to a court the need for the letters. Individuals who receive a letter are muzzled; they cannot speak to anyone about it, not even an attorney.

The idea at the core of the Patriot Act—that everyone and anyone is a suspect—found practical application in the extension of the Immigration and Nationality Act. After 9/11, arrests and deportations of Muslims from Arab countries increased dramatically. Thousands were detained with no charge, kept in secret places; their names weren't released, and they were prohibited from communicating with their families or seeking legal assistance.[34] The Patriot Act nurtured a political culture that unleashed prejudices and abuses against Muslims and Arabs in the United States. In 2003, such detentions were described as "indiscriminate and haphazard" by the Justice Department's own inspector general, and there were significant instances of physical or verbal abuse against Muslims and Arabs arrested by Justice Department officials for minor offenses, subjected to beatings and unwarranted invasive physical searches.[35] Such behavior typically leads to scapegoating, and after 9/11, any male older than 16 from any of 18, mostly Arab countries, was required to report yearly to the INS and to provide any change in address or employment. They also had to tell the government names of any U.S. citizens they knew; those names became part of a database.

Far beyond its stated intent to pursue terrorists, the administration's broader goal is to extend state repression over a cross section of Americans, to target individuals and organizations without connections to terrorism. "Within six months of passing the Patriot Act…the Justice Department was conducting seminars on how to stretch the new wiretapping provisions to extend beyond terror cases."[36] Ashcroft spoke often of using the act's extensive investigative tools to go beyond the pursuit of terrorist threats to include conducting criminal investigations. Its provisions authorize the FBI to engage in searches to determine what people are reading in libraries and bookstores and to subject them to surveillance, whether or not material is related to terrorist conspiracies. Librarians were put in the position of being agents of the state. In one study, during just a few months in 2002, more than 400 library directors said they had been requested to provide data about their patrons; about half did, and half refused. According to section 215, the government has the authority to conduct searches of reading material to engage in fishing expeditions. While official denials from Ashcroft and the Justice Department were emphatic that the concerns of librarians were without merit, extensive secrecy surrounds the use of section 215; a freedom of information suit filed in 2003 to obtain names and statistics about it was unsuccessful: "because of the mandated gag order against all parties in a section 215 warrant, it is impossible to know the extent of the Department's surveillance on private citizens."[37]

The Patriot Act also undermines the formal right to associate and engage in political dissent, allowing the Bush administration to present a false picture of popular support for its policies. One example: a practice begun early on, was the use of free speech zones. A university student was arrested by the Kalamazoo, Michigan, police because he wouldn't go to the "free speech zone" a couple of hundred yards away from President Bush's supporters. His sign said, "Welcome…Governor Bush," merely signifying that he didn't accept the results of the 2000 presidential election. The monopoly of speech by those in power is a police state feature. Individuals who wanted to attend appearances of the president or vice president were prescreened, required to provide names, addresses, birthdates and social security numbers: information that often was compiled in a database. If individuals weren't known to Republicans, they were also required to sign loyalty oaths; if they refused, they couldn't attend the rallies. Antiwar activists and administration opponents were subjected to scrutiny at airport check-ins with some being informed that they were on the federal "no fly" list as potential terrorists.

The government associates political dissent with terrorism. For individuals and organizations in a post-9/11 America, opposition to Bush administration policies was all that federal agencies needed to conduct surveillance. Peace groups found that documents known as Spy Files turned out to have been shared with other municipalities and "the FBI Joint Terrorism Task Force . . . created after 9/11 . . . had been conducting surveillance against peaceful protestors throughout the country."[38] In post-9/11 America, the police state measures of the Bush administration have the unique distinction of coordinated support from all parts of the federal government. Both Congress and the president's antiterrorism measures are part of a larger fight to destroy what remains of democracy, eliminating the relevance of the Constitution and civil liberties. As in the 1960s, the 9/11 political climate of terrorism reactivated local law enforcement efforts in the surveillance of political dissent, with police identifying and documenting individuals who attended peaceful protests that should have been fully protected by the Constitution. The Denver police labeled as "criminal extremist" the Quaker group—the American Friends Service Committee, Amnesty International, and a local group that monitored law enforcement. Civil disobedience was now a criminal activity. For example, three nuns, active in the antiwar movement, entered an Air Force base near Greeley, Colorado, painted crosses in their own blood on a Minuteman III missile silo and held a prayer vigil. "They were arrested, handcuffed, left on the ground for three hours and then jailed for seven months before trial. The nuns claimed they were using symbolic free speech to protest America's potential use of weapons of mass destruction and the impending war against Iraq . . . [they were] charged with sabotage and with obstruction to national defense under the Patriot Act provisions . . . The government said it wanted each of the protesters sentenced to at least six years imprisonment, the minimum under the Patriot Act."[39]

In city after city, there was a return to past practices of local law enforcement, clamping down on those who protested administration policies. A 2003 peaceful antiwar demonstration outside the New York headquarters of the Carlyle Group investment firm, connected to the Bush and Bin Laden families, resulted in the arrest and detainment of

70 participants. In 2004, a subpoena delivered by a local sheriff's deputy to Drake University in Des Moines demanded the names of people who had attended a student antiwar forum on its campus. With the Patriot Act, the federal government has the right to acquire and submit to a court the names of those under investigation, as well as whether or not they are suspected of involvement in terrorist activities. The university, in accordance with the Patriot Act, is under a gag rule not to disclose that subpoenas had been issued. So it functions as a useful tool to silence those who seek to exercise rights under the First Amendment and who oppose the administration. The act's definition of domestic terrorism refers to acts intended to influence government policy by intimidation, including various forms of peaceful dissent. Individuals and organizations opposing the administration's policies through civil disobedience will be identified as domestic terrorists.

Using the broad definition of domestic terrorism, the federal government prosecuted Greenpeace for peacefully protesting the illegal export of mahogany from Brazil. Greenpeace didn't interfere with the movements of the company it was protesting. Nonetheless, if it had been found guilty, it could have been declared a terrorist organization by the Justice Department. The judge dismissed the case, but the Bush administration was sending a message to chill civil disobedience. The Patriot Act arbitrarily labels organizations as terrorist and makes everyone a potential enemy of the state. Such was the case with TIPS, the Terrorist Information and Prevention System, under which Americans are supposed to watch each other and report "any suspicious behavior." Similarly, the Total Information Awareness Program (TIAP), a super database, would gather and store numerous tidbits of information. Although the program was eventually curtailed, government efforts to monitor everyone continued.

The Transportation Security Administration's plans for CAPPS (Computer-Assisted Passenger Profiling System) put airlines in the position of assessing risk on all Americans who fly, requesting that airlines inquire about how passengers purchased tickets, with whom they traveled, and itineraries. MATRIX, the Multistate Anti-Terrorism Information Exchange, replaced the Total Awareness program, providing local, state, and federal government with a method of merging into one database all government and private records from drivers' and pilots' licenses, boat and plane registrations, and property ownership documents, to bankruptcy filings, listings on terrorist watch lists, professional licenses, and criminal history. MATRIX gathers these data, generating a profile to develop stereotypes of terrorist suspects, failing to consider valid reasons for a particular profile. The government pursued additional means to gather data and conduct surveillance. In December 2003, the FBI in Las Vegas requested electronic copies of all customer lists of casinos, hotels, travel and car rental agencies, and airlines using McCarren Airport. The experiment was believed to be designed to see how well federal agencies could develop a database based on these data. The police state was evolving to invent superior means of social control.

Congress had not completely ceded authority to the White House. Some of the Patriot Act provisions were to sunset in 2005, such as extending time for secret warrants issued by the FISA court, expanding the purpose of FISA warrants, and sharing information between law enforcement and the CIA. But its most troubling parts were permanent. The Bush administration and some members of Congress introduced the Interdiction of Criminal Terrorist Organizations Act or Victory Act, in Patriot II. By equating criminal and terrorist activities, it expanded the powers of law enforcement as well as the definition of criminal acts. Since lack of knowledge is no excuse, the Victory Act assumes guilt before innocence. Another section further erodes due process protections, giving the attorney general the power to subpoena outside the court system. Other sections allow federal law enforcement to subpoena electronic communications and personal records without having to show cause in court. Under consideration was a bill that would expand the use of national security letters, eliminating any possibility of a legal challenge. Congress passed the Victory Act, and President Bush signed it into law, allowing the FBI more freedom to conduct surveillance and secretly gather personal information, especially credit card records and others from financial institutions, now defined as banks, jewelers, pawn brokers, casinos, and car dealerships.

The Department of Homeland Security, created as a result of the Homeland Security Act, operates without legal limitations or judicial oversight. Its director has the freedom to share information without determining its validity. The department has the right to access and data mine contents from Internet service providers and to engage in secret surveillance. This information is shared with federal, state, and local agencies, but the public is denied access. The permanent state of emergency is the sole means of legitimizing such control, whereas in a viable democracy, the people and institutions would question and prevent such abuse of power. For example, if the secretary determines that a public health emergency exists, he has the power to require that a particular group or the entire nation must be vaccinated. But no clear standards define what constitutes such an emergency. The department also protects the powerful, while taking whatever measures it deems necessary for the masses; if a vaccine is used in an emergency, its manufacturer is exempt from legal liability, while meetings about such policies are strictly secret.

The Patriot Act and the Department of Homeland Security created a police state climate that we either ignore or accept as the price paid to live in post-9/11 America. In public and private places, Americans now see armed, uniformed security forces; private security guards; off-duty police officers; state and local police forces; specialized police forces; National Guard troops; armed forces reservists; and active duty military personnel. At airports, everyone is treated as a potential terrorist suspect. Americans have been socialized to accept surveillance, screening, and the checking of their personal belongings.

In such a climate, there is greater acceptance of the authority of law enforcement and security personnel. Accountability in the courts is lacking. Police misconduct convictions are rare. It is extremely difficult to bring civil actions for such misconduct, and the Patriot Act diminishes the court's role. The secrecy surrounding surveillance has not been counterbalanced by courts using Judicial Review. The near suspension of many civil liberties—the virtual elimination of probable cause, assumption of guilt, withholding from the accused the nature of charges and preventive detention—are all police state attributes. Routine government operations have been classified as secret, and not long after 9/11, President Bush issued an executive order, effectively denying access to presidential records. The Freedom of Information Act was diluted. Under the Patriot Act, the government has the authority to engage in secret searches of persons and organizations expressing their right to political dissent. Funding security becomes a primary concern. Congress partnered with the White House in a $40 billion appropriation, funding federal, state, and local preparedness initiatives to fight, investigate, or prosecute terrorism and to boost security and repair facilities and systems damaged by the attacks. Three out of five items funded supported surveillance and security. The administration could tap an additional $10.6 billion from the FY 2002 Emergency Budget Supplement for homeland security.

As the administration pledged to fight terrorism, it would begin making its case against Iraq, using a standard ploy to whip up a nationalist frenzy to support a war. As the drumbeat got louder, the administration and the corporate media promoted blind patriotism and the message that questioning the war was "un-American." Police states engage in wholesale political repression to ultimately employ the coercive might of the state. The war against Iraq is consistent with the police state practice of confronting perceived threats from without and within. The permanent war-making economy manufactures and exaggerates those threats. The police state that America has become uses the military-industrial complex to build and maintain its global empire, and the Office of Homeland Security (OHS) plays an important role, overseeing and investigating possible terrorist threats, insuring the protection of important infrastructure, and evaluating the effectiveness of security measures. The OHS works with state and local governments to evaluate how they detect, prepare for, and prevent terrorist attacks. Its formation represented a major reorganization of American government; it became part of the executive branch and one of the biggest cabinet departments, consisting of agencies from the Immigration and Naturalization Service, the Customs Service, the Coast Guard, the TSA, the Federal Emergency Management Agency, and many others. The purpose of this reorganization was to give prominence to it and its goals of controlling America's borders, coordinating state and local governments, responding to emergencies, developing technologies to detect weapons, and evaluating intelligence gathering. America was becoming a garrison state, preparing to mobilize and react with force to halt any perceived terrorist threat.

The war on terrorism neatly fit the needs of the military-industrial complex. In December 2001, the Senate approved Pentagon spending of more than $300 billion. One month later, President Bush requested another $48 billion for defense spending. Military spending, the terrorist threat, and empire building work well together; Bush's defense spending proposal was the largest jump since Vietnam.[40] Not long after 9/11, the government also put in place measures to persecute individuals, mostly men of Middle Eastern background, between the ages of 18 and 40; federal and local police questioned 5,000 of them about their work, salaries, activities, telephone use, and people they knew.[41] In the aftermath of the attacks, there were more than 100 cases of harassment against Arabs or Arab-Americans at airports; FBI agents and local or state police also turned up at their homes, schools, and workplaces to question them. Political dissenters also were targeted. Faculty attending teach-ins and seminars at colleges and universities were criticized or denounced by administrators. Attorney General Ashcroft loosened restrictions on the FBI, giving it a freer hand to spy on individuals and organizations, recalling the extent of surveillance under Cointelpro. After 9/11, federal agencies conducted private surveillance of computers and Internet use.

Video cameras and security monitors became ubiquitous in public areas, including airports, highways, shopping centers, and at automatic teller machines.

The government also changed its use of political trials, which historically made examples of political or social dissenters. After 9/11, trials were used for propaganda purposes to prove the administration's victories in the war on terrorism. The following cases show how the administration attempted to create special criteria outside the normal due process standards, to judge defendants' actions. Yaser Esam Hamdi was an American citizen, born in Baton Rouge, in September 1980. In 2001, he underwent weapons training in Afghanistan. He eventually turned himself in to the Northern Alliance and was transferred to American military authorities and Guantanamo Bay in January 2002. Hamdi came under the administration's view that all Guantanamo Naval Base detainees caught in Afghanistan were "unlawful Enemy Combatants."

Like Hamdi, Jose Padilla, also a U.S. citizen, traveled to Egypt in 1998 and to Pakistan and Saudi Arabia in 2001. He met al Qaeda Lieutenant Abu Zubaydah in Afghanistan and discussed possible terrorist attacks against the United States. Padilla learned to use explosives with the intention, with other al Qaeda operatives, to construct and explode a "dirty bomb" in the US. He was arrested upon arrival in Chicago. Padilla also was characterized as an enemy combatant. As both cases traveled from lower Circuit Court to the Supreme Court, they illustrated how the Bush administration put itself in the unique position of interpreting the meaning of due process, subverting due process and creating new standards.

The executive branch consistently argued that it could best decide how to deal with wartime emergency measures. The term enemy combatant was a convenient justification for its exercise of unlimited power in wartime. The administration sought to define the war on terrorism as so unique that the executive branch must not be subject to any legal restraints. One potential obstacle was the courts. Rulings in these cases show how the courts can halt police state practices; they also show their limitations. A key constitutional issue is the centuries-old legal principle, the writ of habeas corpus, the legal proceeding to challenge possible unlawful imprisonment. The Great Writ, as it is often called, begins with a right of those imprisoned to have their day in court to determine whether or not their loss of liberty was justified. In the Hamdi and Padilla cases, the administration's position was that petitions for habeas corpus should be denied due to the enemy combatant label and the submitted statement of Michael Mobbs, special advisor to the undersecretary of defense for policy. Mobbs generated a summary of documented records concerning Hamdi's capture and Padilla's ties to high-ranking al Qaeda members. In the 4th Circuit Court, Judge Doumar agreed with arguments by Hamdi's attorney that the vagueness of Mobb's declaration and its disregard for Hamdi's due process rights were insufficient to imprison him; the government had not proven its claim that he was an enemy combatant. In Doumar's words, to accept the government's claim on face value would amount to a "rubber stamp," a violation of habeas corpus. He strictly adhered to the premise that the government would have to bear the burden of proof that Hamdi was an enemy combatant, by providing evidence, including all of his statements and notes from interviews, and identifying those who interrogated him and the American officials who decided he was an illegal enemy combatant and their criteria. Doumar also decided that the Mobbs statement was inadequate to determine the legality of Hamdi's imprisonment.

But the Bush administration wouldn't comply with Circuit Court Judge Mukasey's request, whose decision illustrates the difficulty courts had in ruling against police powers. Mukasey's ruling deferred to some degree to the administration's contention that Hamdi could be held as an enemy combatant, removing from the government the legal burden of proof; it also assumes this arbitrary definition is legally valid. Mukasey abided by the Constitution in ruling that the government must provide Hamdi legal counsel. But the court ruled that Hamdi's petition for a writ of habeas corpus should be denied, accepting on face value the Mobbs declaration. The court argued since there was basic agreement from Hamdi's petition and Mobb's declaration as to the facts of the case, then Hamdi was an enemy combatant. The ruling accepted that Bush's wartime powers under Article II of the U.S. Constitution allowed him to legally detain persons caught on a battlefield. The administration filed a request to Judge Mukasey to overturn his earlier ruling and deny Hamdi access to counsel. The statement the government provided from Vice Admiral Lowell Jacoby, the Defense Intelligence Agency director, who advises the president on national security issues, justifies denying the right to counsel to prevent jeopardizing intelligence-gathering. But Mukasey denied the request.

There appeared to be progress in Padilla's appeal to the 2nd Circuit Court of Appeals, which overturned Mukasey's ruling, denying that the administration had the constitutional authority to imprison "U.S. citizens on American soil outside a zone of combat." The government would have to release Padilla unless he was charged with a criminal offense, in which case, he would have a right to an attorney. The Bush administration sought legal cover for its novel notion of enemy combatants as revelations of torture began to be made public. Through Supreme Court appeals in the Hamdi and Padilla cases, the administration sought support for its view that the danger of terrorism warrants the suspension of law; but the rulings sent officials scrambling to rethink how to undercut the rule of law without relying on the courts. The Court's 5-4 decision avoided direct confrontation over whether an American citizen could be detained far from a battlefield, but it ruled against the claim that he could be held as an enemy combatant. It concluded that the president had the authority to detain individuals identified as enemy combatants, a partial victory, but it also ruled, to the dismay of many in the White House, that anyone so detained must have an opportunity to challenge this designation before a neutral decision maker. So long as a writ of habeas corpus is in place, even a person defined as an enemy combatant cannot be detained indefinitely. Still, the rulings gave the administration wiggle room, for they did not specify the procedures to guarantee habeas corpus, how long an enemy combatant could be detained, or what kind of court is best suited to hear such cases.

Rasul v. Bush provides additional proof of the administration's attempt to sidestep international laws on torture. Only eight days after arguments were presented, the photographs of abuses carried out by American soldiers on prisoners at Abu Ghraib were published, revealing potential violations of international and domestic laws. The administration argued that such statutes only apply to torture taking place outside the United States, so allegations of torture at the Guantanamo Base were not covered, since it was within the territorial jurisdiction of the United States. A majority of justices supported the petitioners' arguments that federal courts have the legal jurisdiction to hear writs of habeas corpus from Guantanamo detainees. They referred to the right of habeas corpus and the fact that the detainees were in U.S. territory, not near hostilities and, most important, that the detainees should not be placed in indefinite detention due to the distinct geographic location of their confinement. The Court sided with international law in stating that federal courts have the legal jurisdiction to hear a habeas corpus writ from anyone detained by the United States anywhere in the world.

In light of the ruling, attorneys representing detainees sought access to their clients and pressed for judicial review of their status as enemy combatants, while the administration again attempted to nullify the ruling. Attorneys were allowed to meet with detainees, but access was limited to litigants, indicating that the administration hoped to limit the ruling's scope; it also worked with the Defense Department to create another means, in military instead of civilian courts, to examine habeas corpus claims. This was a departure from the traditional means to apply this right. Instead of a civilian court and a lawyer, each detainee was provided with a "personal representative," a military officer who would represent each detainee, challenging the detainee's status as an unlawful enemy combatant before a Combatant Status Review Tribunal (CSRT). Standard legal procedures were further diluted with violations of attorney-client privilege. Meetings between attorney and client were subject to audio- and videotaping and a "classification review" of information obtained by the detainees' attorneys. Once a gag order was in place, an attorney could not disclose anything about a detainee without the expressed consent of government officials. Attorneys were required to turn in anything said that presented a national security threat, indicating the built-in prejudice against detainees who hadn't been formally charged with any terrorist acts. Attorneys had to undergo elaborate security clearances. The process put detainees in legal limbo, charged as unlawful enemy combatants and denied legal standing as prisoners of war, which would have provided them with protection under the Geneva Conventions. Contributing to this legal limbo were the Administrative Review Boards, ARBs, which supplemented the CSRTs, conducting a secret review to determine the detainee's intelligence value or threat to the United States. Like the CSRTs, they bore a mere semblance of legality. Since detainees were placed outside of international law, not under the Geneva Conventions, and since all evidence is secret and cannot be challenged, no clear determination of their status as enemy combatants can be made.

The trials of selected "high-profile terrorists" who appear to personify the danger at hand manifest some attributes of political trials, highlighting the noble cause of fighting terrorism while demonizing the defendant and magnifying the threat that he or she represents. Political trials, like the *U.S. v. Moussaoui*, were supposed to provide the administration with the means to legitimize extreme measures. Zacarias Moussaoui was identified by government prosecutors as the "twentieth hijacker." With this "show trial," the government wanted the appearance of a legal proceeding without giving the defendant his legal rights. Prosecutors refused to give Moussaoui's attorney access to al Qaeda members in detention overseas to testify favorably on his behalf. This violated the Federal Rules of Criminal Procedure, which

allow a defendant to question witnesses who may provide information essential to his defense. One witness, Ranzi Binalshibh, who was
charged with Moussaoui as another 9/11 conspirator, was being held
with other possible witnesses in a secret location. The government's
refusal to comply with the judge's order to videotape depositions from
the detainees undercut its case by prohibiting the government from
connecting Moussaoui to 9/11. On appeal to the 4th Circuit Court,
Judge Brinkman's ruling was upheld: by denying access to witnesses,
the government was violating Moussaoui's Sixth Amendment rights.
Nonetheless, the 4th Circuit Court of Appeal reversed Brinkman's
ruling on the elimination of the death penalty because Moussaoui's
attorneys could make use of written "substitutions" for videotaped
depositions gathered from various classified "intelligence reports" of
the detainees' interrogations. The strange turn of events, the denial
of Moussaoui's Sixth Amendment rights and his sudden entering of
a guilty plea to all the charges, in particular, those which made him
eligible for the death penalty, indicates the political nature of this trial.
Moussaoui may have changed his plea to guilty because he may have
wanted the Supreme Court to review his case. Also, questions can be
raised as to whether or not he wanted to be a martyr for the cause of
Islam or whether he was mentally unstable. Whatever his motives, the
case is one example of many where the government took away a due
process right, then claimed success against terrorists.

In other political trials, such as the "American Taliban" case, hysteria served as the motive to suspend procedural due process. After 9/11,
Osama Bin Laden sought refuge in Taliban-controlled Afghanistan.
President Bush demanded that the Taliban surrender bin Laden to the
United States. With the United States at war, it was only a matter of time
before a scapegoat would be found to demonstrate the U.S. fight against
the Taliban. With great fanfare, Attorney General Ashcroft announced
that a grand jury in Alexandria, Virginia, where many such cases began,
had indicted John Walker Lindh, a 21-year-old, who Ashcroft said
had "dedicated himself to the killing of Americans." Ashcroft charged
Lindh with "taking up arms" and tied him to the 9/11 attacks. The
government's case appeared clear cut; it held that after hearing of the
9/11 attacks, Lindh remained with his al Qaeda fighting unit. After
discovering that the United States was directly supporting the Northern
Alliance against al Qaeda and the Taliban, Lindh's unit surrendered to
the Northern Alliance in November in Afghanistan and was taken to
the Qala-I Janghi prison compound, where Lindh was later interviewed
by the CIA and another U.S. government employee. Shortly thereafter,

Taliban detainees in the compound attacked the interviewers, over-whelmed the guards, and took weapons. One interviewer was killed; Lindh was injured and retreated with other detainees. The intention was to make Lindh an example and to use illegal means to prove that the United States was winning this war on terrorism. In the government's distorted presentation of the facts, there were grains of truth. Lindh had gone to Afghanistan to study Islam. He joined the Taliban to fight the Northern Alliance. Lindh was in an al Qaeda training camp in the summer of 2001 but was caught only after the United States was at war against Afghanistan. The prosecution didn't produce evidence of Lindh's involvement in plans to kill Americans or participation in planning the attacks. Nonetheless, he was indicted on charges of conspiracy to kill American citizens, conspiracy to provide material support to terrorist organizations, and supplying services to the Taliban. Lindh's treatment and the denial of procedural due process contributed to the "show trial" atmosphere, demonstrating the lengths to which the government would go to convict him. He was bound and gagged in a Navy vessel in a small cargo container. His attorney's efforts to instruct interrogators not to question Lindh in his absence were fruitless. Lindh realized that the best he could hope for was a plea; if convicted, he faced multiple life sentences and six additional ten-year sentences. In accepting the plea agreement, Lindh accepted a sentence of 20 years. Ashcroft and the administration claimed victory in the prosecutions of Moussaoui and Lindh. They weren't just waging a pro-paganda campaign to sell the war on terrorism; they were using show trials to make a travesty of the law, a far more ominous goal.

Police states use the cover of the courts to undertake an assault on due process. Using them to manufacture an obsessive fear of terrorist conspiracies, the government was sending the message that Americans must remain in a state of emergency, willing to embrace extreme mea-sures. The Lackawanna Six provides an example. In September 2002, six American citizens of Yemeni descent were arrested in Lackawanna, New York, and indicted on the charge of operating an al Qaeda cell. In keeping with a key Patriot Act provision, they were charged with giving material support to terrorists; they admitted to attending an al Qaeda training camp in Afghanistan. In the words of Michael Battle, the federal prosecutor, without the Patriot Act, these men would not be considered terrorists, and he had no evidence that they were planning anything harmful.[42] But, as Ashcroft had said, "we must prevent first and prosecute later." Preventive detention is key to police states. The Patriot Act trumped any legal notion of probable cause.

The Lackawanna case demonstrates how incidents with any loose association to the incident would be transformed into grand conspiracies. The spark began with an anonymous tip to the Buffalo FBI that these individuals had attended an al Qaeda training camp. At first, the men lied upon questioning about their trip to Pakistan, then one broke down and confessed, leading the FBI to arrest the others. The tipster had only told the FBI of the trip to Pakistan; there was no mention of involvement in terrorist activity. Political hysteria accelerated when a Guantanamo Bay enemy combatant, captured while fleeing Afghanistan, referred to a terrorist cell in Buffalo. Now the FBI had information supporting the anonymous tip. The Patriot Act played a central role in bringing these men to trial where they would face charges of providing material support to terrorists and "training with weapons" in a terrorist camp, which carried a sentence of 30 years or identification as an enemy combatant and disappearance in a military prison. Under tremendous pressure, the defendants accepted plea bargains, with sentences between seven and ten years. The hysteria generated by the Patriot Act strongly favored the prosecution through the use of secret sources, effectively undercutting the rule of law.

The trial of the Portland Seven is a striking example of how the testimony of a single prosecution witness can suffice in charging defendants with a conspiracy to kill Americans. In this case, Maher Hawash's testimony was used to pressure the accused to plead guilty. Hawash, a naturalized citizen from Palestine, was charged with conspiracy to provide assistance to al Qaeda and the Taliban. He agreed to plead guilty to a lesser sentence, seeking to enter Afghanistan to provide this assistance. With Hawash's testimony, two brothers, Ahmed and Muhammed Bilal, and four other defendants pleaded guilty to conspiracy and illegal weapons charges. In fact, they had traveled to China and attempted to visit Afghanistan but were denied entry. They had to admit as part of the plea agreement that they were "prepared to take up arms and die as martyrs if necessary, to defend the Taliban government in Afghanistan." Ahmed Bilal received 10 to 14 years; Muhammed received 8 to 14 years. The other coconspirators charged, Patrice Lamumba Ford and Jeffrey Battle, also pleaded guilty and were sentenced to 18 years on the charge of conspiracy to wage war against the United States. Another defendant, October Martinique Lewis, Jeffrey Battle's ex-wife, was charged and convicted with wiring money to the defendants. The trial proves how little it takes for the government to gain convictions based primarily on conspiracy charges and overt criminal acts. While the conspiracy charge is so general as to apply to any group, with the overt act, the government argues, the actions are intended to produce illegal results. Nonetheless, these defendants had never entered Afghanistan nor taken up arms against the United States.

The case of the Alexandria Eleven was based largely on guilt by association. Eleven men were charged with violating the Neutrality Act, which prohibits supporting any organization that is against a U.S. ally. They were accused of membership in Lashkar-e-Taiba, which opposes India's control over the Kashmir region. An essential part of the government's case was the organization's close ties to al Qaeda, making the defendants material supporters of terrorism. According to the prosecution, the defendants made statements that they were preparing to fight for Muslim causes, to support an enemy of the United States. But according to the defense, the closest they came to "arming themselves against the United States" was their participation in the popular game of paintball. For this, two of the three were given prison sentences of eleven and one-half years and four years. One of the alleged "ringleaders," Royer, as well as Ahmed-al-Hamd, agreed to plead guilty to the use of firearms. He admitted to receiving weapons training in a Lashkar-e-Taiba camp. The fact that Royer had weapons in his possession was sufficient to make it a federal crime and a Patriot Act violation. As an alleged mastermind, he received 20 years while Al-Hamdi was sentenced to 15 even though the Lashkar group wasn't banned, and during the period of the alleged crime, India and Pakistan had already ceased hostilities. The government equated this war on terrorism with a war against Islam, as it had previously repressed other outsiders. A defense attorney argued, "After September 11, Attorney General Ashcroft compared his mission in fighting terrorism to Robert Kennedy's mission in fighting the Mafia. The then-Attorney General was going after those who 'spat on the sidewalk.' Ashcroft can take pride in the fact that he has terrorized these Muslims and their families for less than that.'"[43]

Another assault on the rule of law was the prosecution of attorneys who represented clients charged with terrorist acts. In October 2002, Attorney General Ashcroft announced at the site of the World Trade Center attack the indictment of an attorney he called a terrorist. Lynne Stewart, who had represented clients accused of engaging in terrorist acts, was indicted on the charge of aiding and abetting a terrorist organization. Not only was the indictment unprecedented, it was the first time that part of the indictment charged her with interfering with prison officials taping her meetings with her client. In the name of fighting terrorism, Ashcroft had, in October 2001, made it possible for the government to listen in on what had long been protected: the sharing of confidential information between attorney and client. Ashcroft ordered the Bureau of Prisons to record meetings between federal inmates and their attorneys and introduced other measures to short circuit attorney-client privilege, such as Special Administrative Measures (SAMs), which reshaped interactions between those in custody and the outside world, notably by restricting attorneys' access to clients. In the past, attorneys had no restrictions as to the length of time of such visits, and they were free from surveillance by prison officials. SAMs narrowed how attorneys could represent their clients; they became advocates, counselors, and advisors only with regard to the particulars of the case. The government could tape attorney-client meetings; it became the final arbiter of attorney-client interactions.

This dramatic change began with the pioneering taping of Stewart's conversations with her client. Under the Patriot Act, Stewart was subjected to surveillance as a result of her representation of Rahman, who was suspected of a terrorist plot to bomb New York City's infrastructure. It has been a mainstay in U.S. law that the attorney-client privilege of confidentiality is not to be used to protect communication that fosters criminal acts. If such communication occurs, the government has the right to seek a wiretap or search warrant from a federal judge. But with Ashcroft's SAMs, any attorney-client communication can now be assumed to foster a criminal act. The government bears no burden of proof that an illegal intent and action is underway. Stewart's indictment was one step toward a larger goal to extend SAMs to all attorney-client communications. Stewart went to trial, indicted on two counts of aiding and abetting terrorism, under the Patriot Act. This indictment is novel and shocking for it alleges that the fact of her representation made her a member of a terrorist organization. The message to the legal community was: "Don't represent anyone accused of terrorist activities, or you face possible indictment as a terrorist."

The wider application of the Stewart case was to limit how attorneys represent their clients, especially given the roundup and detention of terrorist suspects sent to Guantanamo Bay. Once defined as enemy combatants, they are in legal limbo until tried before a military tribunal. The accused have limited options. If the defendant can pay for a civilian lawyer, the lawyer has to be approved by the Pentagon under strict rules, which violate attorney-client confidentiality. Attorneys who represent clients at Guantanamo must "obtain and pay for their own security clearances and they cannot represent anyone without having clearance, they must agree to never talk about anything they see, hear or do while at the base unless it is precleared by the Pentagon, all of their contacts with their clients will be monitored and audio- or videotaped; they will only be allowed to see the evidence the Pentagon allows them to see, and some of their proceedings against their clients may take place out of their presence, if the Pentagon deems it to be in the best interest of national security."[44]

Such initiatives happen in the context of an extensive concentration of power within the executive branch, enabled by Congress, which complied with administration demands in November 2001 for broad wartime powers to fight terrorism. With this authority, Bush proceeded to enact through executive order the "Detention, Treatment and Trial of Certain Non-Citizens in the War Against Terrorism," the references of which are so abstract and arbitrary that any noncitizen can be identified by the president as a member of al Qaeda or supporter of terrorist acts against the United States. As captured suspects began arriving at Guantanamo Bay in 2002, it began functioning as a police state facility where all legal precedent regarding prisoner treatment was dismissed, replaced with procedures designed to humiliate and dehumanize them. Among those captured and imprisoned "the great majority were captured either by the Northern Alliance, tribal warlords, or Pakistani intelligence officers during raids on villages, mosques and houses where supposed combatants were indistinguishable from innocent civilians.[45] Ironically, the United States undercut any possibility of capturing actual terrorists by relying heavily on widely publicized bounties, paying up to $5,000 and $20,000 for members of the Taliban and al Qaeda, respectively.[46] It was a strong incentive to turn in almost anyone.

CHAPTER 6

Actions Taken against Enemies of the State

The administration's intention to transport al Qaeda and Taliban prisoners to Guantanamo Bay was announced on December 27, 2001, by Defense Secretary Donald Rumsfeld. The next day, the memo by John Yoo of the Office of Legal Counsel enabled the administration to create a legal fiction, to place prisoners outside the U.S. court system. The memo prevented prisoners from using habeas corpus and argued that in leasing Guantanamo Bay from Cuba, the United States had jurisdiction and control over the base. Another memo by Yoo and special counsel Robert Delahanty excluded prisoners alleged to be members of al Qaeda and the Taliban from protections of Article 5, which says that captured members of either group have the right to be identified and treated as POWs. It argued that members of these groups cannot be considered POWs because they are terrorists, exhibiting the mindset that only the administration can determine which individuals are members of terrorist organizations. It wasn't written to enable the capture of actual terrorists; it was designed to apply to anyone in custody, regardless of the evidence.

Prisoners in Guantanamo's Camp Delta were confined to wire mesh cell blocks, except for a short exercise period and shower. They were shackled when they left their cells and subjected to bright lights all day; guards kept a 24-hour watch, and prisoners had to be observed every 30 seconds. In March 2003, Camp Four was established to process prisoners most willing to participate in thought reform; better conditions included dormitories, and prisoners ate and exercised together. Intelligence gatherers quickly concluded that there were no major players among the hundreds of prisoners. An intelligence analyst that the CIA sent there met with interrogators and determined "that many of the prisoners had no meaningful ties to terrorism."¹ Still, there was a determination to gather intelligence of any kind.

On October 17, 2001, General Tommy Franks, in command of military forces in Afghanistan, had ordered the troops to follow the Geneva Conventions, especially Article 5; military lawyers worked to apply it to Guantanamo, when the initial prisoners captured in Afghanistan were sent there. All indications were that the military would hold Article 5 hearings. Instead, on January 19, 2002, Rumsfeld countermanded Frank's order, insisting that prisoners he considered members of al Qaeda and the Taliban not be offered Geneva Convention protections. On February 7, Assistant Attorney General Bybee finished a legal memo, providing the president with authority to suspend the application of Article 5 because the prisoners had been identified as war criminals. That day, Bush spoke of a "new paradigm" in the war on terrorism. So Geneva Convention protections determining one's status as a POW and Article 3 did not apply. Prisoners were referred to as "enemy combatants," a concept foreign to the Geneva Conventions.

The elimination of legal precedent motivated the administration. In seeking guidance from the Office of Legal Counsel, Alberto Gonzales's asked if interrogation methods were limited by the 1994 federal antitorture statute. There was an interest in just how far interrogations could go before they were outside the law. At Guantanamo and elsewhere, the CIA had custody of individuals they considered high-ranking al Qaeda members; operatives wanted to know if they could employ certain interrogation techniques without risking prosecution. One step made their actions criminal: a simple redefinition of proper interrogation techniques. As a result, the extraction of intelligence surpassed what could be undertaken according to the Geneva Conventions and went toward prohibited practices that constituted torture. Gonzales's question was answered on August 1, 2002, with the Yoo and Bybee memo, which legalized torture, redefining it by making practitioners guilty only if they acted with intentional malice. The criminal aspect of their definition appears in the section that exempts any violation of the law and provides immunity from prosecution if the actions were taken as a result of presidential directives. In Yoo's words, "Congress cannot tie the president's hands in regard to torture as an interrogation technique...it's the use of the commander in chief function. They cannot prevent the president from ordering torture."² Such authority, they argue, makes the president both a lawmaker and interpreter of law. They chose to ignore Article 1 of the Constitution, granting Congress the authority to pass the antitorture statute; for Yoo and Bybee, wartime imbues the executive branch with dictatorial powers, placing the presidency beyond the reach of law. They also misunderstood the Supreme Court's Youngstown ruling that limited wartime presidential power. In other memos, Yoo argues, the president as commander in chief has the authority to act without the limitations established by the Congressional Authorization for the Use of Military Force, passed on September 14, 2001. This blatant disregard for law leads directly to criminal practices at Guantanamo.

That disregard began incrementally. Brigadier General Rick Baccus, in charge of military police at Guantanamo, took seriously Secretary Rumsfeld's initial directive to ensure prisoners were treated according to the Geneva Convention principles. Baccus established a working relationship with the International Committee of the Red Cross, which was given complete access to Guantanamo. He insisted on reminding military personnel and prisoners of the relevance of the Geneva Conventions, clarifying that he wanted prisoners to be treated humanely, allowing them more showers and exercise periods and soliciting reports of any mistreatment; he refused to allow aggressive interrogation techniques. But radical shifts in policy soon occurred: Major General Geoffrey Miller replaced Baccus, and Rumsfeld redirected interrogation procedures. Miller sought to win the war on terror by producing "actionable intelligence." Lieutenant Colonel Gerald Phifer of the interrogation team sought guidance from the Pentagon, requesting sign-off on aggressive interrogation techniques. In response to resistance from detainees, increasingly harsh methods were prescribed, from category 1 to 2, which introduced more extreme interrogation methods, including solitary confinement for 30 days or more, the hooding of prisoners for up to 20 hours, sensory deprivation, removal of comfort and religious items, forced nudity and grooming, prolonged stress positions, and taking advantage of prisoners' phobias. Under category 3, interrogators could lead detainees to believe their loved ones were in imminent danger; detainees could also be subjected to experiments related to cold weather or cold water exposure and interrogators could "use a wet towel and dripping water to induce the misperception of suffocation."[3] Phifer's memo included a statement from Lieutenant Colonel Diane Beaver, a military attorney, who referenced the Army Field Manual, concerning how interrogation practices should conform to the Geneva Conventions. Her conclusion reflected the administration's perspective that the Geneva Conventions do not apply to the Guantanamo interrogations. Beaver determined that all methods are permissible if there is no intent to cause bodily harm. Torture became official state policy.

Approval for interrogation techniques amounting to torture was the same within each federal agency involved in legal matters. When Phifer's memo reached William J. Haynes, general counsel for the Department of Defense, he sent a memo to Secretary Rumsfeld, urging him to accept for use categories 1 and 2 and the use of mild non-injurious contact of category 3. Further refinements continued in response to concerns raised by Alberto Mora, the Navy's general counsel, and Dr. Michael Gelles, chief psychologist for the Navy Criminal Investigative Service. They knew that these techniques were unlawful, but they were silenced when Rumsfeld put a temporary halt on category 2 techniques and the technique authorized from category 3.

A working group examining legal policy and operational issues related to the interrogation of detainees was established in effect, to legitimize torture, supporting its conclusions with references to the Yoo-Bybee torture memo. It approved additional techniques, including more extensive isolation, sleep deprivation, unlimited interrogations, hooding, environmental manipulation, removing clothing, and threats to transfer to countries that practiced torture. Rumsfeld approved 24 such techniques at Guantanamo Bay, and in 2003, he issued a blank check to use any method so long as it had received prior approval from the Secretary of Defense. With a wink and a nod, interrogators had approval on existing techniques and a license to invent. In another demonstration of police state policy, the government, not the courts, makes the final determination on prisoner treatment; the military had the right to subject prisoners to almost any kind of treatment. Such techniques didn't appear out of nowhere. When Guantanamo officials requested approval for more extreme methods, they bore a striking resemblance to SERE techniques, including shackling in stress positions, forced standing, psychological stress, and scenarios designed to convince the detainee that he or his family would soon experience death or pain. The Senate Armed Services Committee on June 17, 2008, released documents regarding the use of SERE techniques.

The rationalization to use SERE at Guantanamo was a 26-year-old detainee considered of some importance, Mohammed Mani Ahmad Sha'Lan Al-Qahtani or Detainee 063. He was suspected of having connections to the United Flight 93 hijackers; there was concern over what intelligence he might provide, and that his relative could be part of another terrorist attack. During questioning, he refused to provide information. The next step was to enlist SERE personnel. Administration officials took a keen interest in this interrogation; Rumsfeld himself was reportedly involved. Other officials, including David Addington; Alberto Gonzales; William Haynes; Patrick Philbein, an associate of John Yoo; and Jack Goldsmith of the General Counselor's Office, toured Guantanamo and all seemed interested in Qahtani, indicating a conspiracy to coordinate efforts, putting aside national and international laws to engage in torture. With full knowledge of the techniques used, Haynes, who had discussed Qahtani with Diane Beaver, advised Rumsfeld the interrogation methods were legal. FBI agents witnessed the treatment Qahtani underwent and reported that he behaved as though he'd been the victim of "extreme psychological trauma."[4] Such treatment wasn't an isolated incident. Another FBI agent recalled seeing detainees chained to the floor without food or water for nearly a whole day or more, having soiled themselves, or in rooms where temperatures could exceed 100 degrees; some had pulled out their hair.[5] Qahtani was chained to the floor and deprived of sufficient sleep. He "was also forced to strip naked, wear a leash, and perform dog tricks. He was forced to wear a bra and thong underwear on his head. He was deprived of the opportunity to use a toilet after having been force-fed liquids intravenously."[6] He was tortured so relentlessly that even interrogators didn't know what to believe; he recanted his statement about working for al Qaeda one day after confessing. Perpetrators began acting sadistically, with an intense desire to obtain total control over him. Practitioners of torture experience a sense of omnipotence, the result of the lack of legal restraint, which led to their inability to recognize that nothing was gained from such tortures: "the Pentagon proclaimed that it was all worthwhile, a Defense department spokesman told Time Magazine that he had become a valuable source of information."[7] But high-ranking officials eventually admitted that the treatment amounted to torture, and Qahtani's statements were inadmissible in a court of law. Susan Crawford, a senior Pentagon official in charge of determining who is to be tried, concluded that Qahtani's treatment amounted to torture. This was revealed in the *Washington Post*, on January 14, 2009, her first interview after being named convening authority on Military Commissions. Vice President Cheney in a December 17, 2008, interview on ABC Television admitted to authorizing torture. In spring 2008, President Bush told ABC News that he had given his approval to top aides to engage in harsh interrogation techniques.

Despite its long history directly assisting the executive branch, the FBI's standards contradicted the president's executive order, which authorized the use of military dogs, stress positions, sleep management, loud music, and hooding. An FBI e-mail in 2004 stated that agents witnessed the U.S. military engaging in harsh interrogation of inmates, violating FBI standards of conduct; it included a clear statement as to how to proceed after revelations surfaced in Abu Ghraib. The president insisted, nonetheless, that harsh interrogation techniques would continue; on March 8, 2008, he vetoed congressional legislation that would have banned water boarding, stripping prisoners naked, subjecting them to extreme cold, and mock executions. He remarked, "this is no time for Congress to abandon practices that have a proven track record of keeping America safe," noting that if the administration were to "restrict the CIA to methods in the Army Field Manual, we could lose vital information from senior Al Qaeda terrorists and that could cost American lives."[8]

Torture was the product of a government that ruled above the law, assuming the right to dehumanize and degrade others without justifications. Guantanamo detainees were redefined as enemy combatants to be tried in Military Commissions, temporary tribunals that replaced civilian courts during a state of national emergency and imposed martial law. Two months after 9/11, Bush authorized Military Commissions to try noncitizens for violating the laws of war and others; they were to operate outside procedural due process. Salim Ahmad Hamdan was among the first charged. Allegedly Bin Laden's driver and bodyguard, he was captured in Afghanistan, turned over to the U.S. military, and transferred to Guantanamo. Hamdan appeared to fit the criteria for trial by Military Commission. He was formally charged with conspiracy to attack and murder civilians, destroy civilian property, and participate in terrorist acts. Using a petition for a writ of habeas corpus, Hamdan challenged his trial by Military Commission as a violation of the Uniform Code of Military Justice and the Geneva Conventions. The Bush administration sought to prevail in the courts while also attempting to circumvent Supreme Court rulings, especially any aspect that questioned detainee treatment. Hamdan's military defense lawyer, Navy Lieutenant Commander Charles Swift, challenged the legality of Military Commissions. Federal District Judge James Robertson agreed, concluding that since the third Geneva Convention is included in the Laws of War, Hamden's lack of status as a prisoner of war negates fairness in a Military Commission trial. Robertson ruled that Hamdan's Military Commission was illegal, because it violated the Uniform Code of Military Conduct, stipulating a defendant must be present at his trial and have access to all evidence against him. The administration successfully appealed to the Circuit Court of Appeals, which ruled that by granting the president the use of force, Congress also gave him the authority to create Military Commissions. The court asserted that the Geneva Conventions were not enforceable, and that even if they were, Hamdan had no rights since he lacked prisoner of war status, and the Geneva Conventions don't apply to nongovernmental organizations such as al Qaeda. In the Supreme Court appeal, the litigants asked who has the authority to establish Military Commissions, Congress or the president? Was Hamdan someone who should be tried by a Military Commission? To what extent did Common Article 3 of the Geneva Conventions apply to Hamdan? There was also the question of the defendant's right to be present and confront evidence against him. In a 5-3 decision, with many nuances, the Supreme Court sided with the defendant on the important legal issues. The ruling would strike down both the possibility that Hamdan would be tried before a Military Commission and the legal justification for the commissions; the Court held that they had not been authorized by Congress, and they denied the right to a fair trial, especially in allowing for the admission of evidence acquired by torture and refusing to allow the defendant to be present at trial or view the evidence against him. Most important, the court struck down the Detainee Treatment Act as not applicable to this kind of pending case. It clearly supported the application of the Common Articles of the Geneva Convention as relevant in the U.S. war on terror. According to the Supreme Court, Article 3 is meant to provide protection for all prisoners caught during wartime.

But at every turn, the administration maneuvered to function above the law. This was the situation with the 2006 Military Commissions Act, one of the most blatant assertions of unilateral power of the executive branch. While the Supreme Court's ruling in Hamdan called attention to constitutional principles, the executive branch was well aware that the Court interprets the Constitution but cannot compel compliance to its rulings. Thus, it engaged in an end-run around the Hamdan decision. The Military Commissions Act of 2006 was an essential part of the Bush administration police state; it was used to evade the Hamdan ruling, making a mockery of law. The essential parts of the Act put before Congress included indefinite detention without trial and without the ability to seek habeas corpus review, the use of hearsay evidence, no right to a speedy trial, unlimited punishment of detainees, the use of any evidence regardless of how it was gathered, and the inability for detainees to rely on the Geneva Conventions for individual rights.[9] The early version of this legislation was sponsored by Steven Bradbury, then head of the Justice Department's Office of

Legal Counsel, who echoed the administration's view that the Hamdan ruling didn't address the right questions on the Geneva Convention. The administration reinforced this view throughout negotiations and the arm twisting of members of Congress to pass the act, which had many troubling provisions, including broadening the enemy combatant definition:

A legal resident in America could be so labelled for making out a check to a supposed Islamic charity. Once identified as an enemy combatant, a person was subject to summary arrest and indefinite detention without the habeas appeal route. Habeas corpus was barred for all detainees in U.S. military prisons. The UCMJ's provisions for a speedy trial and for protection against coerced self-incrimination are specifically declared inapplicable. No provision exists for judicial review of any aspect of the new Military Commissions. No appeals are allowed in the MCA that invoke the Geneva Conventions or other humanitarian laws as sources of rights and protections. Coerced evidence would be permissible if the military judge thought it was reliable. The President has the power to interpret the meaning and the application of the Geneva Conventions. Offenses enumerated in the final version of the MCA were narrowly drawn, for example, the notion that the rape of a detainee is a form of torture is rejected.[10]

While the MCA establishes procedures for persons accused of violating the rules of war, the overwhelming majority of detainees and others caught fall outside of these guidelines; they aren't charged with violating any laws so their status remains unchanged. This is disturbing for it places detainees outside of legal procedures. Above all, the MCA eliminates the one recourse that detainees had—habeas corpus—their only opportunity to have their case heard in court. They are denied access to federal courts with jurisdiction over habeas corpus petitions. The CSRT replaces habeas corpus, but it was clearly outside the norms of civilian courts. Cases were built on hearsay evidence that prisoners couldn't see; any documents they saw were considered practically useless. The MCA's clearest police state feature gives the president the authority to make anyone, even U.S. citizens, living inside or outside the country, enemy combatants and imprison them indefinitely. A person defined as an alien unlawful combatant, who faces a trial by military commission, is denied the legal protections afforded in the Geneva Conventions and so cannot speak of being tortured or having been subjected to excessive treatments. The MCA also violated the constitution by prohibiting non-U.S. citizens from being able to challenge legal grounds for being detained. It also "violates the Geneva

Convention...by watering down protections of Common Article 3 and by effectively granting retroactive amnesty to U.S. officials who have tortured detainees. It violates the Fifth Amendment by allowing evidence obtained by coercion and the Fourth Amendment by admitting evidence seized without a warrant. And it violates the Sixth Amendment, by allowing hearsay and classified evidence which the accused can only see in summary form."[11]

The administration also became obsessed with discovering the thoughts of citizens and noncitizens, to identify additional unlawful combatants using the NSA's secret surveillance of mass communication. Truman had used it to spy on the Russians, but now, the NSA was intercepting and gathering data in the hope of locating a tidbit of a conversation or message among the phone calls, faxes, or e-mails that travel through telecommunications switches and microwave transmissions. Vice President Cheney's involvement with and inspiration for the NSA program to spy on Americans demonstrates his central role in the developing American police state. He was the driving force in expanding the program, briefing very few in Congress and keeping it nearly entirely under wraps. Since the 1970s, Cheney had been driven to respond to what he considered the diminishment of presidential power. He admired presidents, such as Lincoln, Wilson, and FDR, who exercised excessive power in times of national emergency, such as intercepting telegraphs and other communications. In the post-9/11 state of emergency that he saw in America, the president had the right to ignore law and the Constitution. The NSA's surveillance program had roots in Cheney's experience overseeing the agency as Pentagon Secretary for Bush senior.

With America moving toward a police state, even prior to Bush's inauguration, the NSA was already behaving like a power-hungry federal agency; NSA documents advocated that it aspired to a much more potent role in the commercial communications realm, regardless of privacy and legal issues. It was a kind of mission creep. Shortly after the 9/11 attacks, Cheney began exploring with CIA director Tenet and NSA director Michael Hayden how to involve the agency. They knew that under current laws, the NSA did not have the legal authority to monitor and conduct surveillance on Americans. Its post-Watergate role was to conduct counterintelligence surveillance and wiretap foreign embassies. Hayden met with key staff members to begin to fundamentally alter the NSA's no-spying-on-Americans orientation. The agency began making connections between surveillance of overseas and domestic communications. It had been the FBI's role to monitor and spy on Americans suspected of political dissent. After 9/11, the NSA forged a closer relationship with the FBI, with Hayden loosening restrictions at NSA to provide the agency with thousands of new leads on people to pursue in the United States with even remote connections to electronic communications with Afghanistan.

In October 2001, President Bush authorized expanding NSA's mission to conduct surveillance inside the United States, in part by creating a closer working relationship between the NSA and telecommunications companies. Whether it was surveillance of overseas or domestic telecommunications, the NSA needed industry's assistance. But there were legal obstacles, such as the 1978 FISA law, which Bush was prepared to override; he authorized a secret executive order, granting NSA authority to conduct surveillance and spy on Americans. He told a different story in public in Buffalo in April 2004, while promoting the use of the Patriot Act in prosecuting the Lackawanna Six. He characterized the legislation as making it easier for officials to share intelligence and to listen in on communications between terrorists, taking care to note it wouldn't happen without a court order.[12] But no court orders were obtained as the NSA went about spying on Americans. There was some understanding within the government that wiretapping without a court order was illegal. Justice Department lawyers were deeply troubled by the program. But once warrantless wiretapping began, the administration was determined to continue it in secret, standard police state procedure; the NSA increased controls on who could be wiretapped to make the program more acceptable so it could continue without Justice Department interference.

The Bush police state had so concentrated power that members of Congress formally charged with oversight on security were reduced to receiving carefully edited bits of information. When information wasn't censored, they were prohibited from sharing it. The fact that the members of the so-called Gang of Eight (who received briefings from Cheney and Hayden) were so restricted and agreed to these restrictions indicates how far procedural democracy had diminished. The White House so completely monopolized the control of information to which members of Congress had a constitutional right that they couldn't take notes, which would provide historical proof of the briefings and couldn't discuss them with staff members; they even worried about talking to one another. Congress, again, became an effective enabler, allowing the executive branch to concentrate power without resistance. In its defense, it was responding to the shock of 9/11. Congress, like the American people, agreed to go along. When Senator Rockefeller of the Gang of Eight raised concerns, the White House ignored them. Internal democracy had diminished so much that even the FISA court, a secret court with no accountability, was looked upon with disdain. Jack Goldsmith, the assistant attorney general in the OLC spoke of Addington's desire to eliminate the FISA court; Addington constructed the terrorist surveillance program to largely bypass it. The program, first used to intercept communications between the United States and Afghanistan, now had no geographic limits. Yoo's legal analysis supported it, making the case that NSA authorization to intercept a broad range of private communications was a president's prerogative as commander in chief, justified by Congressional authorization of military force to protect the country from terrorist attacks. The extent to which the administration was willing to surpass FISA was demonstrated by its unwillingness to accept even those instances when FISA rejected requests for surveillance: "beginning with the arrival of George W. Bush in 2001, the judges modified 179 of the 5,645 requests for court ordered surveillance and rejected or deferred at least six—the first outright rejections in the court's history—between 2003 and 2004."[13] And FISA knew nothing about the NSA's warrantless program—even though the court can accommodate urgent NSA and FBI requests for warrants 24 hours a day. What little it would learn came during a meeting between presiding Judge Royce Lamberth and key Bush administration officials. The meeting was characterized by practically no participation by Lamberth who promised not to tell his colleagues on the court about it; he was told that the program was the result of a presidential decision; his opinion was not solicited.[14] The warrantless eavesdropping program is based on the police-state assumption that everyone is a suspect, so all writing and speaking must be closely monitored. Even the FISA court knew that the NSA program was without merit, a fishing expedition. Approvals were done by NSA staff, not by judges. "The NSA would become judge, jury and eavesdropper all in one."[15] Little remains of procedural due process safeguards. The NSA acts as a court, to interpret law, and can determine what constitutes acceptable criteria upon which to conduct surveillance. It is not probable cause, it is "reasonableness," a far more arbitrary standard than the Fourth Amendment.

Once suppressive measures begin, they gain momentum and accelerate. The NSA program, Operation Highlander, prompted surveillance on Americans if an NSA supervisor believed the person on the other end of the line was a member of a terrorist organization. "But these people were not members of Al Qaeda, and they weren't talking to terrorists. Nevertheless, the standard operating procedure was to keep recording them and not delete the numbers. They were...hesitant to ever block phone numbers or drop them from the system: There were no really clear cut rules."[16] The NSA assumed the right to invade the privacy of citizens—many of whom were members of the military or contractors, whose personal calls back home were monitored—because it had been given the power to do so. With a war against Iraq looming, the Bush administration had Secretary of State Colin Powell attempt to persuade the UN to authorize the use of force. As the UN debated, the NSA stepped up eavesdropping of UN members, most of all, Secretary General Kofi Annan and Security Council members. The purpose was not just to learn of opposition to the resolution: it was a calculated tactic to manipulate how members would vote. "The agency...could pick up indications of what they needed such as a highway, a dam, or a favorable trade deal and, in a subtle form of bribery, the U.S. could provide the country with a generous aid package to help pay for the construction."[17]

Inside the United States, the NSA expanded police state practices by working with corporate America, which had much to gain. The NSA, which needed permission to access the companies' switching facilities, established ties to the industry through the National Security Agency Advisory Board. With the exception of Qwest, access was granted by the major telecommunications companies, such as AT&T, which allowed the NSA to use Narus Insight Intercept Suite, which gathers up Web mail traffic of all kinds. These data are fed into a powerful computer known as Narus Insight: "packets containing target names, addresses, keywords and phrases would be kicked out and forwarded to the NSA for further analysis."[18] While administration officials gave the green light to expand surveillance, Congress also assisted when the House Intelligence Committee recommended working more closely with industry. The NSA gained greater power and importance while the industry gained much greater profits. Both believed they had a right to go outside the law to accomplish their goals. The police state partly resulted from institutional ties between the NSA and these companies. Thousands of new employees were hired; between 2001 and 2008, the agency workforce expanded by 40 percent. The agency partnered with industry to launch new means of thought control, which facilitated searches of Internet service providers. Other devices helped intercept telephone calls and text messages and allowed the NSA to monitor all international and domestic communications. There was the technical problem of sifting through the vast quantity of communications, sorting out which ones indicated those between terrorists. Such data mining, referred to as link analysis, amounts to the NSA's use of technology to construct guilt by association, acquiring vast quantities of billing information from companies and using its staff and computers to hone in on targets. To connect who was saying what, the NSA enlisted the support of the major telecoms providing international service, such as AT&T, MCI, and WorldCom. It was rationalized as a kind of preventive thought control, which was to occur without the intrusion of the FISA court. Sidestepping the FISA court was regarded as necessary to keep the warrantless eavesdropping program secret; even it demanded a bare minimum probable cause requirement, which the NSA was unwilling to provide. Now, anyone, a friend or neighbor, with any association direct or indirect, with a would-be terrorist suspect, would have its international communications subjected to warrantless wiretapping. The next step was collaboration with the FBI, which would further investigate individuals in question, assuming that they were guilty. Such thinking was counterproductive, and agents received thousands of leads each month, practically all of which turned out to be meaningless—a pizza shop or a babysitter. "The result was frequent complaints to the bureau's NSA liaison that the unfiltered and unanalyzed data was flooding them and keeping them from pursuing more productive work."[19] This fanatical pursuit was self-destructive and ineffective: "of the approximately 5,000 NSA warrantless taps conducted between September 2001 and December 2005, fewer than ten Americans a year drew enough suspicion to move on to the next level."[20]

Even FBI Director Robert S. Mueller worried that the program did not have "a proper legal foundation." Jack Goldsmith in the OLC considered the program "a legal mess," and in early March 2004 sent Attorney General Ashcroft a memo titled "Review of Legality of the NSA Program." Goldsmith convinced Assistant Attorney General James Comey to side with him on the program's possible illegality. For all of his misgivings, Ashcroft, under White House pressure, had renewed it each time. But now largely due to Goldsmith's and Comey's concerns, he decided that he wouldn't sign. When Ashcroft suddenly became ill, officials rushed to the hospital to get him to sign it. Comey was officially in charge and refused to sign it; there was almost a mini-rebellion by top Justice and FBI officials who threatened to resign over the administration's support for the program. What happened next illustrates how far the government had been transformed into a police state, for ultimately law and the Constitution did not matter. In spite of clear statements by the Justice Department and the FBI, Bush would eventually reauthorize the NSA program, negating the authority of the Justice Department and the attorney general's office, the official guardians of law and protectors of the Constitution. The administration cloaked the program's legality in the authority given to the president by Congress to use force in the war against terrorism. By ignoring the fact that congressional authorization didn't include secret warrantless surveillance programs, Bush felt he had all the authority he needed. The administration was deeply committed to pursuing this war on terrorism outside of constitutional limits.

The events that followed the program's exposure by the *New York Times* illustrate how the American police state adapted to changing circumstances. Hayden and the NSA worried that exposure would lead to questions about its legality. In spite of the ACLU lawsuit against the NSA, the White House, as it had before, would find a way around the district court ruling. In August 2006, the court ruled against the administration's claims that Congress had given the president the prerogative to act on his authority to use whatever means available to confront al Qaeda. The court considered the NSA program illegal for evading the FISA court and violating the Fourth Amendment. It concluded that the program should be terminated. Undeterred, the administration appealed; it also tried other strategies, one was to appear to concede to the FISA court's authority. Under the new approach, the NSA would target for surveillance any group of foreigners that it had probable cause to believe were members or associates of a terrorist organization. The NSA concluded it didn't need permission from the FISA court to tap foreign communications, only if the communication goes through a telephone in the United States. In such cases, then, the NSA could engage in surveillance immediately, provided the agency makes an emergency application to the FISA court in three days. Thus, the administration could appear to comply with the FISA court when it hadn't.

The 2006 Congress called for an investigation into the NSA's association with the telecommunications industry. In response, the administration maneuvered to protect its unlimited power to monitor the thoughts of U.S. and non-U.S. citizens. Congress was under pressure to renew the Protect America Act. With fear mongering as the key tactic, the administration, with Republican congressional support, bullied and intimidated Democrats to associate the act's renewal with immunity from prosecution for the telecoms. With this new version, the administration further weakened the FISA court. The bill, for the first time, gave the NSA authority to eavesdrop without a warrant, not just on overseas communication but also on U.S. citizens who communicate overseas. In a small concession, the NSA would still have to obtain from the FISA court permission to target Americans domestically. With passage of the immunity provision, the Bush administration had perverted the law so that now, illegal activities are legal, even if they conflict with the courts and the Constitution.

The administration was not as successful in the courts. So when frontal assaults to impose its extremist views were unsuccessful, it tried a backdoor approach. A prime example is the effort by Attorney General Gonzales and his aides to proceed with a clandestine campaign to remove U.S. attorneys with the assistance of his chief of staff, Kyle Sampson, who enlisted White Counsel Harriet Miers, her aide William Kelley and Deputy Attorney General Paul McNulty. Sampson conducted an assessment to determine which of the 93 U.S. attorneys should be fired. The rationale was based on insufficient loyalty to the president and not the extent to which these attorneys supported rule of law. Eight prosecutors were listed. The action was without historical precedent. While U.S. attorneys are appointed and can be fired at any time by the president, only a small number have ever been removed. The firings were part of a larger strategy to staff the Justice Department with pure ideologues who would follow the administration's agenda. The acting head of the civil rights division, Bradley Schlozman, made a concerted effort to fill the ranks with right-wing attorneys affiliated with the conservative Federalist Society. The climate was ripe for weeding out attorneys and prosecutors identified as liberals.

Such actions underscored the executive branch belief that all power should be concentrated in a Unitary Executive. In executive orders and signing statements, President Bush used this term more than 100 times. With signing statements, in particular, the executive branch took over functions reserved in the Constitution for Congress and the Supreme Court. It's no coincidence that presidents began making greater use of signing statements as the government moved toward becoming a police state. Until the Reagan administration, signing statements were rare. In 1984, when Reagan signed the Competition in Contracting Act, he issued a signing statement, essentially an order to federal agencies not to implement a particular section of the law. The implication led to a court challenge by a bidder, who would have won a contract had the government obeyed the law. In 1985, a federal judge ruled that the administration had to follow all of the act's provisions. That Attorney General Meese was initially willing to refuse to follow a court order

marked a turning point. Reagan used signing statements with a total of
95 sections of bills, the most of any president until then.[21] With signing statements, presidents could make and interpret law. A Meese aide
had assigned Ralph Tarr, head of the OLC, to construct a history of
signing statements. Tarr concluded that they "give [the White House]
an additional tool—the threat of a potential signing statement—with
which to negotiate concessions from Congress."[22] President Bush, Sr.,
used signing statements to reinterpret 232 sections of bills. Officials
began viewing them as more powerful than the veto when "defending
prerogatives from congressional meddling."[23] This trend continued.
Walter Dellinger, head of the Clinton administration's OLC wrote:
"If the President may properly decline to enforce a law, at least when
it unconstitutionally encroaches on his powers, then it arguably follows that he may properly announce to Congress and to the public
that he will not enforce a provision of an enactment he is signing."
Clinton used signing statements with 140 sections of bills.[24] With 9/11
as the rationale, Bush administration officials believed they had a right
to issue signing statements. In many ways, they allowed the executive branch to assume government's entire function, making Bush a de
facto dictator. Other federal agencies were solicited to work with the
White House in using signing statements to expand its power at the
expense of Congress.

In the Bush administration, Cheney made sure that all legislation
arrived at his office, where Addington conducted a detailed reading.
The two thus acted as guardians and promoters of excessively expanding presidential authority over issues that previous presidents never
attempted. Addington was consumed with the need to add signing
statements to anything Bush signed into law, and Bush set the record,
adding 1,132 signing statements to laws that Congress passed. In one
way, Bush used them like a line-item veto, even though the Supreme
Court concluded that they are unconstitutional. Signing statements
help concentrate formal power in one person who rules above the
law by decree. It's no coincidence that the Bush administration used
the Unitary Executive theory to rationalize signing statements, all of
which included Bush's assertion that so long as the legislation was in
keeping with his power as a Unitary Executive, he would sign it into
law. Future Supreme Court Justice Samuel Alito explained the principle as one that gave "the president not just some executive powers but
the executive power—the whole thing."[25]

There were general patterns to Bush's signing statements. He used
them partly to implement a unilateralist foreign policy, excluding

Congress or to override bills it had passed. When Congress prohibited U.S. troops from engaging in combat in Colombia, where the United States was helping the government fight narcotics-funded Marxist rebels, Bush invoked his power as commander in chief with a signing statement, refusing to abide by those restrictions. He used them to reinforce his erroneous interpretation of his constitutional authority as commander in chief, to exercise power without legal restraint from Congress, behaving like a dictator. He used signing statements in August 2004 and December 2005 to override Congress when it twice attempted to place legal limits on intelligence gathering and protect Fourth Amendment rights, prohibiting the use of intelligence that wasn't legally gathered. He used them to undermine law by, in effect, creating new law, acting as supreme lawmaker. Congress passed a bill in 2006 prohibiting the opening of first class mail without a warrant unless it was suspected that it contained a bomb. "Bush's signing statement said that the executive branch could, nevertheless, open mail without a warrant when specifically authorized by law for foreign intelligence collection."[26] He used signing statements to take over the functions of other branches of governments, as if they didn't exist; for example, Bush used one in October 2006, when, after Hurricane Katrina, it was revealed that Federal Emergency Management Agency director Michael Brown was an expert in horse racing, not emergency management. Congress legislated that the president nominate candidates to lead FEMA who had at least five years of relevant leadership experience; Bush's signing statement said that since he headed the executive branch, he had the power to make such appointments and thus didn't have to abide by that requirement.

This concentration of power through the use of signing statements eclipsed the authority of the other branches by maintaining secrecy in areas in which Congress had a constitutional right to be informed. After signing a 2004 law requiring that scientific information prepared by government scientists and researchers immediately be provided to Congress without censorship or delay, Bush added a signing statement, allowing him to withhold that information if he determined that it could hinder foreign relations, national security, or executive branch operations. By denying such information, essential to constitutional interactions between the president and Congress, these signing statements provided Bush with dictatorial powers. In creating the Department of Homeland Security in 2002, Congress said that its oversight committees must be provided with information about vulnerable chemical plants and airport screening of baggage as well as uncensored reports about immigration visas. Bush's statement held that he had a constitutional right to hold back and alter such information. And after Congress passed whistle-blower protections for employees at the Department of Energy and the Nuclear Regulatory Commission, Bush issued a signing statement, which implemented the bill without these protections.

Bush's aspirations to absolute power extended Unitary Executive theory beyond even what its advocates, such as Steven Calabresi, had intended. Calabresi had contended that the decision not to execute a law was "a tricky thing," and that it should only occur if a president—and others— are convinced that a law is unconstitutional.[27] But Bush used signing statements to expand and concentrate the president's authority without limitations. He no longer had just the option of vetoing a bill or signing and enforcing it. With signing statements, the president makes a conscious decision to ignore parts of the law he considers irrelevant, enforcing only the parts he chooses to enforce. After signing the Detainee Treatment Act in December 2005, designed to prevent prisoners from receiving degrading inhumane treatment, Bush's signing statement concluded that the new law would be understood, "in a manner consistent with the constitutional authority of the President to supervise the Unitary Executive branch and as commander in chief and consistent with the constitutional limitations on the judicial power."[28] Bush would determine what the law was and how laws should be carried out. This interpretation resulted in the eventual widespread mistreatment and torture of prisoners.

Signing statements contributed to making Bush's authority absolute in the renewal of the Patriot Act. For all the revelations about warrantless surveillance, Congress did eventually renew the Patriot Act with provisions intended to protect the privacy of Americans. But Bush's signing statement cited the president's constitutional authority "to supervise the Unitary Executive branch" and hold back information from Congress if he thought it would hinder foreign relations, national security, or the executive branch's constitutional responsibilities. Bush decided if and when information would be provided to Congress and what remained secret. When Congress passed legislation mandating that the Department of Defense provide a detailed report on intelligence gathering, Bush issued a signing statement that said that the DoD should disregard the law. Bush also used signing statements to keep secret CIA "black sites," where prisoners were tortured. In spite of congressional legislation mandating that Congress be informed about them, Bush maintained in a signing statement that he alone has the right to inform Congress of their existence.

The post-9/11 permanent state of emergency and preparations for the Iraq war helped fully develop the American police state. The idea of a permanent global war on terrorism and the manufacturing of Iraq as a direct threat gave the administration what it considered a license to use extreme methods. Russell Tice, an NSA whistle-blower, revealed on Keith Olbermann's MSNBC program on January 22, 2009, that the NSA was spying on American journalists and news agencies, gathering credit card and financial data on Americans. Tice spoke of how they sucked in everybody, and at some point, they may have cherry-picked. Overseas, there were fewer constraints. In Iraq, everyone was identified as a terrorist. It was the mentality of the colonizer taken to an extreme. Actions in Iraq and Afghanistan would even surpass the violations of international law at Guantanamo Bay.

Extremism and fanaticism inside the administration were supplemented by opportunism and the involvement of outsiders, such as Ahmad Chalabi, who, in the early 1990s, led the Iraqi National Congress, determined to overthrow Saddam Hussein. He found an eager audience with former officials involved in the Gulf War under Bush senior. They had had limited success with the Clinton administration. Under pressure from congressional Republicans, Clinton signed the Iraq Liberation Act, allocating funds to train and arm the Iraqi opposition. A much more determined effort developed when some of the same former Bush administration officials assumed important positions in George W. Bush's administration, including Defense Secretary Rumsfeld; his deputy Paul Wolfowitz; and Douglas Feith, an undersecretary of defense. They were determined to overthrow Hussein with preemptive action. Richard Perle, assistant secretary of defense under Reagan, was appointed chairman of the Defense Policy Board, which advised the Pentagon. Ahmad Chalabi had personal ties to Wolfowitz, Perle, and eventually Rumsfeld; Feith; and Scooter Libby, who became Cheney's chief of staff. While Perle and others, such as pundit William Kristol, produced articles urging Hussein's ouster, Chalabi's war plans were being circulated to a Pentagon planning group with Wolfowitz's support. Other intelligence gatherers were not convinced, particularly the CIA. Senior administration officials sought to establish a 9/11-Iraq connection, but CIA analysts hadn't found any. Then Wolfowitz and Feith established their own intelligence-gathering unit, the Counterterrorism Group, to manufacture a connection. With assistance from Chalabi and his Iraqi National Congress in exile, it would neutralize the CIA's hesitation. CIA director Tenet mistrusted Chalabi, but the agency didn't seek to prevent Pentagon officials from using intelligence reports based on information from him and the Iraqi National Congress. Tenet's attitude was to acquiesce in what was becoming a fast track to war against Iraq. The CIA was now in the business of producing intelligence to support going to war.

Cheney took great interest in the intelligence gathering for the 9/11–Iraq connection. He took unusual steps, repeatedly visiting CIA headquarters, meeting with analysts to question them or push for greater intelligence to justify waging war. He traveled to Kuwait and Egypt seeking support for an invasion, while American military forces built up their regional presence. To make the strongest possible case, it was essential to establish that Hussein possessed weapons of mass destruction and was capable of attacking the United States.

The next step was to manufacture the case to Congress, the American people, and the UN. Bush and Cheney often repeated distorted information about links between the 9/11 planners and Iraqi intelligence officials and about how close Hussein was to developing and using nuclear weapons—it amounted to a cumulative propaganda campaign.[29] As the administration fabricated false statements and evidence, Congress was deceived outright. When Bush met with key members of Congress in September 2002, he urged swift support for his resolution to invade Iraq, purportedly to confront Hussein's nuclear threat. One month later, Bush again emphasized to congressional leaders that Hussein was building nuclear weapons and was capable of targeting the East Coast with biological and chemical weapons delivered by unmanned aircraft.

The Bush administration then engaged in its most daring and distorted selling of the Iraq war, in which CIA Director Tenet, in a closed meeting, began developing an elaborate case that Hussein had the means to construct nuclear weapons. Tenet discussed the interception of aluminum tubes headed for Iraq that he said would be used to build centrifuges that can produce enriched uranium. The so-called blockbuster revelation was that Iraq had attempted to buy large quantities of uranium from Niger, a known uranium producer. In Bush's 2003 State of the Union address, he referred to these reports as evidence that Hussein was trying to develop nuclear weapons. Supported by officials in the Department of Defense and the Pentagon, the administration was isolating critics who questioned Iraq's quest for nuclear weapons. CIA analysts who knew that Iraq didn't possess nuclear weapons were denied access to even those within the administration who might question those claims if they had contrary evidence, primarily Secretary of State Colin Powell. Not long after Powell made his infamous presentation to the UN, the Niger-uranium-Iraq ties were revealed as bogus by the director general of the International Atomic Agency. By manipulating intelligence, the administration reached an essential goal: the achievement of absolute power over people and events. The administration was willing to use unreliable information from Chalabi and another Iraq exile with the code name "Curveball," whose information was critical to the argument that Iraq was creating biological weapons. The administration used it to undercut the findings of UN inspectors who couldn't locate weapons of mass destruction, alleging that they couldn't be found because they were mobile biological weapons. This became an important part of Powell's UN presentation; he received the intelligence through a third party and before the war, intelligence officials had never even met Curveball. The information was provided to a U.S. military intelligence unit, which sent this unfiltered report to all other parts of intelligence services, which accepted the claims without question. Eventually, Curveball's claims were found to have been fabricated, proving that intelligence agencies were all too willing to provide what the administration wanted. According to the independent WMD commission, the incident demonstrated an intelligence failure: analysts were willing to believe in unverified information from a single source just because it squared with their theories.

CHAPTER 7

Exporting the American Police State

In the context of the war against Iraq, which began on March 19, 2003, the most brutal and violent version of the American police state unfolds. Regardless of the administration's ever-changing statements as to why the United States was in Iraq, the goal was to establish an exported police state. In Iraq and Afghanistan, the administration created a system of rule based on detention and interrogation, the justification for which was to confront these "aliens" identified as terrorists. From August 31 to September 9, 2003, General Miller and a number of interrogation specialists were inspecting the Abu Ghraib prison, which Miller viewed as an interrogation center for Iraq. He intended to "Gitmo-ize" Abu Ghraib, and he had the administration's approval to do so. This idea developed out of a working partnership between high-ranking military officers and administration officials. Miller had informed his superiors in the Southern Command post of this intent, and he addressed the Senate Armed Services Committee in May 2004. After Miller completed his inspection, political decisions were made to export police state practices, especially torture. The Department of Defense sent Tiger Teams and others to Abu Ghraib, also used at Guantanamo, to interrogate detainees. Techniques to be used at Abu Ghraib weren't covered by the Army Field Manual. Interrogation teams instructed Abu Ghraib personnel to employ sleep deprivation and dogs to frighten prisoners and break them down psychologically and physically. Miller passed his recommendations to the commander of coalition forces in Iraq, Army Lieutenant General Ricardo S. Sanchez, who authorized interrogators to use methods outside of those in the Army Field Manual, including extended isolation, stress positions, extreme temperatures, and sleep deprivation. The manual's adherence to the

Geneva Conventions was ignored. Interrogators had the discretion to use any method they saw fit. The gulf between methods stipulated as legal in the manual and interrogators' knowledge of them, on one hand, and the methods put into practice, on the other, made these techniques consistent with police state practices. For example, the field manual states that "fear up and harsh methods" violate legal standards used to interrogate prisoners. Nonetheless, in Guantanamo Bay, Mohammed al-Qahtani was subjected to strip searches, made to wear women's underwear, attached to a leash, and made to perform dog tricks. Personnel became socialized to accept these illegal techniques as commonplace since no one protested. In the absence of clear legal restraints, a culture of torture was created. The knowledge of, and failure to enforce, legal guidelines for interrogations was reinforced by administration officials, who appeared to tolerate moving beyond legal interrogations. Secretary Rumsfeld's December 2002 interrogation memo said: "I stand for ten hours a day. Why is standing limited to four hours?" Vice President Cheney remarked that U.S. intelligence "will work on the dark side, if you will and that it would be vital for them to use any means at their disposal." This was more than tacit approval for interrogations to go outside the law. Cheney commented in 2006 that he considered waterboarding a "no-brainer." General Sanchez had accepted General Miller's recommendation to employ methods not in the Army Field Manual. Directives were issued in which "military interrogators in Iraq were informed that the 'gloves are coming off,' that prisoners were to be 'broken,' and that the interrogators should propose 'wish lists' of 'effective' techniques for review."[1] Such messages worked their way down the chain of command, demonstrating that mistreatment of prisoners had been ordered from the top. The high command had given rank and file officers a license to invent.[2] Dehumanization, suffering, even the death of prisoners was excused because it was being done to "enemy combatants." One officer, accused of suffocating a prisoner to death, remarked that the interrogation guidelines didn't take into consideration "the type of people we are interrogating in Iraq."[3]

While death by torture was uncommon, military police and interrogators were increasingly inventive; one female soldier forced a prisoner in his underwear to jump and roll repeatedly in a room heated to 150 degrees Fahrenheit. It was considered routine to handcuff hooded prisoners to railings. With such practices commonplace, there was no reason to question abuse and torture. Such abuse could not be carried out without uniform consent from perpetrators and the officers who tolerated them. A report on abuse at Abu Ghraib stated that detainee abuse was common knowledge among enlisted soldiers at Abu Ghraib, and that while abuse of a sexual nature was seen and documented, it went unreported.[4] There was also a clear division of labor of police state practices. There were reported cases of so-called specialists in special forces units who had a license to engage in sadistic practices. One prisoner subjected to the special treatment was brutally assaulted: "in the fall of 2003, Americans dressed in civilian clothing beat his head and stomach, dislocated his arms, broke his nose, forced an unloaded pistol into his mouth and pulled the trigger and choked him with a rope. He alleged that he had been beaten so severely that he urinated blood."[5] That such practices were not uncommon points to the results of policies suspending laws that are supposed to ensure humane treatment for prisoners. Those laws had been replaced by the brutality of the police state. Such sadism by the task forces was known and reported to administration officials.

If the invasion of Iraq was an example of how the Bush administration expanded police state measures, the documented excessive violence perpetrated on prisoners indicates how dysfunctional a police state is, for nothing is gained from subjecting individuals to pointless violence. The brutal treatment and murder—possibly from hypothermia, according to a medical officers' statement—of Abu Malik Kenami in the hands of so-called interrogators is a tragic example. He was imprisoned with no observed medical problems but died after being subjected to forced exercise as punishment, handcuffing, hooding, and being confined to a cell made for 30 people that was inhabited by more than 60.[6] Such acts reduce victims to a nonhuman state of otherness, while the perpetrators remain devoid of all feelings. How else to explain the treatment of another prisoner, Obeed Hethere Radad, shot to death by a guard in September 2003 after being confined in isolation? "The investigation found probable cause to believe that the specialist had committed the offense of murder."[7]

Sadistic practices were used against captured Iraqi citizens of all ages. Everyone was assumed guilty, and authorities have absolute power and the right to use it. This occurred with an Iraqi teenager, who ended up in U.S. custody in December 2003 and who said that his teeth and jaw were broken when he was kicked by a soldier after being cuffed, hooded, showered with cold water, and forced to exercise. "the boy and his brother were seized as 'subtargets,'...not because they were suspected of wrongdoing but because they were male Iraqi citizens found inside the target's home."[8] Even U.S. personnel stationed at

Abu Ghraib were well aware that Iraqis were rounded up wholesale and that those caught had no terrorist ties, "most of the detainees had just been picked up in sweeps for no particular reason."[9] That this was common practice was confirmed by sworn statements by the Military Intelligence Group and the Red Cross which reported in October 2003 that 70 to 90 percent of Abu Ghraib detainees "were arrested by mistake or had no intelligence value."[10] Still, sadistic practices continued, sanctioned by the administration and stemming from the rank and file. Abu Ghraib soldiers had little to no training in how to treat prisoners. A psychological motivation to abuse can stem from the fact that soldiers who participated were at the bottom of economic and social ladders. By torturing and degrading their prisoners, whom they saw as inferiors, they could elevate their status. When the powerless are given an opportunity to exercise absolute power, they will do so.

The physical layout of Abu Ghraib and the anarchy in daily operating procedure also played a role. Abu Ghraib functioned under the concept of preventive detention, but it was implemented without clear distinctions as to how the prison should distinguish criminal from political offenses. This created a confused atmosphere in which all prisoners were regarded as the same. The camps at Abu Ghraib housed and mixed together a broad cross section of Iraqi society. Only the part known as the "hard site" was set up to house "high-level prisoners" who had fought against U.S. troops. Military intelligence knew that such resistance fighters hadn't been involved in terrorist activities. With the steady influx of prisoners, inadequate record keeping contributed to prisoner abuse and torture; officials could hardly process all the detainees or keep records of their arrests, making any semblance of order difficult, creating an atmosphere in which inventiveness was prized. There were also far too many prisoners in relation to military police, a 75 to 1 ratio. It was difficult to determine which interrogators were contractors, CIA agents, or special forces.

Despite these conditions, there was a general understanding as to how to treat prisoners. General Sanchez had established a basic interrogation policy for Abu Ghraib, allowing interrogators to exercise complete control over prisoners and their food, clothing, and shelter as well as the interrogation room's light, temperature, and physical layout. MPs and interrogators were free to determine how to conduct interrogations, while Military Intelligence (MI) members were present, making sure that interrogations were harsh, even brutal. Members of Other Government Agencies (OGAs), a euphemism for the CIA, also were present as were federal agencies that played a vital part in prisoner torture, another police state hallmark. This will to dominate totally the minds and bodies of Iraqis during the occupation occurred in the context of war, an "emergency situation." With the usual arrogance of a conqueror, torture was a message to the Iraqi people: accept the U.S. occupation. When policy makers responded to the rise in American casualties and growth of a resistance movement, the military, stepped up, sweeps in largely civilian neighborhoods, increasing the number of Iraqi civilians in detention. In obvious denial that the occupation was motivating resistance, the main purpose—seen as a means of halting mounting U.S. casualties—was to punish any Iraqi citizen captured without much concern about whether or not he was part of the resistance. This set in motion a rush to capture, confine, and torture Iraqis. By summer 2003, the first commander, Brigadier General Janis Karpinski, observed that in three months, the number of prisoners had skyrocketed from 25 to 14,000 "security detainees" in a single prison.[11] Iraq had been transformed into a country with more than 100 prison complexes, housing about 20,000. Abu Ghraib was among the largest.

In summer 2003, Karpinski began taking note of the CIA's role in Abu Ghraib. The agency was using part of the prison as a "hard site" to unleash the harshest interrogation techniques that were part of Kurback, SERE, and the CIA's Honduran handbook. Karpinski became aware of the military high command's role in a meeting with General Miller, who made it clear that Abu Ghraib would be the training ground where MPs would learn to work with interrogators. In fall 2003, General Sanchez issued a memo authorizing interrogation techniques outside the Army Field Manual not in use at Guantanamo Bay. The memo authorized techniques used by the CIA to inflict psychological and physical torture, through a collaboration with the military. Techniques included changing the detainee's diet, sleep cycles, and environment, making a pretense that people from another country, not the United States, were doing the interrogations; isolation; exposure to dogs, especially because of the alleged Arab fear of dogs; loud music; screaming; stress positions; use of false documents; creation of fear; disorientation; and shock.

Such techniques, authorized by General Sanchez, who was trained only as a troop commander, indicated that all parts of the government were collaborating to employ torture. Proof that torture had become official policy lay in the fact that there was little difference between what Sanchez had authorized and the techniques in the Kurback Manual and the 1983 Honduran handbook. Both placed a premium on turning the victim against himself or herself through physical and psychological methods. Both the Kurback manual and Sanchez's authorization emphasized that the interrogator must have absolute power, tearing down prisoners while increasing their fear. So two influences shaped the application of torture at Abu Ghraib: the Sanchez/CIA techniques and the torture veterans from Guantanamo Bay. Military police at Abu Ghraib received vivid instruction from pictures and videotapes showing detainee abuse. Once made official, these techniques gained momentum. General Karpinski had objected to the treatment of inmates at Abu Ghraib and resisted efforts to prohibit Red Cross access to interrogations; then she was replaced by two senior intelligence officers reporting directly to Sanchez, Colonel Thomas Pappas and Lieutenant Colonel Steve Jordan. The structure was in place to allow excessive abuse and torture of Abu Ghraib detainees. Under Pappas, the military police were responsible for the initial processing and extensive disorientation of the prisoners to soften them up for CIA and military intelligence interrogations by "punching, slapping and kicking detainees, keeping them naked for several days at a time...this treatment soon moved beyond sleep and sensory deprivation to sexual humiliation, marked by photographing naked male and female detainees, forcibly arranging detainees in various sexually explicit positions...forcing groups of male detainees to masturbate while being photographed."[12] These were methods right out of the CIA's torture playbook. The CIA also insisted that military intelligence interrogators establish conditions for interrogation. Pappas made sure the MPs followed the CIA techniques used to break down the prisoners for interrogations, such as control of the diet, feeding bread and water, subjecting prisoners to extreme hot and cold temperatures, sensory deprivation, isolation for a month or more, stress positions, and the use of working dogs. Various forms of mistreatment, many pulled verbatim from CIA interrogation manuals, were documented by the International Committee of the Red Cross; prisoners were hooded so they couldn't see or breathe, beaten, paraded naked in front of others, and handcuffed for days to bars in painful positions. In one visit, the ICRC uncovered evidence of prisoners who had been mistreated and were suffering from impaired memory and speech, severe anxiety, even suicidal inclinations. Amnesty International also found widespread abuse at Abu Ghraib as well as denial of due process rights, reporting that prisoners could be held for weeks with no charges, unable to see their families or attorneys.

When General Karpinski, the first military commander in charge of Abu Ghraib, became aware that Iraqis were detained for no good reason, she remarked "We're holding these prisoners, many of them without any evidence other than the one page arresting report by some young soldier from one of the infantry or armored divisions, 'caught looting,' or else, she said, you have a target individual and a good grid coordinate on his last known location and the division's or the brigades would put an operation together to go out and apprehend this individual. Well, if he's in the middle of a card game or a dinner, he's got thirty of his closest friends around him, they're not always clear who the individual is, they just know that this is the grid coordinate location. So they arrest everybody there."[13] Karpinski, who reviewed files of prisoners who could be eligible for release, knew that of those Iraqis rounded up, there was little evidence of their participation in prior anti-U.S. actions; she noted that "she rarely saw more than the flimsiest hint of any association with insurgent activities in the files."[14] But ultimately, all that mattered was capturing Iraqis, confining them, and forcing them to confess under torture to whatever interrogators had in mind.

Abu Ghraib was a system designed to torture: a matter of proper command and coordination. General Pappas demanded that prisoners identified as "high value" be isolated and placed under the authority of MI on Tier 1A, in which torture became common. Once directives were issued from military command, torture became routine, largely due to the actions of the military police, who distanced themselves from their actions. MP Sabrina Harman kept a diary of her experiences, describing how she coped with the brutality and death, noting one day "I saw my first dead body. I took pictures!"[15] Dead bodies were a curiosity. Other entries contained detailed descriptions of bodies at the morgue. "She had her picture taken at the morgue, leaning over one of the blackened corpses, her sun-flushed cheek inches from his crusted eye sockets. She is smiling—a forced but lovely smile and her right hand is raised in a fist, giving the thumbs up."[16]

The daily routine reinforced MPs' compliance. They didn't have to think about the consequences of their acts. It became a simple matter of getting the job done. The day-to-day practices of a police state culture are geared toward dominating and controlling the minds and bodies of others. Sometimes, that meant preventing prisoners from consistently sleeping. The chain of command reinforced the psychological separation of MPs from prisoners. Military intelligence officers were vigilant in ensuring torture was carried out, instructed to play very loud music, pour water on prisoners, bang on garbage cans, scream through megaphones, and switch lights on and off to totally disorient prisoners. For MPs, it became solely a matter of discipline, shutting down one's emotions, following orders to avoid reprimands from superiors. This is the lower rung of bureaucratic implementation of torture in a police state. Contributing to the MPs' compliance was their lack of knowledge as to the functions of the MI people, whom they called OGA or ghosts because they weren't easily identified and often didn't wear name badges. MPs were also confused as to the status of prisoners but were well aware of the OGA prisoners. The MPs had to accept directives from MI interrogators without question; they complied because the directives often changed day to day and prisoner to prisoner. The MPs' understanding that the prisoners were less than human was reinforced by the policy that they knew practically nothing about them except for their five-digit numbers. They further dehumanized them by creating nicknames based on physical characteristics. MP Sabrina Harman illustrated how one grew numb to events at Abu Ghraib. "In the beginning, she said, you see somebody naked and you see underwear on their head and you're like, oh that's pretty bad—I can't believe I just saw that. And then you go to bed and you come back the next day, and you see something worse. Well, it seems like the day before wasn't so bad."[17]

The psychology of some personnel stationed at Abu Ghraib, such as Corporal Charles Graner, fit right into the prison's brutality. Where would police state practices be without the willing participation of a Charles Graner? He wasn't about to pass up the opportunity to have absolute power over someone. Graner was given free rein to unleash his aggression on prisoners. He had already experienced a total institution as a corrections officer at SCI Greene, a super-max prison in Greene County, Pennsylvania, where he had grown accustomed to working in the prison's high-stress environment. There were indications that he was prone to violence in his personal life, too. Once stationed in Abu Ghraib, he learned quickly that he could express his rage, subjecting prisoners to physical and emotional abuses. In the infamous Abu Ghraib photograph, Graner put a strap around a prisoner's neck, forcing him to exit the cell, while his girlfriend, Lindy England, held the strap. The MPs knew from basic training that they had a duty to disobey an immoral order, or that if their immediate superior was the source of the immoral order they could report the abuse further up the chain of command. They did not. All the MPs knew, at the most basic level, was that what they were doing was lawless. Harman would later explain that this was the reason she took all the photographs. The MPs went along because they wanted to go along. Perhaps Lindy England put it best: "It was standard operating procedure."[18] There was understanding from the top of the chain of command down to the MPs that brutality and torture at Abu Ghraib was policy. So what passed as standard operating procedure is no different from criminal acts causing physical harm. Yet in spite of evidence of the criminal nature of such offenses, by and large, all the perpetrators remained above the law. "No soldier ever served jail time. No civilian interrogators ever faced legal proceedings. Nobody was ever charged with torture or war crimes, or any violation of the Geneva Conventions. Nobody ever faced charges for keeping prisoners naked or shackled. Nobody ever faced charges for holding prisoners as hostages. Nobody ever faced charges for incarcerating children who were accused of no crime and posed no known security threat. Nobody ever faced charges for holding thousands of prisoners in a combat zone in constant danger of their lives. Nobody ever faced charges for arresting thousands of civilians without direct cause and holding them indefinitely, in communicado, in concentration camp conditions."[19]

The reintroduction of extraordinary rendition provided additional proof that America is now a full-fledged police state, identifying with other police states by forming alliances with them. The process of seizing, transporting, and making people vanish without a trace has to be one of the police state's most oppressive features. With extraordinary rendition, police state methods become globalized. In the context of the global war on terrorism and the creation of "emergency situations," any person identified as a terrorist suspect is fair game. People became subject to renditions, not just in locations where the war on terrorism was already raging but in countries where the United States wanted to introduce it, such as Bosnia, Croatia, Albania, the Sudan, Somalia, Kenya, Zambia, Pakistan, Indonesia, and Malaysia. Once seized, prisoners were shipped to other police states, including "Egypt, Syria, Morocco, Jordan, Afghanistan, Uzbekistan, and Thailand."[20] Officials called the program "extra legal." Prisoners captured and detained by foreign governments found themselves outside of all national and international law prohibiting mistreatment and torture; they were allowed no contact with an attorney or a courtroom. Renditions allowed the CIA and the military to kidnap anyone, even without evidence of that individual having knowledge of terrorist activities. The simple power to accuse was all that was necessary to abduct someone. The Bush administration used extraordinary renditions to put individuals outside Geneva Convention protections, which strictly prohibited the use of torture to extract information. No prisoner held according to Geneva Conventions guidelines could be forced to provide anything other than the most basic information. Also dismissed was Article 3 of the UN

Convention on Torture, which states that a prisoner cannot be transferred to a country where they could be tortured. The Bush administration knew full well that prisoners were being sent to countries with a history of human rights abuses; Egypt, for example, an important U.S. ally, has a notorious reputation as "torture central." There were numerous CIA flights to Cairo after 9/11. During the U.S. intervention in Afghanistan, the military also played an important role in renditions involving sending prisoners to their home countries. This was a violation of international law, for anyone going through the process of being repatriated was required to have a hearing to determine if being repatriated meant mistreatment in his country; many such prisoners became victims of abuse and torture. President Bush cemented these police state practices after 9/11 by creating a state of emergency. His memorandum of notification, signed on September 17, 2001, made the CIA a super-secret police force, capable of acting on its own, seizing and transferring prisoners elsewhere to confine and interrogate them. This was a pattern in the growth of the American police state; authoritarian agencies had one purpose: expansion and increased control over their missions. The CIA's role in rendition became self-perpetuating.

During the invasion of Afghanistan, the CIA and the military solved the problem of what to do with the ever-growing mass of prisoners by expanding their missions, creating secret detention facilities. Some were built to contain prisoners identified as "high-value detainees." By creating various secret site classifications, the CIA was rationalizing the numbers and kinds of prisoners detained. Still, the treatment was the same: interrogations and torture around the clock. One black site in Afghanistan was known as the salt pit. Interrogations were performed by U.S. personnel. Conditions were so primitive, the food and water of such poor quality, the cells dark and damp, it would be hard to believe that the real purpose was to extract information. This was demonstrated by the experience of Khaled-el-Masri, who was removed from his cell by masked men; he was repeatedly interrogated but was never questioned about specific crimes or acts of terrorism. Deemed uncooperative, Khaled was returned to his cell, where he was left alone for weeks at a time. Conditions in his cell were far below any livable standard, and he was moved to and from interrogations in chains. Khaled asserted that he "was roughed up in interrogations,...photographed nude and both injected with drugs and given suppositories against his will; later, went on a hunger strike, he was fed forcibly."[21] The abuse of Khaled is rooted in an assumption of guilt by association for he belonged to a mosque that recruited Muslims to fight, and his associates included its leader, who gave anti-Western sermons and supported global jihad. At best, it was circumstantial evidence, but it was all that was needed for the Bush administration to suspend law. Khaled's abuse was one example of many in which torture was undertaken for a thought crime, even though there was no overt planning or carrying out of terrorist acts.

With extraordinary renditions, the administration expanded state power, directly coordinating decisions from the White House to other participants. According to CIA officials, "Everything we did down to the tiniest detail, every rendition and every technique used against prisoners in our hands, was scrutinized and approved by headquarters. And nothing was done without the approval from the White House— from National Security Advisor Condoleeza Rice herself and with a signature from Attorney General John Ashcroft."[22] The planning and carrying out of individual renditions also required approval from the CIA's Counterterrorist Center, which had to conform to procedures established by the attorney general and the National Security Council. Alterations in implementing renditions meant informing the official in charge of the Counterterrorist Center and sharing it with the relevant oversight committees in Congress. That the official authorization of extraordinary renditions and the entire process was illegal, there is no doubt, neither is there doubt that these renditions and torture weren't primarily motivated to gain information. The purpose of deporting Khaled and others to CIA black sites was not to acquire actionable intelligence; interrogators quickly discovered that brutality and torture were unsuccessful in extracting information. For example, Manadel Al-Jamadi, an Abu Ghraib prisoner, died under CIA interrogation on November 4, 2003. He had no paperwork, he was a "ghost prisoner" of the CIA. Sergeant Tony Diaz was on duty in the MI block along with another MP, Jeffrey Frost. One hour after Al-Jamadi had been processed, MPs were ordered to shackle him, handcuffed, to a window. Within an hour, Diaz and Frost were called in to help. Al-Jamadi was unresponsive, even after repeated attempts to revive him. Diaz raised the hood. "His face was totally messed up—huge black eyes and bruises everywhere. One eye was swollen shut, and the other was open...He wiggled the finger close to the prisoner's nose but the eye stared right past it, and it occurred to Diaz: this guy is not even alive."[23] Harman and Graner were on duty that night, when the commanding officer in charge informed them that a prisoner had died of a heart attack. It would be an eventful evening, because that night, Graner and Sergeant Frederick came up with the idea to abuse a prisoner they had nicknamed Gilligan. The abuse was captured in the infamous photo of the hooded man with a poncho cape, arms outstretched. After this prisoner Al-Jamadi was abused, he was kept in the shower on the floor next to bags of ice, to preserve his remains. Harman noticed ice draining from under the door. She entered the shower room and photographed the bloody body. She immediately knew what the commanding officer had told her was a lie. Harman was surprised by the extent of his injuries: bruises on his knees, thighs, and wrists and blood coming out of his nose and ears; a tooth was chipped. "You had to look close. I mean, they did a good job cleaning him up. The gauze on his eye was put there after he died to make it look like he had medical treatment because he didn't when he came into prison."[24] Al-Jamadi had been tortured to death by the CIA. After his ribs were broken, he was put into the Palestinian hanging torture position. In the morning, his body was taken from Abu Ghraib with a fake intravenous drip in his arm, an attempt to mask his death, later determined to be from asphyxia. That no one was ever officially charged with torturing him to death; arresting him without charge; denying him medical treatment; bringing him into Abu Ghraib, unregistered as a ghost detainee; and then smuggling him out of the prison amounts to an official government policy to torture prisoners to death. The Al-Jamadi example is not about the war on terrorism. In December 2002, two prisoners, Dilawar and Mullah Habibullah, in Bagram, Afghanistan, were tortured to death. Dilawar underwent similar tortures as Al-Jamadi, including shackled stress positions for prolonged periods. The personnel behind their deaths were not only not disciplined, they were rewarded: Bagram commanding officer Captain Carolyn Wood returned with her unit to Iraq, where she helped formulate interrogation policies at Abu Ghraib, based on methods used in Afghanistan.

The use of black sites and torturing to death as official government policy exhibits a twisted form of police state social engineering. The U.S. government policy of kidnapping persons with no formal charges is a policy of state-sponsored disappearances. The secret black sites are a global network, expanding the American police state's geographic impact. "The U.S. military admitted to as many as 14,000 prisoners being held elsewhere."[25] This secret invisible population remains in a permanent state of political limbo—without rights—subhuman. This is a global network of police state-style institutions in 20 countries, in Europe, Asia, and the Middle East, connected to their intelligence agencies, an alliance of nations engaging in police state practices. To nations involved in renditions, international law and human rights agreements don't exist; these nations become a global police force operating outside the law. The secrecy of the sites maintains the facade that the U.S. government abides by principles of procedural democracy. At the same time, the few visible camps—Guantanamo and Abu Ghraib—serve another propaganda function, demonstrating the administration's absolute power in the war on terrorism and manufacturing fear in the American public, through photographs of orange-suited prisoners, handcuffed, blindfolded, and subjected to harsh interrogations.

For all the shock and disgust expressed in response to the images of Guantanamo and Abu Ghraib prisoners, the abuse and torture practices were never meaningfully addressed. The photographs reveal a basic truth: that specific forms of torture are acceptable. There is something of a perverse delight in taking these photographs as the way to acknowledge and document the pain and suffering of others. The photographs provide documentary evidence of how well the perpetrators performed their tasks. Since release of the Abu Ghraib photographs did not lead to significant prosecutions for obvious war crimes or gross violations of international law, the photographs sent an ominous permanent message: Torture is a most useful police state measure; whomever the government identifies as an enemy who stands in the way of an expanding police state will face torture as state policy. The breadth of the term terrorist is useful in permanently excluding anyone from legal protections and allowing for use of brutal techniques. Prisoners are disposable assets. The administration's ideology was that it was in a permanent state of exclusion from the law. So it had no problem ignoring the antitorture statute that in 1994 made the UN Convention Against Torture part of the U.S. criminal code. In a strange public relations stunt, President Bush, in an April 2005 press conference, stated that the U.S. government would use "diplomatic assurances" that individuals subject to rendition would not be tortured. In practice, government officials and the CIA knew that it was nothing more than verbal assurance by the host government that torture was off the table. Such assurances from a country like Egypt, where torture was endemic, were almost comical.

Another tool enabling the international expansion of the American police state are private armies and unprecedented growth of privatized military firms. These firms embody supermilitarism, selling war making to the highest bidder. Mercenary armies enable empire building by outsourcing services previously performed by the military and freeing traditional combat forces to conquer and control territory. Mercenaries are as old as war itself; what's new is how the United States uses them to serve an antidemocratic function. The trend has accelerated with every post-cold war military operation. As terrorism replaced Communism as the chief global menace, demand increased to confront threats from individuals and organizations moreso than from standing armies. The lines between freedom fighters, civilians, terrorists, and criminals blurred; all were suspected enemies of the state. By the end of the cold war, ex-soldiers constituted a ready labor force, and massive amounts of weapons were for sale.

After 9/11, privatized war making allowed the Bush administration to use the military as the democratic expression of U.S. national security interests while a private army performed some police state measures. These firms, unconcerned with the rule of law and the Geneva Conventions, can target anyone as an enemy of the state, functioning as secret "shock troops" without accountability. They allowed the executive branch to carry out secret operations unilaterally. "Congress only has authority over official authority, not over private entities."[26] With privatized military firms, violence without restraint is inevitable. They treat resistance as a license to take revenge. In Iraq, mercenaries unleashed a steady stream of violence in many instances, against civilians. At Abu Ghraib, private military employees were deeply involved in abuse and torture. The administration's partnership with private military firms was no accident: all of the translators and as many as half of the interrogators at Abu Ghraib were private contractors; they were implicated in nearly 40 percent of abuse incidents at the prison.[27] There is ample evidence that private armies in Iraq had a license to shoot and kill without repercussions not just Iraqis but also U.S. marines, killing for a sadistic thrill, "contractors set video of themselves shooting at civilians to Elvis' song 'Runaway Train' and put it on the Internet, the alleged joy ride shootings of Iraqi civilians by a Triple Canopy supervisor."[28]

Blackwater was granted its first government contract during the Clinton administration. From Clinton to Bush, the expanding police state resulted partly from use of these firms, which fit the strategy of expanding state power overseas. The U.S. government's power was being measured by its ability to reshape global relations. Rumsfeld wanted to transform the military to fight quick, compact wars, using fewer troops, high-tech weapons systems, and increased reliance on the private sector. Rumsfeld's colleague and ally was Dick Cheney, who, as head of Haliburton, had made the company a primary provider of support services for the military overseas. The police state grew by incorporating corporate firms into war making. The U.S. government made foreign policy outside the public sector, without Congress and without assessing the wishes of the American people. Domestic and international politics were defined as the imposition of the administration's will by force; the new norm is to have no accountability to the public. Blackwater claimed that its soldiers were civilians and thus weren't subject to the Uniform Code of Military Justice; it also said they were immune from civil litigation. First hired to protect occupation officials, under Paul Brenner, Bush's envoy early in the occupation, Blackwater was later granted special privileges. The most important of these was the Brenner decree, issued on June 28, 2004, which immunized contractors in Iraq from prosecution. When Rumsfeld's small mobile military proved unable to maintain control in Iraq, Blackwater filled the void with the "contactor brigade," recruiting private soldiers through a division called Greystone Limited. These individuals weren't acquainted with the treatment of civilians in wartime; they came from countries with histories of military rule and gross human rights abuses, such as the Philippines, Chili, El Salvador, Panama, and Peru. Some had served in Pinochet's brutal regime. The personnel filling positions in Blackwater had the idea that might makes right, a philosophy that it demonstrated after Hurricane Katrina, which devastated New Orleans in 2005. Hired by the Department of Homeland Security, Blackwater's employees operated outside legal guidelines, unimpeded by adherence to the First and Fourth amendment rights of citizens. Blackwater operatives moved in and out of neighborhoods, free to stop anyone and take any action without questions.

In Iraq, Blackwater soldiers functioned as shock troops, sending the message that force can and will be used; and killing of civilians is an option. Blackwater's intrusion into the city of Fallujah was intended to send the message that this private army could control the city. This didn't happen. U.S. troops had killed Iraqi civilians, and the citizens of Fallujah took revenge on the contractors. Blackwater's mercenaries tried and failed to use shock troop techniques on Fallujah. More alarming was Blackwater's attempt to assume command of regular U.S. troops in Najaf. In the midst of the fighting, there were accounts of Blackwater's men giving orders to American soldiers, even on when to fire. These instances reveal the extent to which a private army became a functioning part of the occupation while being able to lobby for the use of more powerful weapons.

While there were few formal checks on the CIA and the FBI, none existed on Blackwater. It acted as a private army for special operations, such as extending American empire building, especially to gain access to oil reserves. It's no coincidence that Blackwater was dispatched to the oil-rich Caspian region to assist in establishing a base. The Clinton and both Bush administrations knew the importance not only of gaining control of the oil but of shaping regimes in the ex-Soviet republics, through which the oil would flow. The push was on to set up a pipeline from Tajikistan through Afghanistan, hence the American interest in supporting Kazahistan and Azerbaijan. For the Clinton administration, this meant supporting the antidemocratic regime in Azerbaijan. From Azerbaijan's capital, Baku, a large pipeline would ship oil to Tbilisi, Georgia, then Turkey and the port city of Cehhan, where it could be sent to the United States and other Western nations. With a military presence, the United States could exercise control in these ex-Soviet republics and Russia. But the pipeline would be vulnerable to attacks, given its proximity to Chechnya and Iran, which harbored strong anti-United States, anti-Western sentiments. Two factors were essential: friendly regimes and a mobile fighting force. The first requirement was met when President Bush reestablished U.S. military aid in 2003 to Azerbaijan and provided supplemental military aid to Kazahistan. Blackwater trained an elite Azerbaijan fighting force to protect American oil interests and prepare to establish a base for staging possible attacks against Iran. Blackwater partnered with the U.S. government to conduct empire building at the expense of democracy. Blackwater also may have played a role in renditions; many of its planes were spotted at airports believed to be involved in the program. Its planes operated out of Bagrum, the U.S. torture institution in Afghanistan. It may be a coincidence, but given Blackwater's super-secret contracts and ties to the CIA, a role in renditions wouldn't be surprising.

Inside the United States, Blackwater was well suited to an authoritarian role, using force against the masses. In New Orleans after Hurricane Katrina on August 29, 2005, Blackwater acted as an invading army in enemy territory: "150 heavily armed Blackwater troops dressed in full battle gear spread out into the chaos of New Orleans...Some patrolled the streets in SUVs with tinted windows and the Blackwater logo splashed on the back; others sped around the French Quarter in an unmarked car with no license plates. They wore khaki uniforms, wraparound sunglasses, beige or black military boots and had Blackwater company IDs strapped to their bulging arms. All of them were heavily armed—some with M-4 automatic weapons capable of firing 900 rounds per minute or shotguns."[29] A private army had taken over the streets of New Orleans, armed with weapons suited to a war zone. While the residents desperately needed food, water, and shelter,

Blackwater provided men with guns. This set a dangerous precedent: the domestic use of mercenaries who acted above the law, with no understanding of the rights of citizens and legal procedures; it appealed to the Bush administration's goal of further instilling police state measures inside the United States. With Blackwater in New Orleans, the administration sidestepped the Posse Comitatus Act, which prohibits U.S. troops from assuming the role of law enforcement officials.

One year later, the use of a private army in Iraq had reached an unprecedented level, evidence that even military force had become a tool to be used by political elites. "By Rumsfeld's last day in office, the ratio of active-duty U.S. soldiers to private contractors deployed in Iraq had almost reached one to one, a statistic unprecedented in modern warfare."[30] It was the ultimate realization of the Bush administration police state: A private government run by the few now had its own private army, the complete subversion of democracy. It exhibited a will to dominate and an obvious hostility to principles of human rights and rule of law, especially through its secret recruitment of soldiers "in some of the shadiest human-rights abusing locales on the planet."[31]

For all that has transpired under the Bush administration, what is the future of the American police state? The past may offer some guidance. After 9/11, with the so-called war on terror, the administration operated as a state within a state. By creating the essential national emergency and the fear to go with it, the Bush administration, in a short period, achieved the ability to wield absolute power with congressional approval. Congress legitimized this police state by generating legal fictions, legislation violating the Constitution. The administration then had a free hand to encroach upon all parts of government, whether it was the Justice Department or the CIA, to meet its goal of fighting terrorism while using government to dominate the thoughts and actions of U.S. and foreign citizens. One thing seems certain in tracing the history of how America became a police state: the final version formed during the Bush administration was extreme. The policies it enacted domestically and overseas exceeded those of previous administrations. But such extremism would prove self-destructive. During the second G.W. Bush term, police state practices were becoming dysfunctional. Officials began acknowledging in private that torture wasn't producing reliable intelligence. Insiders began to question accepted policy. Ashcroft and Comey's resistance to reauthorizing the Patriot Act was a recognition on some level of the breakdown of official policy, as were Goldsmith's efforts to undo the Yoo torture memo. Both the media and the American public were shocked by the police state policies, from the torture exposed at Abu Ghraib to the NSA surveillance program. As much as the power of the police state depended on excessive secrecy, it wasn't absolute. Whenever the secrecy and oppressive measures were exposed, support diminished. Yet, for all the revelations, so much remains hidden, allowing such practices to continue. Most troubling is the historical record. If the historical advance of the police state tells us anything, it is that once in place, oppressive police state practices generally remain. Toward the end of the Bush administration, some of the more extreme police state practices began to be scaled back, a trend that continues with the Obama administration. This trend can be viewed as a moderation, not an elimination of the police state. When the police state is fully developed, self-destructive tendencies appear. Whether it was the war on Iraq or the economic meltdown, the Bush administration, for all of its authoritarianism, became unable to govern. This led to a questioning of certain elements of the Bush administration police state. A regime based on a rigid chain of command did not tolerate asking questions or offering alternatives; as a result, there was a breakdown; extremist policies were proving unworkable. The police state of the Bush administration became dysfunctional.

Various courts had questioned the administration acting outside the rule of law. The Supreme Court 5–4 ruling in *Boumediene* asserted that the detainees at Guantanamo should have a right to habeas corpus, ruling against the use of Combatant Status Review Tribunals. Several justices challenged the premise that the administration had the right to determine the meaning of the Constitution. A majority of justices also was clear in challenging the administration's key assumption that the government has the right to suspend due process in a national emergency. Also called into question was the practice of implementing "arbitrary imprisonments" without due process. The court's ruling in *Boumediene* undercut the justification for the Military Commissions Act of 2006, which legalized the removal of habeas corpus rights. The Court understood that if that provision remained, detainees who went to trial would appear in a kangaroo court.

In another case, Ricardo M. Urbina of the federal district court ordered the release of 17 Chinese prisoners, members of Western China's Uighur Muslim minority, who had been in Guantanamo Bay for seven years. Like so many Guantanamo prisoners, they were never charged with any crime. The general charge was guilt by association. The Justice Department had determined that members of the Uighur Muslim minority belonged to a group identified as a terrorist entity; therefore, no proof of terrorist involvement was necessary. The judge's ruling was influenced by the Supreme Court's *Boumediene* ruling, allowing detainees a right to have federal judges review the reasons for their detention. In fact, since *Boumediene*, of 23 detainees who had habeas corpus hearings in federal court, the government has won only 3. But while federal courts and the Supreme Court questioned the administration's arbitrary suspension of due process, they were essentially powerless when Congress and the administration sidestepped the rulings.

Less than one month before the Obama administration came into office, Congress released an important Senate panel report, connecting abuse and torture at Abu Ghraib, Guantanamo Bay, and other sites to top Bush administration officials. The report, issued by Senators Carl Levin and John McCain, provided the first in-depth look at the interrogation techniques that the administration authorized. Of particular significance was the report's linking of policies formulated by Rumsfeld to officials at the Defense Department. It concluded that the abuse and torture of Abu Ghraib prisoners was not due to a "few bad apples" but was authorized by Rumsfeld and other top officials; it also contained details on the use of SERE. But federal court rulings and the Senate panel's findings limited which police state practices became public. The government's willingness to investigate police state measures that remained secret was still a question.

CHAPTER 8

The Future?

A glimmer of hope seemed to appear shortly after President Obama took office. His administration issued an executive order, outlining in broad terms the intention to close Guantanamo Bay within a year. It called for a ban on torture, ordered the CIA to close secret prisons, and review the cases of Guantanamo prisoners. It also required that Defense Secretary Gates ensure that within 30 days, conditions at Guantanamo would follow the Geneva Conventions. There were indications that aspects of it were followed. But a closer look exposes limits and resistance to reforming police state practices. While the executive order signified a general policy statement, officials in the Obama administration were looking into including a loophole that would allow the CIA to use interrogation methods not authorized by the Pentagon. The administration also has not addressed the use of extraordinary rendition and leaves the door open to enhanced interrogation techniques. Appearances can also be deceiving, as in the policies being adapted by Obama's attorney general, Eric Holder, who ordered a review of Bush administration claims of state secrets to withhold information from defendants to circumvent lawsuits. According to Justice Department spokesman Matt Miller, the attorney general directed Justice Department officials to review claims of state secrets that could be used only in legally appropriate situations. And consider Justice Department actions in a San Francisco federal appeals court over a lawsuit regarding the CIA's extraordinary rendition program. *Mohamed et al v. Jeppesen Dataplan* was a lawsuit brought by the ACLU, regarding terror suspects who were abducted to other countries to be interrogated and tortured. Banyan Mohamed, an Ethiopian national, was abducted in June 2002 from Pakistan to Morocco, where he was detained and tortured for 18 months. During the Bush administration, the ACLU's lawsuit was thrown out of the courts on the grounds of state secrets. In the San Francisco courtroom, Eric Holder's Justice Department invoked the same argument. So, according to the Obama administration, the CIA still had the right to carry out extraordinary renditions. Also troubling was the gulf between executive order 13491 and its implementation. The order clearly stated that the United States will abide by domestic laws and international obligations. But the Bush administration loophole that there's no guarantee that persons sent elsewhere would be free from abuse and torture continued in the Obama administration. Like its predecessor, the Obama administration was not following the International Covenant on Civil, Political Rights ratified in 1992, which prohibited sending individuals elsewhere to face degrading treatment and torture. Executive Order 13491 also states that the CIA shouldn't establish detention facilities, imprisoning people for indefinite periods. Nonetheless, its vague language refers to short term and transitory periods, which could turn out to be indefinite. And incoming CIA director Leon Panetta saw Executive Order 13491 as a virtual blank check to use extraordinary renditions, noting during his confirmation hearings, "I will seek the same kinds of assurances that they will not be treated inhumanely." This is no different from Bush administration policies: a wink and a nod to would-be torturers. When questioned about the execution of prisoners who were subjected to rendition during the Clinton administration, Panetta responded, "I think that this is an appropriate use of rendition." So despite official statements, a degree of continuity exists between some Bush administration policies and those of the Obama administration. The ACLU sued the government to release Justice Department memos regarding CIA interrogation methods authorized from 2002 to 2005 and used at CIA black sites. Their release, in April 2009, points to the forces at work in the Obama administration. In many ways, these memos were the "smoking gun" as to the illegal nature of the Bush police state. Political pressure was brought to bear on the Obama administration from organizations determined to use the courts to expose the extremism and fanaticism of the Bush police state. The memos reflect a willingness to unleash sadistic, cruel techniques because the victims were identified as less than human; this explains why the memos discussed repeated use of torture even without tangible benefits leading to actionable intelligence. The memos characterize the techniques as having been used with cruel detachment, a technocratic experiment, and yet the torturers were well aware of the outcome. Torture, as practiced and described in the memos, is the insanity of a police state, the committing of an act over and over and expecting a different result. Such was the case with the ongoing torture of Zubaydah; the memos said that he had been waterboarded 183 times, indicating that the CIA was not primarily interested in seeking information. It also demonstrates how inured state officials had become to the suffering of others—White House officials, the leadership of the Senate, and the House intelligence committees never researched the origins of the techniques they approved. They acted unaware of the SERE program and unaware that the United States had prosecuted the use of waterboarding as a war crime after World War II, even that the practice started during the Spanish Inquisition. While officials chose to ignore torture's history, CIA director George Tenet was investigating how SERE might be used against terrorists. He ignored the assessments of SERE trainers that such techniques could increase a prisoner's resistance or lead to unreliable information. All levels of the administration were in agreement about using torture. Even when dissident voices questioned its use, focusing on the moral and legal issues, such as Philip Zelikow, Secretary of State Rice's policy representative to the NSC, his misgivings were ignored.

That it took a lawsuit by the ACLU to force the release of the Justice Department memos was a troubling, early indication of the Obama administration's reluctance to confront the police state practices it inherited. Administration officials seemed well aware that the memos were the tip of the iceberg. Even CIA Director Leon Panetta concedes that release of the memos was only the beginning. Equally troubling was Congress' response, in particular, Representative Leahy's proposal for a Truth Commission, which in many ways, would result in a legal whitewash, providing documentation of events and little else. A Truth Commission would, in the end, accomplish little more than the Church Committee after Watergate, preserving the authoritarian nature of executive power, leaving untouched the excessive secrecy and illegal activities of antidemocratic federal agencies.

The Obama administration's response to the memos was similar to the initial response to exposures during Watergate. In both instances, there was initial resistance to enacting even superficial reforms. Attorney General Holder said, "It would be unfair to prosecute dedicated men and women working to protect America for conduct that was sanctioned by DOJ." In a well-planned public relations move, President Obama visited the CIA personally to reassure the agency with a "move forward" message. Once documents were released, he appeared to backtrack, responding to criticism that he was essentially letting off the hook rank and file torturers and raising the possibility of an investigation of White House attorneys who signed the memos. Obama then officially deferred to his attorney general, claiming that it was up to him to make a final determination.

The Obama administration followed historical precedent in not directly addressing police state practices, especially in its great reluctance to address the overall criminal nature of the Bush administration in waging its war on terrorism. The Obama administration, like others before it, has so far avoided dealing in any meaningful way with the erosion of democracy. At least, post-Watergate reforms attempted to confront the concentration and abuse of power within the federal government. But the Obama administration has avoided meaningful reform. Consider its lack of response to the Levin report. The 230-page document contains numerous references documenting rampant criminal activities coordinated from top to bottom, especially the illegal use of torture. The report reveals that torture began in December 2001, almost one year before the writing of the infamous Justice Department memos, authorizing its use. Also that month, the Defense Department gathered information from its Joint Personnel Recovery Agency, which had trained military personnel subjected to extreme interrogation through SERE; the program was employed against detainees at Guantanamo Bay, Abu Ghraib, and Bagram. In response, Obama advocated a 9/11-style commission, remarking that he worried "about this getting so politicized that we cannot function effectively and it hampers our ability to carry out critical national security operations." The mantra of a police state is that security always trumps civil liberties. The report also refers to how authorization defied national and international laws. One section reveals how a September 7, 2002, memorandum that President Bush signed amounted to the suspension of the Geneva Conventions. Back on October 11, 2001, Major General Michael Dunleavy, then Commander of Guantanamo Bay, had requested permission to employ enhanced interrogation techniques. The Levin report and other sources say his request reached Haynes, who suggested that Rumsfeld authorize 15 interrogation techniques. Rumsfeld did, and Guantanamo officials soon established standard operating procedures for SERE techniques, including stress positions; forced nudity of detainees; and slapping, pushing, and hurling them against the wall. A few months later, the report says that enhanced interrogation methods became standard operating procedure elsewhere.

The report further proves how the Bush administration's use of torture as state policy amounted to a criminal conspiracy of like-minded authoritarians, proving that it functioned as a police state. John Yoo of the Justice Department Office of Legal Counsel wrote the memorandum granting authority to government officials to use torture and participated in meetings organized by Counsel to the President Alberto Gonzalez and David Addington, counsel to Vice President Cheney; the topic was how to use the August 2002 memos authorizing torture and to develop legal foundations for CIA interrogation techniques. The Levin report clearly establishes that the administration turned the law upside down, reinterpreting laws that prohibited what the government was authorizing. Michael Chertoff of the criminal division of the Justice Department had, in fact, advised CIA general counsel Scott Muller and his deputy John Rizzo that the August 1, 2002, memo gave interrogators immunity from prosecution when they torture. Despite this evidence, the Obama administration still appeared unwilling to acknowledge the criminality pervading all levels of government and its contribution to a police state.

In police states, medical professionals allow others to experience pain and suffering. The Levin report refers to events that took place on April 16, 2002, three and one-half months before the Yoo-Bybee memos were written. A military psychologist had devised a means to use interrogation methods originally employed by Chinese Communists during the Korean War. In May 2009 on National Public Radio, Bryce Lefever had no problem justifying his recommendation of torture as nothing more than a natural reaction of SERE psychologists to the 9/11 attacks.

Also troubling was the American Psychological Association's extensive support for the torture program; it stated: "Psychologists have a critical role in keeping interrogations safe, legal, ethical and effective," but the Levin report said psychologists had the opposite effect. In March 2002, psychologists were in the forefront, introducing waterboarding and other SERE methods, running training courses in torture at Guantanamo Bay. OLC memos illustrated how psychologists rationalized their roles, asserting that the techniques did not violate statutes because they didn't lead to lasting mental harm. The presence of medical professionals was supposed to safeguard against any permanent harm being inflicted on victims. Psychologists who participated in torture subscribed to the mistaken belief that they could shield themselves behind APA ethical standards, which in the end, proved akin to hiding behind a Nuremberg defense. Like the Nuremberg defendants, psychologists became complicit in torture when simply following orders. But the Nuremberg defense only partially explains the role of psychologists; they were in a close working partnership with federal agencies, devising and implementing torture techniques as well as observing them.[1] Although the Church Committee recommendations proved inadequate to halt the evolution of an American police state; at least various reforms were put forth and for a time taken seriously. The Levin report merely recorded the past administration's violations of the law.

The Obama administration's position that amnesty should be granted to those who tortured as well as those who authored the torture memos, itself violates national and international law; it also ensures that such policies will likely be repeated. The Bush and Obama administrations have accepted the doctrine of following the orders of superiors, a defense rejected at Nuremberg and the My Lai massacre trial. In avoiding widely acknowledged national and international statutes on torture, the Obama administration is now complicit in accepting the use of such measures. Its failure to address the Bush administration's criminal nature indicates that the police state is truly permanent.

As of summer 2009, the rejection of a special prosecutor could be seen as stemming in part from unwillingness among congressional Democrats to confront the police state policies of the Bush administration out of fear that they, too, could be found complicit. In a May 8, 2009, article in the *Washington Post*, intelligence officials released documents pointing to evidence that House Speaker Nancy Pelosi had been briefed in December 2002 on the use of harsh interrogation techniques on al Qaeda suspects, in particular, Zubaydah. Other Democrats briefed in 2002 included Senators Graham of Florida and Rockefeller of West Virginia, and, in 2003, Rep. Harmon of California. These revelations indicate that members of Congress knew about the use of torture and that Senate and House intelligence committees were briefed on the use of harsh interrogation techniques. Another indication of how difficult it is to roll back police state policies are the discussions about reactivating Guantanamo's military commission system, yet another reversal of the Obama administration's suspension of the commissions after the inauguration. There is an eerie similarity between the reasoning of Obama administration lawyers and arguments made by the Bush administration. "The more they look at it," said one Obama administration official, "the more commissions don't look as bad as they did on January 20." While the Obama administration issued public statements toying with the idea of piecemeal reform of the Bush police state, it also preserved many of its elements, indicating a preference for a modified police state. Evidence appears in the Obama administration's acceptance of Appendix M of the Army Field Manual, which permits the use of techniques, which the administration believes should be used in the war on terror, such as solitary confinement, perceptual or sensory deprivation, sleep deprivation, inducement of fear, sensory overload, and temperature or environmental manipulation. The administration also preserved the category of enemy combatants, leaving open the possibility of continuing to use extraordinary renditions. And there are still functioning CIA black sites. Obama and Holder have both said waterboarding is torture, a crime according to U.S. and international law and yet, as of summer 2009, there were no indications that the administration was investigating for possible prosecution any Bush administration officials.

Regarding the return of habeas corpus for prisoners at Bagrum, the following remark by a federal judge shows that the Obama administration has not made a clean break: "Having considered the matter, the government adheres to its previously articulated position." The Obama administration also did not embrace the rule of law regarding the ACLU suit against Jeppesen Dataplan Inc., a Boeing subsidiary, essentially the CIA's travel agent in the extraordinary rendition and torture program. It invoked essentially the same defense in U.S. Circuit Court as the Bush administration, that state secrets must be protected to protect national security.

The Obama administration merely modified police state practices. In May 2009, Attorney General Holder stated that the administration's review of 30 prisoners about to be set free should again be reviewed as part of a larger number of 60 prisoners also about to be released. Close to 40 were about to be released since their case files had been examined by a number of military review boards at Guantanamo; others were to be released based on court rulings. Instead, the administration intervened, believing it had the right to second-guess both the courts and the military review boards, acting as the final legal authority. This action implies that the administration's authority supersedes that of the courts and the rights of defendants to exercise a right of habeas corpus. Most important, such actions delay these prisoners' release, and procedures in place are far from guaranteeing that once released, they would not be targeted again. The administration has accepted its predecessor's abstract definition of terrorism and its reserving of the right to seize and detain anyone, whether a U.S. citizen or noncitizen even in the absence of an association with, or participation in, terrorist activities.

Also troubling is its interest in reviving the military commissions, which sidestep habeas corpus. Accepting preventive detention is another police state carryover; in a statement to the Senate Appropriations Committee, Secretary of Defense Gates described many remaining prisoners at Guantanamo as "the 50 to 100...probably in that ballpark, who we cannot release and cannot try." He said this despite the fact that these individuals were illegally seized, detained, and tortured. The theory behind preventive detention is that the state has the authority to assume total control over individuals and groups, based only on predictions that they pose a possible future danger. While these prisoners remain in legal limbo, they are still subjected to torture. So while the Obama administration evades its legal obligation to investigate, Spain has begun its own investigation, exposing ongoing torture at Guantanamo Bay, documenting such practices as waterboarding, blows to the testicles, detention of prisoners underground in complete darkness while being denied food and water, and being smeared with feces. According to the Spanish inquiry's preliminary findings, torture was implemented during both the Bush and Obama administrations, under the authority of American military personnel and with the active assistance of medical personnel. The Obama administration also has failed to halt the use of IRF (Immediate Reaction Force) squads in Guantanamo, MPs on standby to respond quickly to any emergency to confront, by forced extraction, a prisoner who appears noncompliant or resistant. IRFs became standard operating procedure in May 2003. Once called in, the IRF has a primary role in torturing prisoners during interrogations, routinely gagging and beating prisoners, forcing their heads into toilets, breaking bones, gouging eyes, and slamming prisoners' heads onto concrete floors. Since they can strike any time, their purpose is terrorizing prisoners. There are documented accounts of prisoners who committed suicide in response to repeated IRF abuse. Although hundreds of hours of videotaped recordings documented IRF abuses, they have been destroyed. There has been no abandonment of IRF brutality during the Obama administration.

The administration also has not addressed the ghost prisoners held in CIA black sites, whose status is unknown. Official estimates indicate that the CIA has imprisoned at least 94 individuals, 28 of whom were subjected to torture. Neither administration has made public these prisoners' whereabouts or identities or the extent to which they pose a threat. During the summer of 2006, even after the Bush administration acknowledged that CIA black sites exist and announced the end of the program, prisoners were transferred to Pakistan, Egypt, and Jordan.

To this day, the Obama administration has yet to acknowledge their whereabouts and status; it has neither released the names of prisoners mistreated and tortured at Bagram Air Force Base nor the length of their prison terms; nor are they allowed to challenge their imprisonment. Many of Bagram's prisoners have been detained for six years without access to attorneys.

The Obama administration appears content to preserve the FISA Amendments Act, another police state holdover, which regards all citizens as potential enemies of the state. These amendments give the government the authority to monitor U.S. citizens' telecommunications, mail, and e-mail, without having to identify the suspects' names or groups; all ideas become suspect. The act excludes significant judicial oversight to ensure civil liberties protections. The FISA Court, which is supposed to oversee the program, is a rubberstamp, allowing the government a legal license to engage in surveillance of private citizens. The amendments place no limits on how the government uses and stores the data. They also grant immunity to the telecoms, which partnered with the government to secretly spy on citizens.

Police state culture also is evident in the use of a new system to report suspicious activity in the guise of discovering terrorist plots. In Boston, Chicago, Miami, New York, and Los Angeles, police officers now fill out "Terror Tipsheets," detailing activities that seem to be out of the ordinary. By 2014, federal and state officials will have established a national reporting system using special codes to identify and monitor a broad category of suspicious behaviors: in particular, those subject to police officials engaging in surveillance with binoculars or cameras. Also subject to surveillance, according to these guidelines, are individuals or organizations that espouse extremist views, support terrorism, brag about affiliation with extremist organizations, or display support for known terrorist networks, even possessing posters of terrorist leaders or possessing or soliciting information about sensitive events or schedules of such events.

Public statements by former administration officials, such as Jay Bybee, in which he supported the memos that authorized torture, have been met at the very least, with tolerance while the Spanish government, in particular, Spanish Judge Baltazar Garzon, pursues a criminal investigation into the Bush administration's conspiracy to commit torture, a program that targeted Spanish nationals. Another reaction to the Obama administration's failure to follow its legal obligations was expressed by Manfred Nowak, an Austrian serving as the UN Special Rapporteur on Torture: "the United States had committed itself under the UN Convention Against Torture to make torture a crime and to prosecute those suspected of engaging in it." He said this in response to the Obama administration's decision that CIA officials should evade prosecution for their participation in the torture of terrorist suspects.

If not for the ACLU Freedom of Information Act lawsuit, the existence of additional torture photographs would have remained secret. Prior to assuming office, Obama pledged to initiate policies of openness and transparency. But confronted with choosing politics or the law, he chose the former, speaking and acting much the way his predecessor did, diminishing the importance of the photographs and most of all, mimicking the Bush argument that the abuses were the acts of a few rotten apples, and that those responsible had been prosecuted. Both statements couldn't be further from the truth. Obama's most startling claim, identical to one Bush made, was that the release of these photographs would somehow jeopardize national security. Federal courts have soundly rejected that argument. Failure to release them continues the Bush policy of punishing a few scapegoats at the lowest levels while top officials get off scot-free. The photographs could illustrate just how comprehensive was the Bush administration's systemic pattern of prisoner torture and abuse. These personal snapshots taken by soldiers could provide evidence for investigating prisoner torture and abuse of prisoners. But like its predecessor, the Obama administration did not accept the ruling of the U.S. Court of Appeals for the Second Circuit, arguing that a larger public interest would best be served over any abstract or possible threat to U.S. troops.

Legal grounds for a criminal investigation can be found in various federal laws, such as the War Crimes Act; the Anti-Torture Act; and specific federal laws, which criminalize abuse and mistreatment carried out by U.S. officials in overseas facilities. Common Article 3 of the Geneva Conventions provides legal protection for prisoners, which was not provided due to CIA and military personnel who committed torture on the detainees. Unless circumstances force the Obama administration to act soon, the perpetrators can count on the clock running out as statutes of limitations kick in. This applies to the many possible criminal charges that could be leveled against the Bush administration police state, including the manufacture of evidence to wage an aggressive war; the misleading of Congress; the secret surveillance programs; attempts to cover up crimes through secret memos and executive orders; neutralizing existing laws; and the destruction of evidence, such as tapes documenting torture.

Under Section 371, the Obama administration has five years in which to charge the perpetrators. Regarding the torture statute, 2340A, Bush administration officials could be charged with committing torture and being involved in a conspiracy to commit torture. The clock started ticking on January 20, 2009. In accordance with Section 3286, which was changed during the adoption of the Patriot Act, there are eight years in which to prosecute. It contains strict and significant references to those who commit torture, assist in committing torture, conspire to torture, or commit torture that results in the victim's death. These provisions are very similar to the principles of the Nuremberg Trials. For crimes against humanity, crimes and war crimes as described in subsection 3286, there is no statute of limitations. Furthermore, there are legal grounds to appoint a Special Counsel to investigate. Attorney General Holder could justify such an appointment based on sufficient circumstantial evidence to initiate an investigation, the need to go outside the Justice Department, and the fact that the Department has been so tainted by involvement in possible criminal acts. Above all, the attorney general can justify a Special Counsel on the grounds that it serves the public interest and the rule of law.

It remains to be seen whether or not enough pressure would mount to create a special prosecutor and what would be the outcome. If past history holds any sway, superficial reforms only accelerate the growth of a police state. To be truly meaningful, reforms would have to be implemented so that at the bare minimum, they would change the nature of the state itself, rejecting empire building at the expense of democracy, making America a truly legitimate mass-based democracy. Until the police state's final formation during the Bush administration, there was still a semblance of procedural democracy. But as events unfolded, the other branches of government, which were supposed to check the executive branch's ever-increasing power, actually contributed to further concentrating it. Reformist measures enacted especially after Watergate contributed toward the further growth of power within the executive branch. By far, the most glaring reform was the creation of the FISA court.

The Obama administration is, once again, exhibiting the same historical tendency to use superficial reformism to attempt to curb extremist policies without addressing the root causes of the Bush administration police state. There will not be fundamental changes to the missions of federal agencies whose functions are hostile to mass democracy at home and overseas. Many of the most extremist policies will remain secret unless uncovered by accident or through investigative reporting; and any reforms will be implemented slowly, allowing opposing forces to mobilize and dilute them, forcing the victims to continue to be victimized. While the debate unfolded over what to do with Guantanamo's remaining detainees in March 2009, conditions continued to deteriorate. Many detainees went on a hunger strike, and in response, officials in Guantanamo tied them to chairs and force-fed them. There are accounts that some were beaten for resisting. There are accounts that there are so many detainees on a hunger strike that there is a shortage of chairs so the detainees are being force-fed in shifts. Human rights organizations had sent a joint letter to President Obama, requesting full access to Guantanamo prison; they are still waiting for a reply.

Those entrenched in the police state culture have resisted attempted reforms. The courts complied with Obama's Executive Order, halting the pretrial hearings of Omar Khadr and other co-defendants charged with conspiracy in the 9/11 attacks. Then, on January 29, the Military Commission's Chief Judge Army Colonel James M. Pohl refused to suspend the arraignment of Abdul Rahim Al-Nashiri, scheduled for February 9. The reason? He said that he found the Obama administration's argument, that time was needed to examine all the options, "an unpersuasive basis to delay the arraignment." Pohl's resistance was based on his support for the Military Commissions Act. He argued that the act was legal, passed by Congress, and was still in effect. Such entrenched police state resistance to policy changes was caused by the continuity of personnel from the Bush to Obama administrations. So while President Obama issued public statements to halt the "arbitrary justice" of the previous administration, officials in positions of authority were determined to maintain it. Susan Crawford, who has the power to suspend the arraignments of Guantanamo detainees, maintained close ties to Vice President Dick Cheney and his chief of staff, David Addington. Other Bush administration officials, Sandra Hodgkinson, a deputy assistant defense secretary for detainee affairs and special assistant Tara Jones, simply changed job titles in the Obama administration.

There is little support either from the Obama administration or Congress to expose the excessive secrecy, which masked the Bush administration's illegal activities, particularly, the partnership between the NSA and the phone companies to conduct surveillance on Americans. In July 2008, the Senate by a 69–28 vote granted the telecommunications companies legal immunity, which, even worse, ended up expanding the government's surveillance powers. The passage of that bill gave the executive branch broader authority to eavesdrop here and overseas on U.S. citizens believed to be connected to terrorist activities. While Obama had initially expressed opposition to granting legal immunity, he ended up voting for what he called "an improved but imperfect bill."

The so-called review of Bagram, where so much sadistic violence took place, does not propose closing it or address how to correct its gross human rights violations. Bagram guards routinely assaulted prisoners as revenge for the 9/11 attacks, unaware that the majority of those detained had no al Qaeda connections. The Bush administration refused to release the records of detainee treatment; likewise, the Obama administration has disclosed nothing about it either. There is no discussion of how to provide posthumous justice for two Afghan detainees, Habibullah and Dilawar, who were beaten to death in December 2002, just a reprimand of the Army captain in command at the time of the incidents. One soldier who severely beat Dilawar about 37 times just had his rank reduced despite the fact that he was found guilty of beating and maiming him. While ample evidence exists that the chain of command from Pentagon officials to the White House bore responsibility for what took place at Bagram, no one above the rank of captain has had to answer for it. No questions were raised as to Bush's role in creating the climate at Bagram by issuing an order in February 2002, denying prisoner of war status and basic Geneva Convention protections under Common Article 3, to captured Afghan prisoners. The lack of actionable prosecution proves that the institutional foundations of a police state will remain essentially undisturbed.

The Bush administration police state used force without accountability, a feature reinforced by the frequent use of private contractors, especially mercenaries employed by Blackwater. In particular, there was the September 16, 2007, killing of 17 Iraqi civilians in Bagram's Nisour Square. Despite the Justice Department review, there are no clear indications that Blackwater will be charged, and no legal action has been taken. President Obama has not supported prosecuting Blackwater nor has he sought to ban using such firms in wartime. It appears that Blackwater is above international law regarding the treatment of civilians in wartime. The Iraqi government wants to prosecute Blackwater, but it is immune from prosecution. It remains to be seen if Iraqi courts, under the new United States-Iraqi security pact, will put Blackwater under their jurisdiction. In the post-Bush administration era, Blackwater still operates within a police state culture, securing contracts and positioning itself as a leader in the murky world of privatized intelligence services. Its corporate interests correlate well with those of an American police state. Blackwater has "diversified" into the privatized security business, setting up a division with CIA-corporate types known as Total Intelligence. While Congress has minimal over-sight over CIA operations, there is no congressional oversight over the secret collaboration between Blackwater, the CIA, and the current administration. Blackwater (which changed its name to Xe) is one example of many companies that make up the vast mercenary Army industry. Others, such as Dyncorp and Triple Canopy, sent mercenaries to Iraq and Afghanistan. Unregulated and above the law, they also developed a reputation for targeting civilians and engaging in human rights violations. But halting the use of such mercenary armies might prove problematic for the Obama administration, given how stretched U.S. military forces are.

The ultimate measure of whether or not the Obama administration will roll back the police state will depend on whether or not there are prosecutions of Bush administration officials. Past history says this isn't likely; whether it was enslavement of African Americans; ethnocidal policies against American Indians; or the consistent, sometimes violent repression of dissent, government has generally not been held accountable. While Nixon left office and a few of Watergate's perpetrators were punished, the institutional arrangements involving the FBI and CIA that made Watergate possible remained. The imperial presidency was slowed but not halted. When the Iran-Contra conspirators violated the Constitution, President Bush senior pardoned them.

The Obama administration's impulse to "move on" is most telling. By moving forward, previous administrations helped solidify a police state. If President Obama decides not to prosecute Bush administration officials, he will have effectively contributed to the reproduction of a police state, stepping outside the law, violating his oath to uphold the Constitution, and "take care that the laws be faithfully executed." Remarks by former Vice President Cheney as to his involvement in supporting waterboarding further strengthen the case for prosecution. The Obama administration should investigate and prosecute numerous violations of national and international law, including the Iraq war, the abuse and torture of detainees, and the warrantless surveillance program. The manufactured evidence to support the Iraq war by itself is, according to the Nuremberg principles, evidence that the Bush administration engaged in a war of aggression, a war crime. Lying to go to war is nothing new, whether it was the Spanish-American War or the Vietnam War, but President Obama could send a message to dissuade future presidents from doing so. The abuse and torture of detainees violated the 1994 law passed by Congress against torture, the Geneva Conventions and the Universal Declaration of Human Rights. While stating his opposition to torture, Attorney General Holder has not taken a stand to investigate and prosecute perpetrators despite a legal obligation to prosecute Bush administration officials for violating the War Crimes Act of 1996, which outlaws the torture techniques those officials sanctioned. The Obama administration also should work with Congress to eliminate the Military Commissions Act of 2006, which provided pseudo-legal cover for torture techniques. This would go a long way toward restoring in principle and practice the cherished right of habeas corpus. The president, working with Congress, could then pass a similar version of the War Crimes Act to deter future administrations from engaging in torture. Since the rule of law is at stake, an investigation into how the Justice Department became a political tool of the White House is in order. Although FISA legally justified secret surveillance, it is still relevant to hold the Bush administration accountable for violating FISA. The cozy relationship between the NSA and the telecoms and the extent to which surveillance of U.S. citizens violated the Constitution also should be investigated and prosecuted. Forcing the NSA and the telecoms to reveal the full extent of their surveillance would help remove the veil of excessive secrecy, which characterizes a police state. Likewise, publicly exposing the torture of detainees under the Military Commissions Act would allow the United States to fulfill its legal obligations as a signer of the International Convention on Torture.

Nonetheless, Eric Holder echoes President Obama in stating, "we don't want to criminalize policy differences." Since when is support for a police state a policy difference? If there are investigations without prosecutions and punishments, the Obama administration will enable a police state to continue. There is no doubt that the Bush administration committed war crimes in Iraq, according to the International Red Cross and the Taguba Report. And it is questionable as to whether or not the Obama administration will investigate and prosecute possible war crimes committed by the military during the occupation against unarmed civilians. Early indications are not promising, given the free pass that private contractors Halliburton and Blackwater received. History reveals that prosecution of war crimes by the U.S. military has never amounted to much. Lieutenant Calley was the only person tried for the My Lai massacre, and though found guilty, his sentence was reduced; eventually, he went free. Perhaps Calley was a convenient scapegoat. But an act of courage from the Obama administration and Congress to investigate and prosecute war crimes in Iraq would undo the perception that the United States evaded responsibility for waging a war of aggression. An investigation also would expose the details of war crimes against the Iraqi people and how the war was conducted. Once the infrastructure was destroyed, many children in urban areas died from drinking contaminated water or suffered from acute food shortages and the lack of medical care. Such results are the opposite of behavior expected of an occupying power; they violated the Hague regulations and Geneva Conventions. The United States, as an occupying power, has an obligation to protect civilians, respect their human rights, and avoid reshaping the nation's political and economic systems.

Within the occupation's first weeks, U.S. forces implemented a massive takeover of Iraq's infrastructure, resulting in widespread destruction of museums, libraries, hospitals, schools, and electric utilities. There were irreplaceable losses to Iraq's national heritage. As the United States dismantled the Iraqi army and police, crime increased dramatically. The U.S. military conducted operations in populated areas, resulting in numerous civilian casualties, again violating international law. There was a lack of respect for basic human rights as U.S. forces failed to maintain public safety, conducted mass arrests and layoffs, established checkpoints, closed roads and whole villages, and demolished homes of innocent Iraqis.[2] Infrastructure was kept in a state of disrepair. During the occupation, even the U.S.-appointed health official stated that health services had significantly declined.[3] And the UN Food and Agricultural Agency reported that unemployment and rising food prices kept about 11 million Iraqis "food-insecure."[4]

Even the Obama administration's announcement to withdraw troops by 2010 is not such a significant break with the past. As with other U.S. interventions, the legacy has been to maintain some form of military presence. Consider the large number of military bases that the United States has around the globe, the after-effects of sending troops. Given Iraq's geographic importance as a source of oil and the fact that it now has one of the world's largest U.S. military bases, it is highly unlikely that the United States will eliminate its military presence. For all the corporate media's cheerleading of how successful the troop surge was and the so-called U.S. exit from Iraq, which is supposed to leave the country in better shape, there is ample evidence that Iraq is still suffering war's devastating impact. Its infrastructure is in shambles: U.S. reconstruction monies allocated only $18 billion for infrastructure reconstruction, and large amounts were used to confront Iraqi resistance to the occupation. Unemployment remains at 60 percent. Most Iraqis do not have access to safe drinking water, and children are particularly vulnerable to malnutrition. Iraqis also suffer from daily violence. Estimates of violent incidents in 2007–2008 were essentially unchanged from the presurge years. Around the time of the surge, Iraq was going through the world's worst refugee crisis with estimates ranging from 4–5 million Iraqis, and afterward, there was a dramatic increase of displaced persons. The Iraq Body Counts Assessments estimate that the occupation has caused the death rate to rise, reaching a total of 1.2 million in early 2008.

The 2010 Obama budget included some modest cuts in proposed exotic weapons systems, which were inevitable, given the 2009 economic crisis. Still, the United States continues to outspend many times over what the rest of the world spends on defense. Overall, the Obama administration is requesting more money for the Pentagon than the Bush administration. Its request for $20 billion exceeds what Congress requested. The focus on the economy allows the Obama administration not to pay serious attention to reforming the police state it inherited; it has authorized 17,000 additional troops for Afghanistan, and it's now possible that the United States could face another Vietnam-type quagmire. Also disturbing is the administration's position on military detainees held in Afghanistan. In making its case to a federal judge that they have no right to challenge their imprisonment, the Obama administration has adopted a key Bush administration position that the prisoners can be denied what their rights are in accordance with the Geneva Conventions.

The only real hope to averting full-blown police state practices during another national emergency is to prosecute the perpetrators. Prosecution could send a clear message, especially if the lawyers who set in motion many Bush police state practices found themselves criminally liable. There is legal precedent. In *U.S. v. Alstoether,* lawyers were convicted of war crimes and crimes against humanity for the advice they gave on how to construct legal cover, so as to make the enemies of the Third Reich disappear. Attorney General Holder could take the bold move to investigate and prosecute lawyers who provided the Bush administration's legal cover. An even more compelling case for prosecution can be made if it is uncovered that officials knew of their wrongdoing and sought legal cover. A report from the Senate Armed Services Committee concluded that "senior officials in the United States government solicited information on how to use aggressive techniques, redefined the law to create the appearance of their legality, and authorized their use against the detainees." If, on the other hand, Congress and the president agree to Senator Leahy's proposal for a Truth and Reconciliation Commission, the perpetrators would be given a get-out-of-jail-free card.

Another reason why the Obama administration may only enact superficial police state reforms is that police state culture has become a part of American society. Police state culture is all around us. In many ways, casinos are models of a police state culture in which surveillance is the norm. Las Vegas casinos were in the forefront of using high-tech surveillance in the 1950s through closed circuit television. Today, the casino is the quintessential culture of a police state because everybody is being watched by somebody. The issue is not that there are individuals seeking to rob casinos, it's the idea that everyone is a suspect and must be watched. Americans accept the fact that they are being watched; closed circuit television is everywhere. Drivers in many of America's cities are accustomed to being watched by closed circuit cameras on street corners, on poles, or attached to streetlights, recording all vehicles that pass by. Such monitoring leads to biased judgments of particular behaviors. The purpose of surveillance is so that watchers can take action against individuals who display certain behaviors. This is the goal of facial recognition technology, in which a determination is made based on the program in the camera to identify a specific criminal or terrorist profile. This so-called intelligent technology is at malls, ATM machines, banks, airports, government and public buildings, and schools. The goal of such technology is to control a range of behaviors, which are not criminal in nature. Watching people is ultimately about manipulating their behavior.

Advances such as radio frequency identification (RFID) reinforce police state surveillance; items containing the RFID computer chip emit signals, revealing when and where it was purchased and by whom. Such technology is replacing the barcode. As with all forms of surveillance, the goal of those in the business of watching people is directed toward controlling their future behavior. RFIDs also have uses in passports and other forms of identification, revealing behaviors and movements. Such information can be used to create profiles, classifying individuals, allowing those in authority to reward or punish, based on the classifications. Credit ratings provide pictures of financial behavior as do driving records, medical files, even marital status. The danger lies not only with the centralization and control of such records but with those who have access to them and the power to interpret what these data mean. Police state culture operates on the premise that in order to control people, they must conform to a certain set of behaviors. Corporate and political elites use data to define who we are. As a result, when corporations gather and distribute information, such "selling of information" appears as a neutral activity; it is not. For example, a product called Choice Point can gather and sell myriad records on individuals from motor vehicle, credit, and financial records to results on drug testing and employment background screening.[5] Police state culture seeks to dominate by not only knowing everything about us, through an invisible paper trail but also by tracking our movements. Spy satellites use heat sensing and imaging technologies to monitor and record our activities 24 hours a day; they are powerful enough to see through vehicles and even fortress-like buildings, regardless of conditions.[6] "Keyhole" is a government spy satellite that can view license plates and people walking in the street. The NSA's Echelon Program can monitor and assemble phone calls, faxes, e-mails, and telex messages; it can listen in on any transmission and conversation in the United States, Europe, Asia, and Africa.

Naturally, the computer has been in the forefront of monitoring people at work and at home. Systems bearing Big Brother names like Spy Agent, Web Stealth, Snoopstick, and Silent Watch, monitor the online activities of office workers. One service determines how much work and what kind is being performed on office computers, recording websites visited, e-mail transmissions, documents printed, even keystrokes typed.[7] The profit motive drives such monitoring for employers can determine how to make workers work longer and faster. It is one thing to use such programs when there could be a possibility of harm caused by certain computer practices, it's another when surveillance is used to treat everyone and any activity as suspect. Surveillance for the sake of surveillance is the essence of police state culture: everyone is looked upon as either a possible criminal or terrorist, without some tangible proof. It emerges from fear of the freedom upon which a democratic culture thrives. Democratic freedoms will lead to some abuse, but in a democratic society, the goal should be limiting only those who abuse freedom to prey on others. Democratic societies generate a kind of spontaneous anarchy, an unregulated license to invent novel modes of thought and action. A police state culture fears this, for such freedoms mean those in authority can lose control. Surveillance stresses conformity, the police state culture norm. That's why after the attacks of 9/11, there was a rush to put in place a national ID card or RealID. Under the authority of the Department of Homeland Security, all personal data would be stored in this one card. RealID wasn't adopted, but its purpose would be to determine who diverges from the norm.

A democratic culture allows people a realm of privacy. But in a police state, there is no sense of moving about anonymously in public spaces. Closed circuit TV is pervasive. Facial recognition technology is increasingly sophisticated, allowing police to identify political dissidents from images. Peoples' movements in public are tracked, through their cellular phones, which must communicate where they are to a base station to receive calls. The federal government has justified reasons for this: "in a recent order, the FCC confirmed that...Personal Communications Services (PCS) carriers would be required to disclose to law enforcement agents with wiretap authorization the location of a cell site at the beginning and termination of a mobile call."[8] Individuals are easily targeted inside their vehicles through the use of Intelligent Transportation Systems that help manage traffic, providing constant data on all moving vehicles in real-time. Thermal imaging reveals hot spots in buildings, allowing police to engage in warrantless surveillance not based on probable cause. These technologies invade even how we look underneath our clothing. The use of passive millimeter wave imaging at airports, using electromagnetic radiation of an object, amounts to a body search. Individuals can no longer expect to have privacy even under their clothing.

With the Bush administration, America reached a perfected form of police state, and while the Obama administration may initiate piecemeal reforms, it won't disassemble its essence. So what is the future of the American police state? Toward the end of the Bush administration, there were indications that the police state was becoming self-destructive. A police state's extremist elite politics make it vulnerable to an upsurge of mass democracy and might prove to be its ultimate downfall. We can take comfort in the words of Mahatma Gandhi: "There have been tyrants and murderers, and for a time they seem invincible, but in the end, they always fall. Think of it, always." The Obama administration will correct the self-destruction of the Bush police state through piecemeal reforms. Through this reformism, it may be possible to begin challenging police state practices, recreating and maintaining viable mass-based movements to restore rule of law and respect for the Constitution. Mass-based democracy could eventually craft a government, which rules for the masses, not political and economic elites. The challenge is to build on and expand the outrage against the Bush administration and the electoral alliance, which made the election of Obama possible. Building democracy from the bottom up should involve a state by state effort to construct progressive political movements. In the short run, it would mean maintaining ties to those in the Democratic party, who are responsive to issues that affect the public at large. Actions on specific issues could serve as a starting point to roll back police state practices: significantly cutting the

Pentagon budget; raising questions about the goals of U.S. foreign policy; opposing the sending of troops to Afghanistan; reducing tensions elsewhere, by seeking a genuine solution for the Israel/Palestine question; developing an economy not dependent on oil; holding accountable the financial sector for the ruthless pursuit of profit making; and channeling monies to uplift the downtrodden to create an economy that would truly reach full employment, allowing for greater unionization of workers. Pressure to adopt such measures may well increase as the economy continues to weaken. It is with the possible combination of a dysfunctional police state with a hint of reformism and the rising expectations of mass movements that America will finally rid itself of its police state.

NOTES

1 Growth of State Power and the Assault on Democracy

1. Terry Bouton, *Taming Democracy: The People, the Founders and the Troubling Ending of the American Revolution* (New York: Oxford University Press, 2007) p. 72.
2. Frances Fox Piven, *Challenging Authority: How Ordinary People Change America* (New York: Rowman and Littlefield, 2006) p. 49.
3. Fred Anderson and Andrew Cayton, *The Dominion of War: Empire and Liberty in North America, 1500–2000* (New York: Penguin Books, 2005) p. 190.
4. Howard Zinn, *A People's History of the United States* (New York: Harper Collins, 2003) p. 125.
5. Ibid.
6. Phil Lane, Jr. and Lenore Stiffarn, "The Demography of Native North America" in *The State of Native America*, M. Annette Jaimes (ed.) (Cambridge: South End Press, 1999) p. 31.
7. Sidney Lens, *The Forging of the American Empire: From the Revolution to Vietnam* (London: Pluto Press, 2003) p. 41.
8. Lane and Stiffarn, p. 33.
9. Lens, p. 41.
10. Ibid., p. 46.
11. Carol Hymowitz and Michaele Weissman, *A History of Women in America* (New York: Bantam Books, 1978) p. 277.
12. Ibid., p. 279.
13. Robert Justin Goldstein, *Political Repression in Modern America* (Chicago: University of Illinois Press, 2001) p. 19.
14. Ibid., p. 27.
15. Ibid., p. 35.
16. Ibid., p. 37.
17. Ibid., p. 39.
18. Ibid.
19. Stephen Kinzer, *Overthrow: America's Century of Regime Change from Hawaii to Iraq* (New York: Henry Holt, 2006) pp. 55–56.
20. Ibid., p. 52.
21. Ibid., p. 53.
22. Michael Hunt, *The American Ascendancy: How the United States Gained and Wielded Global Dominance* (Chapel Hill: University of North Carolina, Press 2007) p. 54.
23. Ibid., p. 71.
24. Ibid., p. 75.

2 Eroding Democracy in a Time of Crisis

1. Robert Justin Goldstein, *Political Repression in Modern America* (Chicago: University of Illinois Press, 2001) p. 67.
2. Ibid., p. 79.
3. Ibid., p. 86.
4. Ibid., p. 107.
5. Geoffrey Stone, *Perilous Times: Free Speech in Wartime* (New York: W. W. Norton, 2004) p. 156.
6. Ibid., p. 157.
7. Ibid., p. 182.
8. Goldstein, p. 109.
9. Ibid., p. 110.
10. Stone, p. 221.
11. Ibid., p. 223.
12. Goldstein, p. 152.
13. Frank Donner, *Protectors of Privilege: Red Squads and Police Repression in Urban America* (Berkeley: University of California Press, 1992) pp. 36–37.
14. Ibid., p. 35.
15. Goldstein, p. 183.
16. Weinstein, p. 135.
17. Frances Fox Piven, *Challenging Authority: How Ordinary People Change America* (New York: Rowman and Littlefield, 2006) p. 105.
18. Goldstein, p. 199.
19. Donner, p. 54.
20. Stone, p. 246.
21. Goldstein, p. 250.
22. Natsu Taylor Saito, *From Chinese Exclusion to Guantanamo Bay: Plenary Power and the Prerogative State* (Boulder: University of Colorado Press, 2007), p. 23.
23. Ibid., p. 61.
24. Ibid., p. 111.
25. Ibid., p. 103.
26. Goldstein, p. 273.

3 Accelerating the Assault on Mass Democracy

1. Robert Justin Goldstein, *Political Repression in Modern America* (Chicago: University of Illinois Press, 2001) p. 288.
2. Michael Hunt, *The American Ascendancy: How the United States Gained and Wielded Global Dominance* (Chapel Hill: University of North Carolina, Press 2007) p. 128.
3. Ibid., p. 132.
4. Ibid., p. 141.
5. Tim Weiner, *Legacy of Ashes: The History of the CIA* (New York: Anchor Books, 2008) p. 45.
6. Ibid., p. 87.
7. Hunt, p. 146.
8. Weiner, p. 207.
9. Stephen Kinzer, *Overthrow: America's Century of Regime Change from Hawaii to Iraq* (New York: Henry Holt, 2006) p. 171.

10. Weiner, p. 359.
11. Ibid.
12. Kinzer, p. 191.
13. Ibid., p. 203.
14. Ibid.
15. Goldstein, p. 350.
16. Ibid., p. 351.
17. Ibid.
18. Ibid, p. 362.
19. Alfred McCoy, *A Question of Torture: CIA Interrogation from the Cold War to the War on Terror* (New York: Henry Holt, 2006) p. 23.
20. Ibid., p. 29.
21. Ibid.
22. Ibid., p. 89.
23. Ward Churchill and Jim Vander Wall, *The Cointelpro Papers: Documents from the FBI's Secret Wars against Dissent in the United States* (Cambridge: South End Press, 2002).
24. Goldstein, p. 420.
25. Frank Donner, *The Age of Surveillance: The Aims and Methods of America's Political Intelligence System* (New York: Random House, 1981).
26. Ibid., p. 148.
27. Geoffrey Stone, *Perilous Times: Free Speech in Wartime* (New York: W. W. Norton, 2004) p. 488.
28. Goldstein, p. 439.
29. Donner, p. 232.
30. Weiner, p. 329.
31. Ibid., p. 330.
32. Churchill and Wall, p. 235.
33. Donner, p. 72.
34. Ibid., p. 86.
35. Ibid., p. 88.
36. Ibid., p. 94.
37. Ibid., p. 181.
38. Ibid., p. 348.
39. Ibid., p. 349.
40. Ibid., p. 351.
41. Goldstein, p. 460.

4   Absolute Power at the Expense of Democracy

1. Robert Justin Goldstein, *Political Repression in Modern America* (Chicago: University of Illinois Press, 2001) p. 465.
2. Ibid., p. 466.
3. Ibid., pp. 482–83.
4. David Wise and Thomas Ross, *The Invisible Government* (New York: Random House, 1964) p. 328.
5. Frank Donner, *Protectors of Privilege: Red Squads and Police Repression in Urban America* (Berkeley: University of California Press, 1992) p. 307.
6. Wise and Ross, p. 382.
7. Donner, p. 357.

8. Ibid., p. 362.
9. Goldstein, p. 495.
10. Ibid., p. 496.
11. Donner, p. 358.
12. Ibid.
13. Ibid., p. 362.
14. David F. Schmitz, *The United States and Right-Wing Dictatorships* (New York: Cambridge University Press, 2006) p. 115.
15. Howard Zinn, *A People's History of the United States* (New York: Harper Collins, 2003) p. 572.
16. Ibid., p. 107.
17. Ibid., p. 581.
18. Ibid., p. 604.
19. James Patterson, *Restless Giant: The United States from Watergate to Bush v. Gore* (New York: Oxford University Press, 2005) p. 202.
20. Zinn, p. 604.
21. David Schnitz, *Thank God They're on Our Side: The United States and Right Wing Dictatorships, 1921–1965* (Chapel Hill: University of North Carolina Press, 1999) p. 201.
22. Patterson, p. 212.
23. Ibid., p. 234.
24. Stephen Kinzer, *Overthrow: America's Century of Regime Change from Hawaii to Iraq* (New York: Henry Holt, 2006) p. 273.

5 A Police State

1. D. Cole and J. Dempsey, *Terrorism and the Constitution: Sacrificing Civil Liberties in the Name of National Security* (New York: New Press, 2006) p. 27.
2. Ibid., p. 34.
3. Ibid., pp. 35–36.
4. Ibid., p. 42.
5. Ibid., p. 60.
6. Ibid., pp. 138–39
7. C. Savage, *Takeover: The Return of the Imperial Presidency* (New York: Little Brown, 2008) p. 64.
8. Ibid., p. 65.
9. Ibid.
10. Ibid.
11. J. Mayer, *The Dark Side: The Inside Story of how the War on Terror Turned into a War on American Ideals* (New York: Doubleday, 2008) p. 33.
12. Ibid., p. 34.
13. Ibid., p. 39.
14. Ibid., p. 43.
15. Ibid., p. 46.
16. J. Goldsmith, *The Terror Presidency: Law and Judgment inside the Bush Administration* (New York: W.W. Norton, 2007) p. 181.
17. Ibid., p. 97.
18. Ibid., p. 181.
19. Savage, pp. 93–94.
20. Ibid., p. 94.
21. Ibid., p. 96.

22. T. Gup, *Nation of Secrets: The Threat to Democracy and the American Way of Life* (New York: Doubleday, 2007) p. 50.
23. Savage, p. 102.
24. Gup, p. 34.
25. Ibid., p. 143.
26. Ibid., p. 57.
27. W. Brasch, *America's Unpatriotic Acts: The Federal Government's Violation of Constitutional and Civil Rights* (New York: Peter Lang, 2006) p. 5.
28. Ibid., p. 6.
29. Ibid.
30. W. Michaels, *No Greater Threat: America after September 11 and the Rise of a National Security State* (New York: Algora, 2002) p. 35.
31. Ibid., p. 87.
32. Ibid., p. 146.
33. Ibid., p. 147.
34. Brasch, p. 164.
35. Ibid., p. 65.
36. Ibid., p. 76.
37. Ibid., pp. 88–89.
38. Ibid., p. 111.
39. Ibid., p. 112.
40. Michaels, p. 269.
41. Ibid., p. 275.
42. E. Cassell, *The War on Civil Liberties: How Bush and Ashcroft Have Dismantled the Bill of Rights* (Chicago: Lawrence Hill Books, 2004) p. 44.
43. Ibid., p. 172.
44. Ibid., pp. 83–84.
45. J. Margulies, *Guantanamo and the Abuse of Presidential Power* (New York: Simon and Schuster, 2006) p. 69.
46. Ibid.

6   Actions Taken against Enemies of the State

1. J. Margulies, *Guantanamo and the Abuse of Presidential Power* (New York: Simon and Schuster, 2006) p. 67.
2. Ibid., p. 92.
3. Ibid., p. 97.
4. J. Mayer, *The Dark Side: The Inside Story of how the War on Terror Turned into a War on American Ideals* (New York: Doubleday, 2008) p. 203.
5. Ibid.
6. Ibid., p. 207.
7. Ibid., p. 211.
8. http://www.cnn.com/2008/politics/03/08dash.torture.ap.
9. H. Ball, *Bush, the Detainees and the Constitution: The Battle over Presidential Power in the War on Terror* (Kansas: University of Kansas Press, 2007) p. 179.
10. Ibid., p. 184.
11. M. Cohn, *Cowboy Republic: Six Ways the Bush Gang Has Defied the Law* (Sausalito: PoliPoint Press, 2007) p. 75.
12. E. Lichtblau, *Bush's Law: The Remaking of American Justice* (New York: Random House, 2008) p. 107.

13. J. Bamford, *The Shadow Factory: The Ultra Secret NSA from 9/11 to the Eavesdropping on America* (New York: Doubleday, 2008) p. 113.
14. Ibid., p. 116.
15. Ibid., p. 120.
16. Ibid., p. 131.
17. Ibid., p. 141.
18. Ibid., p. 193.
19. Ibid., p. 267.
20. Ibid., p. 267.
21. C. Savage, *Takeover: The Return of the Imperial Presidency* (New York: Little Brown, 2008) p. 234.
22. Ibid., p. 233.
23. Ibid., p. 234.
24. Ibid., p. 235.
25. Cohn, p. 106.
26. Savage, p. 238.
27. Ibid., p. 243.
28. Cohn, p. 108.
29. J. Dean, *Worse Than Watergate: The Secret Presidency of George W. Bush* (New York: Little Brown, 2004) pp.138–139.

7 Exporting the American Police State

1. J. Jaffer and A. Singh, *Administration of Torture: A Documentary Record from Washington to Abu Ghraib and Beyond* (New York: Columbia University Press, 2007) p. 31.
2. Ibid., p. 33.
3. Ibid., pp. 33–43.
4. Ibid., p. 37.
5. Ibid.
6. Ibid., pp. 39–40.
7. Ibid., p. 40.
8. Ibid., p. 41.
9. T. McElvey, *Monstering: Inside America's Policy of Secret Interrogators and Torture in the Terror War* (New York: Caroll and Graff, 2007) p. 16.
10. Ibid.
11. Alfred McCoy, *A Question of Torture: CIA Interrogation from the Cold War to the War on Terror* (New York: Henry Holt, 2006), p. 132.
12. Ibid., p. 138.
13. P. Gourevitch and E. Morris, *Standard Operating Procedure* (New York: Penguin Press, 2008) p. 41.
14. Ibid., p. 74.
15. Ibid.
16. Ibid.
17. Ibid., p. 106.
18. Ibid., p. 199.
19. Ibid., p. 270.
20. S. Grey, *Ghost Plane: The True Story of the CIA Rendition and Torture Program* (New York: St. Martin's Press, 2007) p. 39.
21. Ibid., p. 89.
22. Ibid., p. 151.

23. Gourevitch and Morris, pp. 173–174.
24. Ibid., p. 180.
25. C. S. Smith, *Bad Men: Guantanamo Bay and the Secret Prisons* (London: Weidenfeld and Nicolson, 2007) p. 230.
26. P. W. Singer, *Corporate Warriors: The Rise of the Privatized Military Industry* (Ithaca, NY: Cornell University Press, 2008) p. 214.
27. Ibid., p. 251.
28. Ibid.
29. J. Scahill, *Blackwater: The Rise of the World's Most Powerful Mercenary Army* (New York: Nation Books, 2007) pp. 389–390.
30. Ibid., p. 409.
31. Ibid., p. 434.

8 The Future?

1. S. Soldz, "Coalition for An Ethical Psychology Calls for Independent Investigation of Ties Between the American Psychological Association and Defense Intelligence Establishment" on http://www.zmag.org. Article 21384, 2209. p. 3.
2. J. Brecher, J. Cutler, and B. Smith, *In the Name of Democracy: American War Crimes in Iraq and Beyond* (New York: Henry Holt, 2005) p. 62.
3. Ibid.
4. Ibid., p. 65.
5. M. Farren and J. Gibb, *Who's Watching You: The Chilling Truth about the State, Surveillance and Personal Freedom* (New York: Conspiracy Books, 2007) p. 63.
6. Ibid., p. 77.
7. Ibid., p. 124.
8. A. M. Froomkin, *The Death of Privacy*, STANFORD L. REV., Symposium 2000, p. 1480.

BIBLIOGRAPHY

Ambrose, S. *Rise to Globalism: American Foreign Policy Since 1938* (New York: Penguin Books, 1985).

Ball, H. *Bush, the Detainees and the Constitution: The Battle Over Presidential Power in the War on Terror* (Kansas: University of Kansas Press, 2007).

Bamford, J. *The Shadow Factory: The UltraSecret NSA from 9/11 to the Eavesdropping on America* (New York: Doubleday, 2008).

Bouton, T. *Taming Democracy: The People, the Founders and the Troubling Ending of the American Revolution* (New York: Oxford University Press, 2007).

Brasch, W. *America's Unpatriotic Acts: The Federal Government's Violation of Constitutional and Civil Rights* (New York: Peter Lang, 2006).

Brecher, J., J. Cutler, and B. Smith, *In the Name of Democracy: American War Crimes in Iraq and Beyond* (New York: Henry Holt, 2005).

Cohn, M. *Cowboy Republic: Six Ways The Bush Gang Has Defict the Law* (Sausalito: PoliPoint, 2007).

Cole, D. and J. Dempsey, *Terrorism and the Constitution: Sacrificing Civil Liberties in the Name of National Security* (New York: New Press, 2006).

Dean, J. *Worse than Watergate: The Secret Presidency of George W. Bush* (New York: Little Brown, 2004).

Donner, F. *The Age of Surveillance: The Aims and Methods of America's Political Intelligence System* (New York: Random House, 1981).

———. *Protectors of Privilege: Red Squads and Police Repression in Urban America* (Berkeley: University of California Press, 1992).

Farren, M. and J. Gibb, *Who's Watching You: The Chilling Truth about the State, Surveillance and Personal Freedom* (New York: Conspiracy Books, 2007).

Goldsmith J. *The Terror Presidency: Law and Judgment Inside the Bush Administration* (New York: W.W. Norton, 2007).

Goldstein, R. J. *Political Repression in Modern America: From 1870 to 1976* (Chicago: University of Illinois Press, 2001).

Gourevitch, P. and E. Morris, *Standard Operating Procedure* (New York: Penguin Press, 2008).

Greenberg, K. (ed.), *The Torture Debate in America* (Cambridge: Cambridge University Press, 2006).

Grey, S. *Ghost Plane: The True Story of the CIA Rendition and Torture Reform* (New York: St. Martin's Press, 2007).

Gup, T. *Nation of Secrets: The Threat to Democracy and the American Way of Life* (New York: Doubleday, 2007).

Hersh, S. *Chain of Command: The Road from 9/11 to Abu Ghraib* (New York: Harper Collins. 2005).

Hilde, T. (ed.) *On Torture* (Baltimore: Johns Hopkins University Press, 2008).

Hunt, M. *The American Ascendancy: How the United States Gained and Wielded Global Dominance* (Chapel Hill: University of North Carolina Press, 2007).

Johnson, C. *Blowback: The Costs and Consequences of American Empire* (New York: Henry Holt, 2000).

——. *Nemesis: The Last Days of the American Empire* (New York: Henry Holt, 2006).

——. *The Sorrows of Empire: Militarism, Secrecy and the End of the Republic* (New York: Henry Holt, 2004).

Kinzer, S. *Overthrow: America's Century of Regime Change from Hawaii to Iraq* (New York: Henry Holt, 2006).

Lane, Jr., P. and L. Stiffarn, "The Demography of Native North America" in *The State of Native America*, M. Annette Jaimes (ed.) (Cambridge: South End Press, 1999).

Lens, S. *The Forging of the American Empire: From the Revolution to Vietnam* (London: Pluto Press, 2003).

Lichtblau, E. *Bush's Law: The Remaking of American Justice* (New York: Random House, 2008).

Margulies, J. *Guantanamo and the Abuse of Presidential Power* (New York: Simon and Schuster, 2006).

Mayer, J. *The Dark Side: The Inside Story of how the War on Terror Turned into a War on American Ideals* (New York: Doubleday, 2008).

McCoy, A. *A Question of Torture: CIA Interrogation from the Cold War to the War on Terror* (New York: Henry Holt, 2006).

McKelvey, T. *Monstering: Inside America's Policy of Secret Interrogation and Torture in the Terror War* (New York: Carroll and Graf, 2007).

Michaels, W. *No Greater Threat: America after September 11 and the Rise of a National Security State* (New York: Algora Publishing, 2002).

Nelson, D. *Bad for Democracy: How the Presidency Undermines the Power of the People* (Minneapolis: University of Minnesota Press, 2008).

Patterson, J. *Restless Giant: The United States from Watergate to Bush v. Gore* (New York: Oxford University Press, 2005).

Piven, F. F. *Challenging Authority: How Ordinary People Change America* (New York: Rowman and Littlefield, 2006).

Pohlman, H. L. *Terrorism and the Constitution: The Post-9/11 Cases* (New York: Rowman and Littlefield, 2008).

Rapley, R. *Witch Hunts: From Salem to Guantanamo Bay* (London: McGill-Queen's University Press, 2007).

Rejali, D. *Torture and Democracy* (Princeton, NJ: Princeton University Press, 2007).

Risen, J. *State of War: The Secret History of the CIA and the Bush Administration* (New York: Free Press, 2006).

Robin, C. *Fear, the History of an Idea* (New York: Oxford University Press, 2004).

Rose, D. *Guantanamo: The War on Human Rights* (New York: New Press, 2004).

Saito, N. T. *From Chinese Exclusion to Guantanamo Bay: Plenary Power and the Prerogative State* (Colorado: University of Colorado Press, 2007).

Sands, P. *Torture Team: Rumsfeld's Memo and the Betrayal of American Values* (New York: Palgrave Macmillan, 2008).

Savage, C. *Takeover: The Return of the Imperial Presidency* (New York: Little Brown, 2008).

Scahill, J. *Blackwater: The Rise of the World's Most Powerful Mercenary Army* (New York: Nation Books, 2007).

Schmitz, D. *Thank God They're on Our Side: The United States and Right-Wing Dictatorships, 1921–1965* (Chapel Hill: University of North Carolina Press, 1999).

———. *The United States and Right-Wing Dictatorships* (Cambridge: Cambridge University Press, 2006).

Schwartz, F. and A. Hag, *Unchecked and Unbalanced: Presidential Power in a Time of Terror* (New York: New Press, 2008).

Singer, P. W. *Corporate Warriors: The Rise of the Privatized Military Industry* (Ithaca, NY: Cornell University Press, 2008).

Singh, A. and J. Jaffer, *Administration of Torture: A Documentary Record from Washington to Abu Ghraib and Beyond* (New York: Columbia University Press, 2007).

Smith, C. S. *Bad Men: Guantanamo Bay and the Secret Prisons* (London: Weidenfeld and Nicolson, 2007).

Soldz, Stephen *Coalition for an Ethical Psychology Calls for Investigation of American Psychological Association Torture Collusion* in Opednews.com, May 4, 2009.

Stone, G. *Perilous Times: Free Speech in Wartime* (New York: W.W. Norton, 2004).

Van Bergen, J. *The Twilight of Democracy: The Bush Plan for America* (Monroe, Maine: Common Courage Press, 2005).

Weiner, T. *Legacy of Ashes: The History of the CIA* (New York: Anchor Books, 2008).

Weinstein, J. *The Long Detour: The History and Future of the American Left* (Boulder, CO: Westview Press, 2003).

Wise, D. *The Government Against the People: The American Police State* (New York: Random House, 1976).

Wise, D. and T. Ross. *The Invisible Government* (New York: Random House, 1964).

Wolfe, A. *The Seamy Side of Democracy: Repression in America* (New York: Longman Press, 1978).

Zinn, H. *A People's History of the United States* (New York: Harper Collins, 2003).

INDEX

LA information can be obtained at www.ICGtesting.com
ed in the USA
)W04s1920100914

3452LV00011B/227/P